PACIFIC SALMON
Management for People

PACIFIC SALMON
Management for People

edited by

Derek V. Ellis

Western Geographical Series, Volume 13

Department of Geography
University of Victoria
Victoria, British Columbia
Canada

1977 University of Victoria

Western Geographical Series, Volume 13

EDITORIAL ADDRESS
Harold D. Foster, Ph.D.
Department of Geography
University of Victoria
Victoria, British Columbia
Canada

Publication of the Western Geographical Series
has been generously supported by the Leon and
Thea Koerner Foundation, the Social Science
Research Council of Canada, the National Center
for Atmospheric Research, the International
Geographical Union Congress, the University of
Victoria and the National Research Council of
Canada.

PACIFIC SALMON

(Western geographical series ; v. 13 ISSN 0315-2022)
ISBN 0-919838-03-0
1. Pacific salmon — Addresses, essays, lectures. 2. Salmon fisheries —
Pacific coast (North America) — Addresses, essays, lectures. 3. Fishery
management — Addresses, essays, lectures. I. Ellis, Derek V. II. Series.
SH346.P33   338.3'72'755   C77-002052-6

EDITOR'S ACKNOWLEDGEMENTS

The editor has received a great deal of encouragement and co-operation from many individuals and agencies during the development of this volume, from the initial exploration of the concept, in summer 1975, to final production, early in 1977. In particular he is grateful for photographs provided by British Columbia's provincial archives, Beautiful B.C. Magazine, R.C. Dixon and the Vancouver Sun. He is also thankful for opportunities to discuss problems of salmon management with many colleagues from the University of Victoria, Environment Canada, the B.C. Fish and Wildlife Department, and the Nanaimo Biological Station.

It is acknowledged with appreciation that production of this volume has been aided by grants from the National Research Council of Canada, and by operational support from the University of Victoria, through the medium of both Geography and Biology Departments.

Derek V. Ellis

University of Victoria
Victoria, B.C.
January, 1977

SERIES EDITOR'S ACKNOWLEDGMENTS

The series editor would like to acknowledge that this book has been published with the help of a grant from the National Research Council of Canada.

Many individuals have combined to facilitate its successful publication and distribution. The layout and design of the cover and contents, together with the photographic work was undertaken by Mr. Ian Norie, under whose direction Mr. Ole Heggen and Mr. Ken Quan reproduced maps and diagrams.

Thanks is also given to the organizations and individuals who granted permission to reproduce photographic materials. Mrs. Alison Griffith has provided valuable assistance in the distribution of this and earlier volumes. The final manuscript was typed by Mrs. Margaret McCulloch, her patience is gratefully acknowledged.

Harold D. Foster

University of Victoria
Victoria, B.C.
January, 1977

PREFACE

Over the past few years there has been a rapid and widespread expansion of enlightened attitudes towards managing resources and planning their development. Two principle components can be identified. The first is recognition that a resource is part of an ecosystem, and that manipulation of any part of the system will have effects ramifying throughout. The second component is an awareness that people also are a part of the ecosystem, and the ramifying effects will reach them in many different ways and times.

This book emphasises the salmon resource system – the fish, the environment, the people, and the social organisation and interactions which nowadays link them together and which overlies the natural ecosystem of simpler times. Its examination of this system unfortunately cannot be comprehensive. The system is too complex for that. In particular there are no chapters specifically devoted to special interest groups – the Indian community, the commercial fishermen, the unions or industry management.

What is presented in Section I is an overview of knowledge concerning the salmon and a review of changing management theories and concepts. Section II of this volume is devoted to consideration of present management practices and considerations. Also included is a conceptual chapter which discusses hindsight reviews particularly as applied to the licence programme in British Columbia. Section III concerns itself with the future, for without such prognostications the book itself would be only an academic exercise of little use to people.

Derek V. Ellis

University of Victoria
Victoria, B.C.
January, 1977

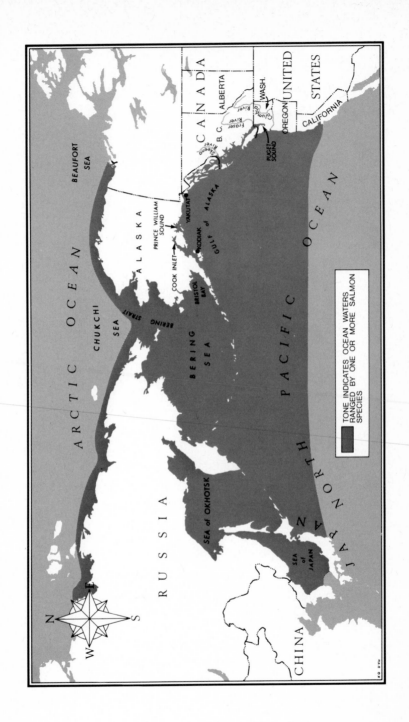

TONE INDICATES OCEAN WATERS RANGED BY ONE OR MORE SALMON SPECIES

TABLE OF CONTENTS

II   PRACTICAL MANAGEMENT

Chapter
4   NEW APPROACHES TO CANADIAN
     RECREATIONAL FISHERIES   103
             P.A. Meyer

5   ENVIRONMENTAL FORESIGHT AND SALMON:
     NEW CANADIAN DEVELOPMENTS   121
             P. Scott and W. Schouwenburg

6   ENHANCEMENT TECHNOLOGY:A POSITIVE
     STATEMENT   137
             J.R. MacLeod

7   HINDSIGHT REVIEWS:THE BRITISH COLUMBIAN
     LICENCE PROGRAMME   148
             Bruce Mitchell

LIST OF TABLES

LIST OF FIGURES

LIST OF PLATES

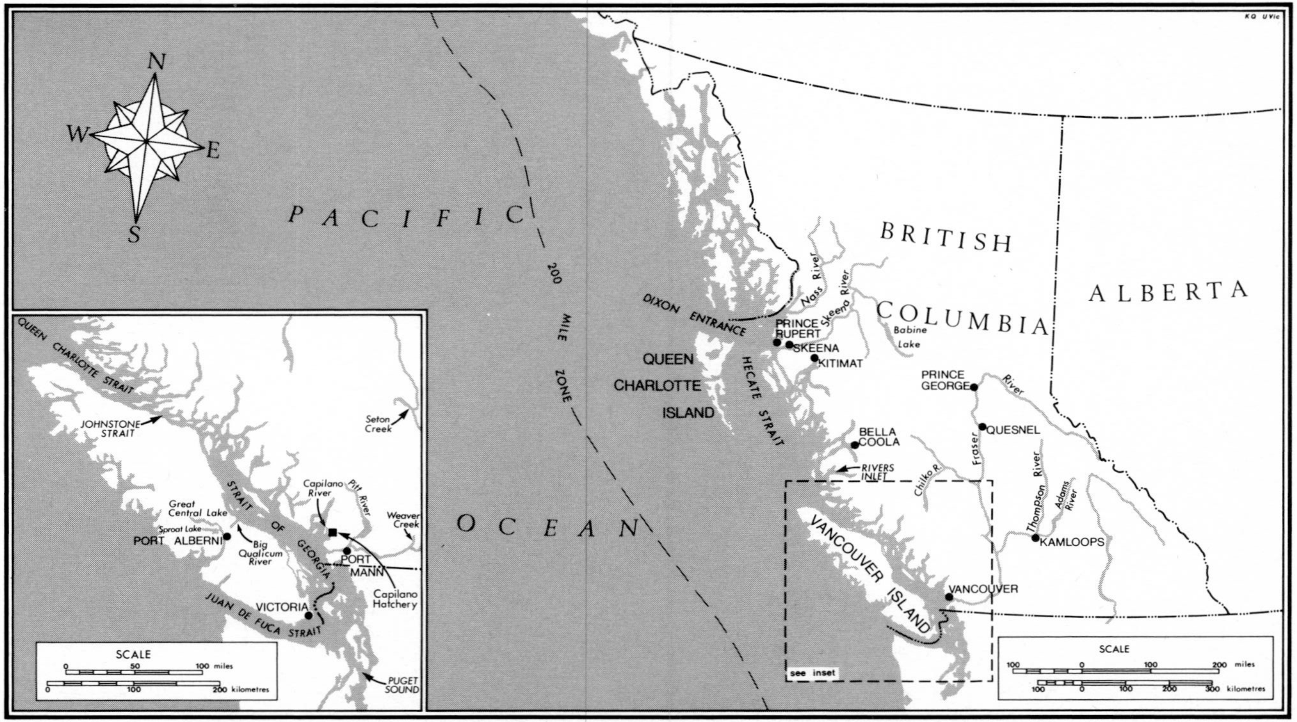

PLATE 1 The British Columbian Regional Interest

SECTION I

EMERGING KNOWLEDGE AND THEORY

"One can only look with sadness and with wonder
at the record of man's use of the
Pacific salmon resources..."

"This (the involvement of biologists in salmon management)
is particularly necessary during a management period
when a philosophy of systems analysis, in which
salmon tend to be regarded as statistically
predictable automata, rather than living,
individually varying animals,
is being emphasised."

"It is ironic that just as the agencies are beginning to
achieve maximum sustained yield (on the Skeena
sockeye at least), the inadequacies of this theory
are becoming widely recognized."

PLATE 2
Seiner

Vancouver Sun Phot

CHAPTER 1

THE FISHERY:
ECONOMIC MAXIMIZATION

James A. Crutchfield

University of Washington

DEFINITION AND SCOPE

The salmon of the Northeast Pacific constitute one of the most valuable fishery resources in the world. Landings in recent years have yielded from $120 million to $200 million to fishermen, and direct employment in salmon fishing in the Pacific Coast states and the Province of British Columbia has averaged approximately 45,000 in the 1970's (Tables 1,1 and 2,1). Because both natural supply and the potential for enhancement are inherently limited, the steady rise in population and income in major countries that consume salmon has raised the real price of salmon (that is, its price relative to the general price level) over the past three decades, and most sharply during the past four years (Table 3,1).

In short, there is money in salmon -- a great deal of money, with every indication that total dollar receipts to the industry will continue to rise even when the carrying-capacity limitations of the natural environment are reached. It is also obvious to anyone who has followed the development of the industry that salmon can be taken at relatively low cost (at least in comparison with the high unit value of the catch in the marketplace). We would expect, then, to find that the high market value of all types of salmon would be translated into highly profitable fishing operations throughout the range of the fishery.

TABLE 1,1

SIZE AND VALUE OF PACIFIC SALMON FISHERIES

Year	Salmon Landings (000 lbs. rd. wt.)		Value of Salmon Catch To Fishermen (millions of dollars)	
	U.S.	Canada	U.S.	Canada
1950	323,324	-	$ 37.4	$ -
1951	376.835	201,960	52.5	28.4
1952	356.007	151,121	45.2	19.6
1953	324,058	190,795	37.8	21.8
1954	334,683	182,614	44.0	23.6
1955	282,005	134,456	40.7	18.5
1956	297,151	116,976	46.2	21.4
1957	266,416	135,848	39.6	18.9
1958	307,499	185,301	45.9	37.1
1959	201,684	109,425	35.7	20.5
1960	235,447	77,593	44.7	18.4
1961	310,398	125,317	52.0	26.2
1962	314,566	167,667	56.4	30.6
1963	294,177	123,668	49.0	22.8
1964	352,246	128,907	56.0	30.2
1965	326,806	95,294	65.2	26.0
1966	387,512	168,849	73.6	38.7
1967	216,664	138,784	48.7	36.0
1968	327,609	182,340	66.4	44.9
1969	267,828	83,348	54.7	27.8
1970	410,119	159,809	99.0	45.1
1971	312,071	139,446	81.0	44.5
1972	216,685	169,384	71.5	50.3
1973	213,009	190,606	127.6	100.0
1974	-	139,869	121.3	74.0
1975	-	80,212	116.3	46.9

Source: Fishery Statistics of the U.S. and National Marine Fisheries Service Databank; Environment Canada, Fisheries, Pacific Region.

TABLE 2,1

EMPLOYMENT IN SALMON FISHERIES

Year	U.S.	Canada
1950	11,082	-
1951	11,024	-
1952	-	-
1953	-	-
1954	-	-
1955	11,741	12,836
1956	9,159	11,851
1957	-	12,999
1958	-	15,263
1959	19,172	15,456
1960	22,036	15,159
1961	24,199	16,805
1962	23,216	16,437
1963	23,853	16,624
1964	23,708	13,300
1965	26,111	13,000
1966	27,814	11,977
1967	26,980	12,117
1968	30,676	12,133
1969	32,111	10,942
1970	34,627	11,647
1971	35,439	10,961
1972	32,755	9,902
1973	-	11,717
1974	-	11,906
1975	-	12,578

Source: Fishery Statistics of the U.S. and National Marine Fisheries Service Databank; Environment Canada, Fisheries, Pacific Region.

TABLE 3,1

WEIGHTED AVERAGE, EX-VESSEL PRICES
ALL SPECIES

Year	U.S. (Current)	U.S. (Real)	Canada (Current)	Canada (Real)
1950	11.6	-	-	-
1951	13.9	16.4	14.1	16.0
1952	12.7	14.6	12.9	15.5
1953	11.7	13.3	11.4	12.8
1954	13.1	15.0	12.9	16.5
1955	14.4	16.5	13.8	17.5
1956	15.6	17.5	18.3	21.8
1957	14.9	16.2	13.9	16.7
1958	14.9	15.8	20.1	22.6
1959	17.7	18.6	18.8	21.7
1960	19.0	19.6	23.6	26.9
1961	16.8	17.2	21.0	21.9
1962	17.9	18.1	18.2	18.3
1963	16.7	16.7	18.4	18.3
1964	15.9	15.7	23.4	22.6
1965	19.9	19.3	27.3	26.1
1966	19.0	17.9	22.9	20.9
1967	22.4	20.5	25.9	23.0
1968	20.4	17.9	24.6	20.7
1969	23.5	19.6	33.4	27.3
1970	24.0	19.0	28.2	22.0
1971	24.9	-	31.9	-
1972	28.0	-	29.7	-
1973	58.0	-	52.5	-
1974	59.0	-	52.9	-

Source: Fishery Statistics of the U.S. and National Marine Fisheries
Service Databank; NMFS, Basic Economic Indicators: Salmon
1974; Environment Canada, Fisheries, Pacific Region.

In fact, precisely the opposite situation prevails. Except for recent years in British Columbia, the salmon industry has been marked by sporadic bursts of expansion in response either to the opening of new producing areas or to prices inflated by sudden spurts of market demand. Each expansion has then been followed by long dragging periods of hardship in which fishing capacity has far exceeded the tolerance of the resource in physical terms and has even farther outdistanced its ability to yield satisfactory incomes to fishermen.

In this chapter, the reasons for this frustrating situation are examined, the necessary conditions for maximizing net economic yield from the resource are outlined, and rough estimates of the potential rents are developed. In the discussion that follows, the term "economic maximization" is interpreted to mean gross returns to fishermen less costs of harvesting and management, properly discounted to yield the largest possible present value. Ideally, the production costs in any time period should be the lowest attainable. Throughout the Northwest, however, although fish traps are in many areas the most efficient method of harvesting salmon, their use is so politically unacceptable that it seems more realistic to confine this discussion of economically efficient capture to numbers and combinations of conventional mobile gear.

Even in this modified form, "maximization," as defined above, is purely a matter of economic efficiency. Society may also have a legitimate concern with such matters as the distribution of income and employment opportunities, the availability and quality of recreational fishing, or the development of isolated fishing communities -- any one of which may involve some sacrifice in net monetary yield from the salmon resources. In the absence of any acceptable common denominator, it seems sensible to define economic maximization in conventional fashion, while fully acknowledging that socially optimal usage of the resource may involve other objectives as well.[1]

5

THE ECONOMIC HISTORY OF THE
SALMON FISHERY

The economic history of salmon exploitation follows the same sorry course that has been noted in other commercial fisheries through- out the world.[2] Because property rights in the conventional sense of the word have been totally lacking, access to the salmon fishery has been regarded as completely free to anyone willing to pay the nominal price for a salmon fishing license and the moderate investment required in vessels and gear.

No single fisherman or group of fishermen has any effective control over the stream of benefits which could be realized by adjust- ing fishing in one period to permit adequate escapement for subsequent cycles; therefore the fishery has tended everywhere to degenerate into a frantic scramble to take fish before competitors can reach them. The results have been catastrophic in both economic and biological terms. In the early days of the fishery, it was all too common to harvest salmon by building impassable obstacles across spawning streams and taking the entire run as it approached the barrier. What matter that this simply closed out fishing within a period of three or four years? There were always other streams to turn to. Eventually it became clear that this murderous kind of exploitation could not be tolerated; yet the fact that no fisherman could expect to benefit in subsequent years from his restraint in the current season made it quite irrational for anyone to withold effort even when the runs of particular river systems were being obviously and critically overfished.

Quite apart from the very real possibility of depletion or extinction of individual races of salmon, open access to the fishery guaranteed that far more investment in labour and capital would flow into the industry than would be required to take any given catch level. Once regulation had begun to protect the physical productivity of the

more important stocks, the basic economic attractiveness of salmon
fishing still encouraged continued expansion of fishing capacity even
though physical catches had stabilised or actually had declined.

As effort continued to mount in the salmon fisheries, regulation became more and more a frantic struggle to keep fishing mortality
within the yield capabilities of limited stocks and to balance the interests of one fisherman group against the conflicting interests of others:
gear conflicts, and ethnic conflicts characterize the relations of
salmon fishermen along the entire length of the Pacific Coast. Since
economic objectives were not seriously considered as a guide to the
regulatory process until very recent years, the overwhelming bulk of
the regulations adopted to protect the salmon stocks either were specifically designed to reduce the efficiency of vessels and gear in order to
control fishing mortality or had that effect as a by-product. This was
hardly conducive to maximization of potential economic benefits.[3]

Overfishing is not, of course, responsible for all of the decline in Northwest salmon yields. Because of their dependence upon
fresh water for spawning and habitat during a portion of their life cycle,
all species of Pacific salmon are vulnerable to competition from other
users of the land/water systems. The development of a Northwest
energy economy geared largely to cheap hydroelectric power dealt a
series of blows to salmon productivity in many parts of the region. More
recently, the onslaught has continued with the massive growth of metro-
politan populations adjacent to spawning rivers, with recreational home
construction in rural areas, and with careless land use policies by real
estate developers and the forest products industry. From an economic
standpoint, the use of artificial measures to augment natural productivity
substitutes more and more costly supply sources for those which previously
came virtually free from nature. Moreover, man's ability to replace
diminishing wild stocks has been limited until recently to the Coho and

Chinook. Some progress is now being made in the propagation of sockeye, pink, and chum salmon, but a great deal remains to be done. Perhaps most important, artificial enhancement can be undertaken successfully only at sites where the water meets stringent quality requirements
for inputs to hatcheries (and where the amount of pollution from their
effluent is tolerable).

In summary, the salmon fishery expanded rapidly from its
inception at the end of the nineteenth century through the 1930's. Each
depletion of preferred species in accessible rivers was followed by geographic expansion to more remote areas and by development of strong
commercial markets for previously low-valued species. By the end of
World War II, the resource was, for all practical purposes, fully developed or overdeveloped throughout its entire range. Despite the subsequent stabilisation of catches in some areas and actual decline in others,
total capital investment and the numbers of fishermen participating have
continued to climb as the increase in salmon prices relative to the
general price level has pulled more and more fishing units into the
industry. The occasional bonanza year has failed to compensate for
the chronically low and unstable incomes of a majority of the salmon
fishermen.

In this process, man has proved unwilling to restrain his
totally wasteful and duplicate inputs of labour and capital to a fully
utilised resource. The result has been a frittering away of benefits
which might have been realized from major advances in fisheries
science, from increased awareness of the biological characteristics of
the Pacific salmon populations, and from the growing flexibility and
sophistication of salmon management. It was not until 1968, with the

PLATE 3
Iron Chink – First Mechanical Processor

introduction of a programme to restrict entry and to reduce excess
capacity in the salmon fisheries of British Columbia, that the first ten-
tative step was taken toward rationalization of the fishery in an economic sense.

ECONOMIC STRUCTURE

Several economic characteristics distinguish all commercial
fishing activities from other primary production, but a few are peculiar
to salmon alone. These include the fact that salmon are anadromous
and spawn only once: therefore no choice is feasible among mixed age
groups or relatively sedentary populations. Except in the ocean-troll
fishery, Pacific salmon are available one time only, and any significant
under - or overharvesting cannot be corrected by alteration of subsequent
fishing effort. It is still more difficult to correct for errors in estimates
of stock and timing, given the fact that the salmon lose economic value
in the latter stages of their spawning run, as the estuarine and riverine
environment saps their quality.

A second characteristic that complicates economic decision
for both harvester and resource manager is the high cost of predicting
salmon runs and the tremendous variation around central tendencies in
the critical spawner-recruit relations which all salmon exhibit. The
industry harvesting Pacific salmon is in continuous short-run disequil-
ibrium. The full size of the run of a particular race can be estimated
only when it actually enters the active fishing stage; and by that time
it is too late either to alter the annual investments allotted to those
stocks or to adjust the total effort directed toward them except through
the "meat-axe" techniques of intra-seasonal area and time closures.

A further economic and biological complication arises from
the present tendency to fish on mixed species and on fish originating in
different river systems. This makes it all but impossible to determine

total fishing mortality on any given management unit.

The combination of characteristics just described limits the salmon fisherman to very short seasons, by area and overall, and forces the industry to make heavy pre-season commitments as to fishing location, processing, and transportation. All of these factors obviously add up to high-risk decisions on the basis of scanty information - by fishermen and resource managers alike - which multiply fishing costs.[4]

In other respects, the salmon industry shares with other fisheries characteristics that set them apart economically from most other types of primary production. An overwhelming majority of the capital and labour employed in the salmon fishery is utilised off-season in other fishing occupations, in non-fishing work for the vessel and crew, or in shoreside work for crew members. To some extent, of course, it is actual availability of the fish which dictates that labour in the salmon industry is only part time. But that tendency has been greatly augmented by management techniques designed to adjust for excess fishing capacity by shortening fishing periods and by restricting movement among fishing areas. Since labour and capital cannot move among occupations without friction and loss of time the effect is, again, to increase the overall cost of salmon fishing.

With relatively few exceptions, the waterfront market structure for salmon is oligopsonistic (that is, the fisherman typically deals with a limited number of buyers who dominate purchases at the few ports accessible to the typical small salmon boat). In addition, the high degree of uncertainty in salmon fishing has led to considerable vertical integration. Some vessels are actually owned by processing companies and manned by skippers and crews subject to the buyers' orders; others are financed by waterfront buyers with the implicit understanding that the firm will have first call on the boat's landings. In general, it is true that the tendency to exploit small-scale, immobile salmon fishermen has been blunted by moderately effective unionization in several segments of the fisheries and by the formation of cooperatives (particularly in Canada).

However, the overriding economic characteristic in the salmon fishery as in most others is the absence of any defined property right in the resource and the resulting "open access." The sorry record of economic waste will persist until measures are taken to hold the inputs of labour and capital to the minimum number of optimal fishing units required to harvest any given catch.

ECONOMIC BEHAVIOUR
OF THE INDUSTRY

Given the common-property status of the salmon resources, the economic behaviour and results are predictable – and unfortunate. As would be expected, the fishery has showed the classic tendency toward overinvestment of capital and labour from its earliest days. In recent decades, as demand has continued to rise, new inputs have continued to enter some salmon fisheries despite general awareness of supply limitations. Higher prices simply meant that the pie could be divided into more and more pieces while returning an income sufficient to hold old participants and to attract new ones whenever the occasional big run occurred.[5]

Economic theory would suggest that over the long run a salmon fisherman would earn, on the average, about the same total income that would be available in his best alternative occupations. While it is difficult to measure accurately the income received by salmon fishermen because of its highly seasonal nature and its supplementary diversity, incomes have tended to be lower than "opportunity" levels.

The reasons are not difficult to define. Because salmon fishing is so highly unpredictable, the occasional big year does occur, even in areas that could be described as heavily overfished. Such abnormally large runs, particularly if they coincide with periods of relatively favourable prices, trigger a flow of new investment in the fishery and frequently involve the construction of new, up-to-date boats, equipped with the most modern gear. When availability of fish and/or prices drop back to more normal levels, the overcapacity tends to persist over long periods, and fishermen's incomes consistently fall below levels that might otherwise be expected. Chronic overcapacity and chronically low incomes would be relieved to some extent if the labour force involved could readily move to other occupations. Unfortunately, a large proportion of those engaged in salmon fishing are culturally, geographically, or economically unable to seek employment where more stable and favourable terms might be available. Particularly in the remote coastal areas of Alaska and British Columbia, this is an acute source of economic distress for non-white fishermen. Since underemployed fishermen are likely to spend a good deal of time maintaining their idle vessels, even a prolonged period of low incomes is of little effect in driving people from the industry. In short, the asymmetry between entry and exit conditions means that new fishing capacity is pumped into the industry during every upturn, but no equivalent reduction occurs when catches or prices are unfavourable.

An important corollary of this argument should be noted. Adequate incomes – that is, incomes comparable to those that people of the same age and educational level could realize in other occupations – are a necessary but not a sufficient condition for an economically efficient fishery. Even if the root causes of chronically low incomes were removed, preferably by restricting entry into the fishery during the occasional boom period and by improving mobility to other areas and other jobs, the industry would still tend to settle into an uneasy long-term equilibrium in which satisfactory incomes would be earned on the

average but which, from society's standpoint, would remain grossly inefficient in that far more vessels and labour than necessary would still be
employed. It has become evident, particularly in the case of the Alaskan and Puget Sound salmon fisheries, that regulation based on a
precarious ability to harness excessive fishing capacity would inevitably
lead to reduced total production. The principal regulatory methods
utilised - closed areas, closed seasons, and gear restrictions - have resulted in unbalanced harvesting of intermingled stocks and of stocks
available sequentially on the various fishing grounds. In Bristol Bay and
in the Canadian-American sockeye and pink salmon fisheries based on
Fraser River stocks, fishing in recent years has been regulated in terms
of one or two days a week and even down to hours in a day. This inevitably strikes hard at whatever stocks are "in the gauntlet" during the
open period, while other population units passing through during the
closed period may be harvested lightly or not at all. Economic as well
as biological waste is an inevitable consequence, since total yields will
consistently fall below the levels that could be achieved if fishing pressure were low enough to permit more selective management.

The economic structure of the fishery has also reduced the total
economic yield available by encouraging "leap-frogging" and the resultant exhaustion of fisheries operating on mixed stocks. Although the
drive to extend net fishing into the open ocean has been curtailed by
law, many of the net fisheries are operating much farther away from the
estuaries of spawning streams than they would choose if freer of competition (and of administrative regulations). The problem of defining the
catch by area of origin and of controlling exploitation on the basis of
management units is obviously complicated by this development. In
addition, the structure of the industry and of regulatory programmes
governing salmon fishing have tended to favour a rapid expansion of
ocean trolling, which always operates on mixed stocks and catches

14

large numbers of immature fish. Those below legal limits are shaken off the hooks under conditions which probably result in substantial mortality; and even those that can be legally retained are taken at such an age and size that almost certainly more marketable weight is lost by early capture than would result from natural mortality if these fish were allowed to mature. The loss in economic return is far from trivial.

Finally, the economic performance of the salmon fishery has been seriously affected by the regulatory methods employed. Since the agencies have, until very recently, lacked any authority to control entry into the fishery or to reduce existing excessive gear, the only recourse has been to curb fishing mortality at the expense of higher economic costs for the fishing vessel. In many cases the reduction in gear efficiency has been deliberate; in others, it is a by-product.[6] In either case, exploitation of the salmon stocks yields a lower net income both to fishermen and to society as a whole.

In technical terms, the barriers to economic maximization of benefits from salmon resources under open-access conditions may be summarized along the following lines.

Figure 1, 1,[7] shows the general form of the function relating fishing effort to sustained yield of any fishery population (Whether the yield-effort relation is asymptotic or humped is not really significant to the analysis.) In the case of the Pacific salmon, a rough version of this function follows from any of the variety of models relating harvestable fish to spawner-recruit relationships over time.

In Figure 2,1,[8] these yield-effort relations have been converted to total receipts and total costs for the fleet working on the resource. An equilibrium of sorts would tend to prevail at a level of effort OE, which equates total and average revenues with total and average costs (including a rate of return on investment sufficient to induce replacement of capital). Assuming (contrary to reality) that the system is

YIELD − EFFORT FUNCTION: STANDARD GEAR

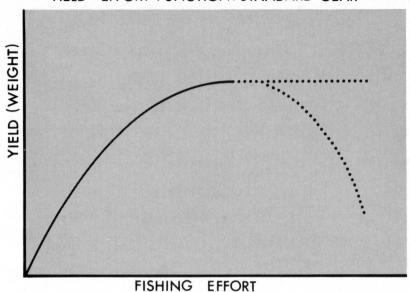

FIGURE   1,1.   Yield-Effort Function: Standard Gear

reasonably stable over time with respect to physical abundance and price, satisfactory incomes would tend to prevail, but at levels of effort which actually show negative marginal yields.

If effort were reduced to OE_2 where physical yield is maximised, a net social benefit (or economic rent) would result. But an even larger return would be realized at OE_3 since at any greater level of effort the increase in receipts falls short of the increased costs necessary to generate them. In the absence of an explicit "rental charge" or direct control over effort, the fishery will invariably generate excess capacity sufficient to dissipate all potential net economic benefit to society − a deadweight loss to the extent that the redundant labour and capital could have been used productively in other occupations.

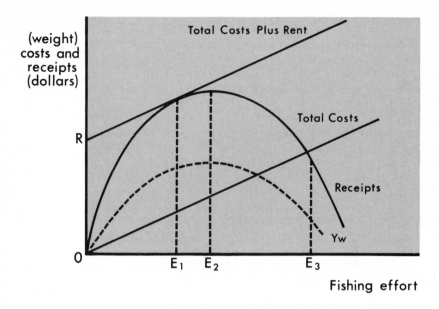

FIGURE 2,1. Yield, Receipts and Costs as Functions of Fishing Effort

The real-world adjustment process is far more complex, for
reasons noted earlier. A given fishery will usually operate on multiple
stocks of salmon, and neither yields per unit of effort nor prices exhibit
the stability assumed in the simple presentation above. Nevertheless,
the motivation and results indicated fit the pattern of salmon exploitation all too well. Capacity in salmon fisheries in the U.S. coastal
states and Alaska has expanded enormously, despite a wide variety of
efficiency-reducing "conservation" measures, during a period when
catches were stable or declining.

In brief, the economics of salmon fishing under common-
property conditions without management would lead self-interested
fishermen to actions which would destroy much of the resource in time

and would severely deplete that which remained. Even with the development of management tools that are moderately effective in protecting the productivity of the stocks, the persistence of excessive capacity in both men and gear causes a deadweight economic loss that constitutes a substantial direct burden on regional economies. It also inhibits the rational management which might otherwise be possible.

MANAGEMENT FOR ECONOMIC OBJECTIVES

The preceding discussion suggests that man as a predator has fallen woefully short of maximizing _anything_ that might be construed as a measure of benefit to himself. In some of the important salmon fisheries, physical yields have fallen to levels well below those that could be realized. In others, yields have been stabilised only by substituting expensive artificially reared salmon for depleted wild stocks. More important, from the standpoint of society as a whole, the inputs of labour and capital utilised at any given level of catch are far above the necessary minimum. It is not surprising, then, that economists concerned with optimal utilisation of the salmon fisheries have pressed hard for a significantly different concept of management.

The primary goal of salmon management surely must be some composite measure of human well-being. This is not measured solely by net economic benefit in the narrow monetary sense, since (as noted earlier) consideration must be given to income distribution effects, employment opportunities, and other social aspects of the activities engendered by commercial salmon harvesting. Nevertheless, economic maximization represents a basic starting point, if for no other reason than that peripheral social objectives can be met more readily if the fishery is on a sound economic footing. While the determination of a yield function – that is, the alternative catches that can be taken from

18

salmon populations with different levels and composition of effort – remains a biological and technical problem, the determination of the right level and composition of effort in terms of cost of inputs and catch values is equally certainly an economic problem. From the standpoint of society as a whole it is just as important to minimize the cost of harvesting as to ensure the right level of harvesting.

Analytically, this means that the level of effort should be such that any further expansion would yield less in additional revenue than the additional cost required to realize it; also, the gear composition and deployment should be such that a given catch in any area could not be taken at lower cost. Superimposed on these formal requirements for efficient resource use must be a recognition of the tremendous variability of the critical spawner-recruit relationship and, therefore, of any function relating effort to yield over time. In short, economic maximization of benefits from the salmon fishery, tempered by whatever additional socioeconomic factors one wishes to consider, must always involve an exercise in second best.[9] The additional costs involved in maintaining adequate capacity to harvest the occasional large runs must be weighed against the costs of maintaining that capacity; and, alternatively, an optimal fleet suitable for the average catch in a given salmon fishing area would inevitably allow some salmon upstream in excess of those required for escapement – a net economic cost. Major economic gains could be achieved if salmon management were to include the right to restrict effort. But such a policy would need to be backed by firm authority to close the fishery when such action might be indicated by the size and timing of specific runs as such information became apparent during the season.

These are essentially modifications of a fundamental principle. The critical point is that both the United States and Canada are spending much more in real resources to capture salmon than they need to.

In the process, they have imposed on salmon management a much heavier burden than it need bear and have doubtless reduced the total physical yield appreciably.

Recognition of these facts has led in recent years to prohibitions on further expansion of fishing effort and to at least limited steps to reduce the excess capacity that already exists. Canada was the leader in this revolutionary change in management strategy and objectives. An innovative programme of license limitation and capacity reduction in the British Columbia salmon fisheries was initiated in 1968. Space precludes a full evaluation of its problems, successes, and limitations. There can be little doubt, however, that even its modest reduction in numbers of vessels has resulted in dramatic improvement in the actual and potential economic benefits from the British Columbia salmon fisheries (and this, despite a perverse tendency to increase investment in new vessels as the older ones are displaced).[10] The evidence need not be sought in theory – it is clearly expressed in the high prices that must now be paid for a right to participate in that fishery. Perhaps equally important, one of the original administrators of that programme has estimated that the unprecedented increase in salmon prices in 1972 and 1973 might easily have resulted in the addition of four thousand or more new vessels to the salmon fishery but for the controls on new entry.

Alaska, facing a far more complex problem of management, has also initiated a moratorium on new licencing and a preliminary programme for reduction of salmon fishing gear. Assuming that it passes legal hurdles now facing it, the Alaska programme is likely to produce the same kind of limited but worthwhile gains that have been witnessed in British Columbia. Even prior to any reduction in the number of licences "grandfathered" into the Alaska salmon fishery, limited-entry permits have been selling at prices ranging from $800 for a trolling licence to $12,000 for a purse seine licence.[11] In British Columbia, where the number of participants has actually been reduced, licences bring far higher prices, despite higher fees and taxes. Active fishermen, in the best position to judge, apparently feel that the permit to engage in salmon fishing has now become a valuable property right.

The State of Washington has also passed legislation limiting the number of salmon licences to those in existence in 1973, but has yet to formulate a plan to reduce what was already excessive capacity at that time. It is anticipated, however, that the limited "buy-back" programme now in operation will be extended to a broader-based system for reducing total capacity in the hands of casual participants.

The cost to society – the difference between what is and what might have been, had even a second-best version of economic maximization been applied in the salmon fisheries – is not readily calculated. Traps have been almost entirely eliminated; less efficient types of gear have proliferated, but even their potential efficiency has been curtailed by legislation or regulation. Thus, nylon gill nets are proscribed; electronic fish finders are prohibited in many areas; vessel and net sizes are limited.

As a first step toward sound management, it would seem useful to indicate the economic benefits that might accrue if fishing capacity throughout the range of the Pacific salmon were reduced to those minimum levels which would be required for taking the harvest in, say, eighty percent of the seasons under present constraints. An exercise of this sort using 1965-1967 data, indicated potential cost savings of $49.5 million.[12] Since the price of salmon in constant 1967 dollars has doubled since then and seems destined to go even higher, the potential economic benefit from limited maximization programmes could easily exceed $100 million annually.

These estimates are heavily biased on the conservative side and should be regarded as minimal. The effects of more balanced harvesting, improved management, and progress in salmon enhancement could increase gross catch values if the top-heavy burden of excess capacity were removed. Many of the more onerous gear regulations could then be discarded, reducing the costs of harvesting still further.

Benefits of these magnitudes, however distributed, loom too large in the regional economies concerned to be disregarded. The experience of British Columbia and of Alaska makes it all too clear that these gains can be won only in the face of stubborn opposition from many participants in the industry (including some who would probably stand to benefit the most from such change). It must be recognized that the present division of the salmon catch among gear types and among fishermen in different geographic areas creates a set of vested interests that are very difficult to alter; but the stakes appear more than ample to justify the effort.

An additional obstacle, of course, is that opportunities for employment are severely limited in many fishing communities, particularly in Alaska and British Columbia. Moreover, the cultural and economic barriers to labour mobility cannot be ignored. It is eminently reasonable that any programme aimed at maximization of dollar returns from the fishery would need also to take into account the minimizing of dislocation and of personal hardship for former participants. It cannot be emphasized too strongly, however, that these constraints on improvement of economic yields must be tested and analysed, not asserted as an act of faith. If ways can be found to ease the surplus labour in isolated fishing villages into other jobs or into other areas where employment opportunities are wider, the fishery should not be forced to bear the full social cost of maintaining incomes for more people than it requires.

THE ECONOMIC IMPACT OF
RECREATIONAL FISHING

Any realistic discussion of maximization of returns from the Pacific salmon resources must take into account the question of recreational fishing. Growth in angler-days has been very rapid throughout the post-World War II period, and projections suggest that this trend will continue (Table 4,1). The demand for outdoor recreation is generally regarded as highly elastic to income, mobility, and leisure time (all of which are, of course, closely correlated). On the assumption that western Americans and Canadians will continue to enjoy increasing per capita incomes and will use part of that additional income to expand their outdoor recreational activities, pressure on quality sport fisheries, such as those for salmon and steelhead, may be expected at least to keep pace. Since there is no evidence that supplies of Chinook and Coho - the principal targets of salmon anglers - can be increased at a comparable rate, the problems of allocating fish among recreational and commercial users will become ever more acute.

Clearly, some common measure of value is needed to deal with these allocation issues, but no really satisfactory method of evaluating outdoor recreation in economic terms has yet been developed. That a number of conceptually invalid techniques have had wide currency (including, inter alia, total expenditures, total costs of provision, opportunity costs of income foregone,etc.) is unfortunate, particularly since they generate very large numbers. Analytically acceptable techniques include carefully worded, cross-checking-type direct interviews to elicit some measure of willingness to pay; and travel-cost models, which substitute costs of travel as a surrogate for prices in order to develop a synthetic demand curve for a particular recreational service. These are, however, costly to carry out and of distinctly dubious accuracy (particularly where the recreation service involved is combined with other

23

TABLE 4,1
RECREATIONAL FISHING

Year	British Columbia		Washington State		
	Catch	Angler Trips*	Catch	Angler Trips	No. of Anglers
1964	253,225	540,225	475,662	1,091,221	302,723
1965	254,200	668,000	938,862	1,278,777	366,801
1966	343,025	690,438	754,857	1,147,579	372,855
1967	283,050	693,625	1,061,583	1,295,579	450,915
1968	320,450	713,750	876,746	1,091,221	428,909
1969	281,050	763,750	876,624	1,215,537	444,734
1970	381,275	839,250	976,223	1,509,835	488,925
1971	539,953	932,348	1,344,818	1,414,837	511,200
1972	317,109	814,130	1,138,926	1,505,245	505,325
1973	354,970	875,205	1,095,360	1,508,290	532,675
1974	483,775	926,305	1,302,818	1,732,156	531,761
1975	447,493	946,765	–	–	–

Sources: Washington Department of Fisheries, Washington State Salmon Catch Report, 1964–1974; Communication from Environment Canada, Fisheries Service, Vancouver, B.C., 1976.

* Boat days x 2.5

24

activities undertaken on the same trip), and they are usually out of date even before publication.[13]

Accordingly, we can talk only in broad generalities about maximization of returns from salmon resources where commercial and recreational users are in competition. It is important, first, to clarify definitions of the outputs involved. Obviously, for a commercial salmon fishery, output is measured in pounds of fish, properly valued. In a recreational fishery, on the other hand, the output is a service (for example, a fishing day) for which success in catching salmon is one, but only one, of the criteria determining the enjoyment of the activity. It is intuitively evident (and certainly borne out by practical experience) that optimal management of a salmon fishery for commercial usage only would call for harvesting a much higher proportion of the total population than would be the case if a prime consideration of management were to ensure optimal catch rates for the growing numbers of anglers. The latter concern would require that far more than the basic minimum of fish be allowed to travel toward upstream spawning areas.

In addition to this inherent conflict in objectives, sport and commercial fisheries are likely to inflict important external costs on one another. Offshore trollers, for example, may not cause sport fishermen any serious difficulty in terms of crowding or gear compatibility, but they do injure many immature salmon which are released, and they do take a great many fish of legal size which would have grown larger and more attractive to anglers had they reached maturity. The net fisheries are even more directly in conflict (at least for Coho and Chinook salmon) since it is obviously impossible to carry on recreational fishing in an area where either purse seiners or gill netters are operating. Quite apart from the competition for the fish themselves, there is literally competition for fishing space.

All of this suggests a real need for a common measure of social value from the two uses if we are to make sense out of the necessary allocation of salmon among anglers and commercial fishermen. This has been a most touchy subject politically in both western Canada and the United States, and legislatures have tended to avoid the problem. But "no decision" about allocation simply means that the division of the catch takes place at random rather than on the basis of a coherent effort to optimize, from society's standpoint, the yield capability of the resource.

An important approach toward reconciling the conflicting interests of anglers and commercial fishermen would be to reorder their respective operations in time and space to the advantage of both. Ideally, one might wish for:

1. A significant curtailment of the troll fishery.

2. An open sport fishery throughout the offshore and inshore areas where salmon are available to anglers.

3. An intensive net fishery operating "behind" the sport fishery to harvest salmon at the point of their entering the spawning streams.

A new gauntlet of this type would offer real advantages to both sides. From the standpoint of the commercial fisherman, harvesting is cheaper in the spawning-stream areas where the fish are concentrated. Although their quality will diminish if they are long in the environment, commercial harvesting can take place rapidly enough to avoid any serious consequences. If these areas were held open for sport fishing alone, far too many unnecessary spawners would inevitably escape upstream, since salmon become increasingly hard to catch with angling gear in the latter stages of their run. On the other hand, sports fishermen angling through the offshore and inshore areas simply could not take enough salmon to present any threat to minimum necessary escapement or to the maintenance of the "inside" commercial operations.

PLATE 4
Cannery Assemb[...]

B.C. Gove[...]

The issues at stake are far from trivial. For example, even rough estimates of the economic value of sport fishing on the Columbia River and on Puget Sound suggest that substantial improvements in net economic benefits can be achieved by some alteration in the allocation of Coho and Chinook salmon.[14] In particular, delaying the bulk of commercial net fishing until salmon anglers have had their turn would greatly stimulate sport-fishing values with very little impact on the total commercial catch. A major part of the value of the commercial catch is in species not readily taken by sportsmen (sockeye, pinks, and chums). In the case of Coho, the net fishery is largely based on mature fish that run late in the season and at a time when poor weather and low "catchability" combine to cut angler activity severely.

Clearly this is an area where additional work needs to be done. It would be particularly helpful to bring into sharper focus the estimated value of recreational fishing. The trend toward charging a license fee for salt-water salmon angling may serve this end. Even in the absence of really satisfactory valuation procedures, cases where the lowest possible estimate of value added by one activity exceeds the highest estimate of that added by the other suggest a need for reallocation in terms of ordinal ranking alone. Opportunities for this kind of improvement in utilisation can be developed fairly readily, area by area, on the basis of existing data and existing knowledge of commercial and sport-fishing effort.

CONCLUSION

One can only look with sadness and with wonder at the record of man's use of the Pacific salmon resources: sadness that extinction of many populations and severe depletion of others has occurred, in some cases long after the need for restraint in harvesting was recognized and after mechanisms to achieve that restraint had been implemented; and wonder that we could repeat, time after time, the gross economic waste from open access to salmon fishing despite the examples, in all fisheries, of the devastating results of such a policy.

Knowledge of the salmon stocks of the Pacific Coast states and of Canada, and formulation of the behavioural models which must underline any rational management programme, have grown apace in the last two decades. But knowledge about salmon resources does not come cheap; and given the tremendous uncertainty that attends the life cycle of the salmon, quantification of the models becomes even more costly. It is therefore critically important, as concerns both the usage of the resource itself and the direction and cost of management and of the necessary information systems, that economic benefits be included as a major element in the objective function of salmon management agencies. Both management techniques and information systems must be evaluated by their effects on value of output and by the economic costs of obtaining those values rather than by biological considerations alone.

It may well be that the corner has been turned with respect to preservation and even some rebuilding of the salmon resources of the Northwest. What remains unclear is whether Canadian and American governments will determine to face, resolutely and patiently, the difficulties involved in moving toward a management regime that will reasonably approximate optimal utilisation of the stocks. Fisheries science has provided far more tools than fishery management has been able to use, given the political timidity and the confusion over objectives that have characterized salmon management throughout this century.

REFERENCES

1. For a discussion of the literature in public sector economics dealing
   with multiple objectives and its application to fishery
   problems, see CRUTCHFIELD, J.A. "Economic and Political Objectives in Fishery Management," Transactions of
   the American Fisheries Society, No. 102 (April 1973),
   pp. 481-491. It should also be noted that the Fisheries
   Conservation and Management Act of 1976 (16 USC 1801),
   which extends U.S. jurisdiction over marine fisheries to
   200 miles, defines optimum yield in terms that embrace
   (but do not specify clearly) economic, social, and biological elements. Confusion over possible meanings of
   "optimal yield" is well illustrated in ROEDEL, P.M. (ed.),
   Optimum Sustained Yield as a Concept in Fisheries Management. Washington, D.C.: American Fisheries Society,
   Special Publication No. 9, 1975.

2. The roots of the economic problems associated with common property
   fisheries were first noted in GORDON, S. "The economic
   Theory of a Common Proprty Resource," Journal of Pol-
   itical Economy, No. 62 (April 1954), pp. 124-142 and
   SCOTT, A.D. "The Fishery: The Objectives of Sole
   Ownership," Journal of Political Economy, No. 63
   (April 1955), pp. 116-124. For sophisticated formal
   discussions of the issues see SMITH, V.L. "On Models
   of Commercial Fishing," Journal of Political Economy,
   No. 77 (March/April 1969), pp. 181-198 and BROWN,
   G. Jr. "An Optimal Programme for Managing Common
   Property Resources with Congestion Externalities,"
   Journal of Political Economy, January/February 1974,
   pp. 163-173 and CLOAK, C.W. and MUNRO, G.R.
   "The Economics of Fishing and Modern Capital Theory:
   A Simplified Approach," Journal of Environmental
   Economics and Management, No. 2 (1975), pp. 92-106.

3. For examples of such regulations and a discussion of their economic effects, see COOLEY, R.A. Politics and Conservation: The Decline of the Alaska Salmon. New York: Harper and Row, 1963; SINCLAIR, S. Licence Limitation - British Columbia: A Method of Economic Fisheries Management. Ottawa: Department of Fisheries of Canada, 1960: CRUTCHFIELD, J.A. and PONTECORVO, G. The Pacific Salmon Fisheries: A Study of Irrational Conservation. Baltimore: The Johns Hopkins Press, 1969.

4. An interesting analysis of the impact of uncertainty about the actual size of predicted runs is presented in MATHEWS, S.B. Economic Evaluation of Forecasts of Sockeye Salmon Runs to Bristol Bay, Alaska. Unpublished doctoral dissertation, University of Washington, Seattle, Washington, 1967.

5. In 1969, following an exceptionally large run of sockeye salmon in Bristol Bay, more than 200 new gill net boats were constructed for use in this badly over-capitalized fishery. A Canadian expert estimated that the very high salmon prices of 1973 and 1974 would have brought at least 4,000 additional boats into the fishery except for licence limitation laws. More than 1,500 new salmon boats, primarily trollers and gillnetters, entered the Alaska fisheries in 1973 and 1974 despite the passage of licence limitation legislation restricting participation to those active before December, 1973.

6. For analyses of the effects of alternative regulatory measures, see CRUTCHFIELD, J.A. "An Economic Evaluation of Alternative Methods of Fishing Regulation," Journal of Law and Economics, No. 4 (October 1961) and ROYCE, W.F. Prospects for Alaska Salmon. Seattle: University of Washington, College of Fisheries, Fishery Circular No. 203, 1964.

7. Adapted from CRUTCHFIELD, J.A. and PONTECORVO, G. The Pacific Salmon Fisheries: A Study of Irrational Conservation. Baltimore: John Hopkins Press, 1969. p. 18.

8. Adapted from CRUTCHFIELD, J.A. and PONTECORVO, G. The Pacific Salmon Fisheries: A Study of Irrational Conservation, Baltimore: Johns Hopkins Press, 1969. p. 29.

9. The importance of these constraints has often been neglected in economic policy prescriptions. See ALVERSON, D.L. "Management of the Ocean's Living Resources: An Essay Review," Ocean Development and International Law Journal, 3, No. 2 (1975).

10. CAMPBELL, B.A. "Licence Limitation Regulations: Canada's Experience," Paper presented at the FAO Technical Conference on Fishery Management and Development, Vancouver B.C., 1972, and published subsequently the Food and Agriculture Organization of the United Nations, Rome, Italy, Publication No. FI : FMD/73/S-12; and CAMPBELL, B.A. "A Review of the Economic Theories of Licence Limitation as They Relate to the Experience of the Salmon Vessel Licence Control Programme in British Columbia," in the British Columbia Salmon Vessel Licence Control Programme, Section IV. Vancouver, B.C.: Department of the Environment, Fisheries and Marine Service, Pacific Region, 1973. For a more critical view, see PEARSE, P.H. "Rationalization of Canada's West Coast Salmon Fishery: An Economic Evaluation," in Economic Aspects of Fish Production. Paris: Organization for Economic Cooperation and Development, 1972.

11. State of Alaska, Commercial Fisheries Entry Commission, Entry Permit Price Survey. December, 1975. (Unpublished)

12. CRUTCHFIELD, J.A. and PONTECORVO, G. The Pacific Salmon Fisheries : A Study of Irrational Conservation. Baltimore: The Johns Hopkins Press, 1969, p. 174.

13. The issues involved are summarized in KNETSCH, J. and DAVIS, R. "Comparisons of Methods for Recreation Evaluation," in KNEESE, A.V. and SMITH, S.C. (eds.) Water Research. Baltimore: Johns Hopkins Press, 1966; SCOTT, A.D. The Valuation of Game Resources: Some Theoretical Aspects. Ottawa: Department of Fisheries of Canada, Canadian Fisheries Reports No. 4, 1965; and CRUTCHFIELD, J.A. "Valuation of Fishery Resources, "Land Economics, No. 38 (May 1962). For examples of good applied work in the field, see SINCLAIR, W.F. The British Columbian Sport Fisherman. Vancouver, B.C.: Fisheries Service, Pacific Region, Department of the Environment, July 1972; and BROWN, G. and MATHEWS, S.B., Economic Evaluation of the 1967 Sport Salmon Fishery.

State of Washington Department of Fisheries Research
Bulletin, Technical Report No. 2, 1970.

14. MATHEWS, S.B. and WENDLER, H.O. Economic Criteria for
Division of Catch Between Sport amd Commercial Fish-
eries with Special Reference to Columbia River Chinook
Salmon. State of Washington Department of Fisheries
Research Papers, 3, No. 1 (1967), pp. 93-104.

PLATE 5

CHAPTER 2

THE FISH: AN ETHOGRAM FOR MANAGEMENT [1]

Derek V. Ellis

University of Victoria

INTRODUCTION

There are problems in biology which must be resolved for
effective management of salmon.[2] These include difficulties of
measuring productivity as the basis for yield calculations. There are
also problems of physiology and pathology which must be solved for
good control of enhancement. But in addition, there are gaps in knowledge concerning ethology or behaviour of the fish. Such problems
underlie for example actual fishing practices and their regulations,
transplantation for enhancement purposes, and guidance of migrants
around dams and water intakes. In this behavioural context it is the
overt, rather than the internal, activities of salmon which are important.

The discipline of Ethology[3] has developed concepts which can
assist the resource manager in appraising consequences of salmon behaviour on decision-making. One such concept is the use of an ethogram, an inventory of the behaviour of a species. If well constructed
this serves as a check-list which can be consulted at times when it is
necessary to ensure that the range of salmon activities has been considered in a management context. An impact matrix can thus be
developed systematically using a well developed ethogram.

THE SPECIES AND THEIR LIFE-CYCLE

The Pacific salmon's life cycle is enacted over vast distances from stream to ocean and over a relatively long time period of some 2 - 7 years. The fish have a most unusual capability to travel from isolated spawning grounds, often located far up the headwaters of rivers downstream to the sea and then to wander over many thousands of miles through the ocean before returning home to their own ground. This is a remarkable feat of navigation requiring considerable capability and accuracy on the part of the fish's sensory and response systems. The complex and extended life cycle exposes the fish to a sequence of environmental problems and fisheries, and each breeding stock has its own unique sequence of difficulties to overcome.

A convenient starting point for an overview of the species[4] and life-cycles is in the stream at which the cycle begins. It is in the bed-gravel, in the fall of the year, that a male and female lay and fertilise eggs. After 2 - 3 months the 2 centimetre long alevins hatch and lie in the gravel for a few more weeks before gradually wriggling their way up to the water flowing overhead. At some stage in the spring, rising water temperatures or other environmental properties in association with their own increasing swimming ability will provoke them to leave the gravel bed and start their free-swimming lives.

At this stage, the life cycles of the five species of Pacific salmon which inhabit North American rivers diverge. The pink and chum salmon for instance immediately swim and drift downstream to the sea, "leap-frogging" along by nightly dashes through the gauntlet of predators. If the estuary is not reached in a single night, they remain in hiding in the river gravel during the day. Once in the estuary they then school up in daylight and feed within its rich and productive ecosystem. In large rivers, such as the Fraser, the schooling occurs before the estuary is reached, and then survival is a matter of continuous swim and drift, day and night, in masses sufficient to take enough of the young past the feeding predators of the large river environment.

The sockeye salmon behave similarly to the pink and chum although the immediate end-point to their spring migration is a lake not an estuary. They will remain feeding there until the next spring or even the following year.

The chinooks and cohos have a very different behaviour pattern. The fry spread out by downstream swim-drifting and upstream swimming throughout the accessible watershed, and cull their food from the organic drift of the river. The two species separate out, however, within their common habitat and thus reduce their inter-specific competition for available resources. Chinooks tend to grow quicker than cohos, so they are the stronger swimmers and utilise faster water where there is less heavily utilised food. The young chinooks may eventually migrate downstream late in their first summer, but the young cohos generally overwinter in their home watershed either in cutbanks, pools or even lakes. Thus they utilise the freshwater resource through the winter before finally flushing out of the system the following spring.

Once in the sea, at whatever age, there is a tendency to stay in the estuary for a while since most salmon arrive there in the spring or early summer and have the annual production season ahead of them. Eventually however the growing fish move offshore into increasingly more distant water, and many of them enter an oceanic cyclical wandering phase, about which insufficient is known. Sockeyes, pinks and chums, and some cohos and chinooks enter the gigantic anti-clockwise oceanic drifts of the North Pacific Ocean. They can direct their wanderings as they forage on fish, nekton and zooplankton near surface to the extent that they return annually to the general area of their entry point to the gyral.

The cyclical pattern of movement ensures that in their spring wanderings they are in the optimum location to find the shortest route to their home estuary. Thus each year maturing salmon in their millions leave the gigantic revolving ecosystem of sea, plankton and fish, and direct themselves towards their home estuary. The pinks generally leave after only one winter in the system, the others after two or more, with the near hundred pound tyee chinooks the last to leave after perhaps seven years at sea.

When maturing adults arrive in the right estuary, travel upriver to the spawning ground is dependent on water quality and quantity in the river channel and consists of upriver swimming with only the minor complication of tributary selection. Often a stock has developed special adaptations or timing to the hydrological patterns of its home watershed. The run may move early or late in its maturity so that the fish spawn immediately on arrival, or they may wait for weeks in a lake enroute. As river flows rise and fall, so barriers to migration appear and disappear or become harder or easier to surmount. Temperatures also may change with amount of melt-water from the interior mountains.

Finally on the spawning grounds, these predators after a life of independent oceanic wandering and hunting must change their life-styles to pair up under conditions of restricted space. The females must dig a redd out of the gravel and in that redd, male and female must simultaneously tolerate close approach of the other and release their sexual products. After several such matings the adults die nearby, but death is a recycling process with remaining body nutrients returned to the home watershed.

THE ETHOGRAM

An ethogram can be ordered in many ways. The system adopted here is a simple two-level hierarchy of six functional categories each broken into a series of incompletely separated sets of actions. The annotations within each category following are an attempt to review the behaviour of Pacific salmon, in the context of raising issues which are significant for management of the resource.

Obtaining Materials and Energy

Any organism must tap a source of materials and energy from the ecosystem if it is to grow from a single-celled fertilised egg and in its turn perpetuate the species. Pacific salmon illustrate a common strategy, that of changing their food source with growth. Initially the embryo, as it grows through the alevin stage lying in the gravel, is dependent on the yolk laid down in the egg by the mother. Soon after leaving gravel for open water, the fry start independent food gathering, although this may be delayed for a day or so for pink and chum fry on their nightly leap-frog journey down to the estuary. The food gathering at this stage consists of opportunistic feeding on virtually any small organic matter, live or dead, which drifts, swims, or even flies past. Such tactics imply that our small 2 cm. long fish have already developed acute three-dimensional vision sufficient to take an accurate fix on moving food, the co-ordination to intercept the drift and snap it up in motion, and the sensitivity to reject the material if not edible. There is even more to their capability since the continual supply of drift food from upstream can be best tapped by individual fish maintaining a fixed station. By returning to such a station after each feeding foray they are prevented from unwittingly drifting downstream. As a result aggressive territorial competition between individuals for prime available space, that is good feeding stations, sets in.

The fry of species which quickly enter large bodies of water, the pinks, chums and sockeyes, feed there in a similar way at first but are not exposed to a unidirectionally flowing habitat. Instead the water medium may be still, or virtually so, or possibly influenced by more or less regularly changing tidal currents. The effects of this on feeding tactics are that the fish must actively seek their food rather than have it come to them. Thus fry in lakes and estuaries can commonly be seen wandering in schools through the shallows, which is a behaviour which balances food-gathering in a productive environment with protection from underwater predators (but not of course from kingfishers and other birds overhead).

Once the juveniles move offshore to lake depths or coastal seas, and then to the ocean, our knowledge of their feeding behaviour is more limited since their actions can rarely be observed directly. It is known that they become true predators in that stomach contents show their prey at sea to be smaller fish (cohos and chinooks) and larger zooplankton or invertebrate nekton, for example, small squids (sockeye, pink and chum). We can speculate that they use the tactics of chasing-type predators utilising organisms smaller than themselves for food.[5] They remain in the top few hundred feet of water, (where the food is concentrated) and they appear to travel individually or at most in loose aggregates which could hardly justify the term schools.[6]

The salmon have also developed a time-related feeding strategy fairly common to those animals which have a far-ranging life-cycle. Prior to the time to start the long return to the breeding grounds, the fish lay down an energy store within their body, the size of which is adapted to their specific needs for the return journey. This last adaptation is a significant management concern, since unusual blocks to

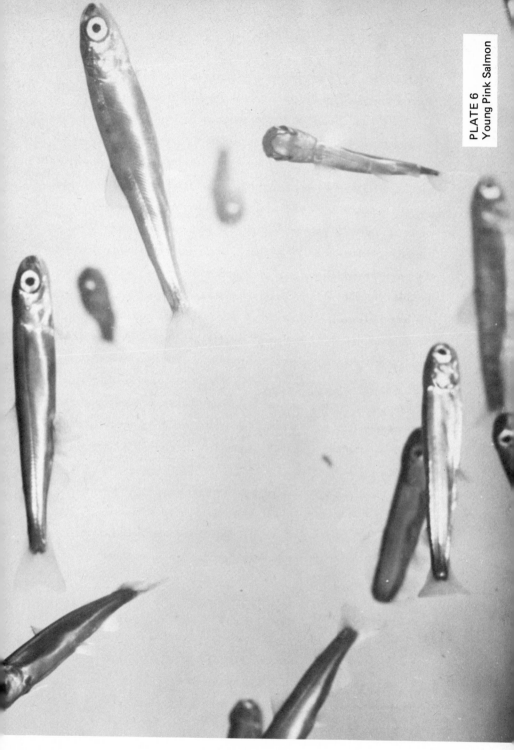

PLATE 6
Young Pink Salmon

D.V. Ellis Photo

the upstream migration whether artificially induced by fishways or
naturally induced by low river flows or landslides can so use up the
programmed energy supply that the fish cannot survive long enough to
reach their spawning grounds and complete the prolonged activities
of mating. Furthermore as feeding stops , lure-type fishing gears sim-
ulating natural prey eventually become ineffective.

To return to the phenomenon of a generalised strategy for
predatory animals, such forms often feed intermittently or periodically
over the 24-hour day-night cycle. There are a number of environmental
circumstances which favour such an adaptation of daily food gathering.
Food for predators is often widely dispersed, either through being in
the form of large animals ranging widely in small groups, or in very
large groups of smaller prey. The predator may need to provide itself
with sufficient energy at one meal to last for some time, and so may
feed to satiation, which by definition precludes further feeding activity
for sometime. Furthermore, environmental factors are also important
since hunting is often dependent on very accurate prey-tracking vision,
and predators that depend on their eyes may be limited to daylight
strikes.

There is a great deal of anecdotal evidence from fishermen
supporting the hypothesis of varying feeding activity in salmon. There
are times and places where salmon simply appear not to be hungry, and
then the skill of the fisherman in provoking a strike is paramount.

Avoiding Predation

For any animal there is the obverse aspect to obtaining food,
and that is to avoid becoming the food of some other animal. Pacific
salmon achieve this by following a number of strategies. Initially
as small fish in streams and estuary, where they are subject to predation

by many other species, they have two escape systems. The first is the emergency response, an explosive, virtually undirected dart-off which is simply too sudden and too fast for the hunting predator to follow. But this must quickly give way, through risk of fatigue, to the second response, that of hiding. Hiding places vary with the size of fish and nature of the predator, from a tangle of underwater vegetation, to holes within a gravel bed, river cutbanks and even the depths of river channels and pools beyond the reach of shallow feeding gulls and bears.

These two responses imply a great deal about the salmon's sensitivity even at the fry stage. They can recognise a predator, and there is advantage to them in responding positively to stimuli indicating depth or other hiding place. Predators generally can be perceived visually by dark shadow, often approaching fast or at least moving in an alert fashion. This stimulus paradigm appears to have generated one of the problems affecting hatchery-reared fish which have often been artificially fed in such a way that large shadows overhead means food. After release to the wild, such a stimulus situation has the totally different meaning of a predator. As a result, it is no wonder that hatchery fish have low survival rates in the wild.

This stimulus paradigm has an even more important biological implication. The natural response has been superceded by an induced one, and we can reasonably conclude that salmon have some capacity to learn,[7] yet another behavioural phenomenon which must be of concern to management, at least in hatchery practice if not gear design and operation.

Learning may also be implicated in the hiding response of salmon. There is survival value for a prey species to know its local habitat so well that on approach of a predator, the dart to hiding place can be well directed and speedy with minimal time devoted to decision-making concerning the route to follow. Salmon introduced into a new environment, whether it be aquarium, river pool or fishway will often engage initially in more or less random wanderings, giving the impression of exploration of, even curiosity about, their surroundings. Fishway design might well benefit from considering this point and its implications for speeding migration through a repetitive structure for which the basic shape can be learned in the first few pools.

Maintaining and Changing Habitat

There are constraints on the space that an animal will inhabit. These range from the simplest, most direct, physical-chemical constraints of the type that prevent most fishes from living out of water; to the almost psychological restraints of a defended territory which some animals will resist leaving to the point of death.[8] Maintaining habitat is the term used here to identify those behaviours which restrain spatial wandering in the various stages during the lifetime of the Pacific salmon. There has to be a complementary term also for the sequence of migrations made by these fish, and so this section deals with both maintaining and changing habitat, behaviours which alternate in sequence.

It is arguable where the first habitat maintenance patterns arise since the initial wrigglings of alevins in the gravel may be insufficient to take them significantly far from the point at which the eggs were laid. However, the first habitat change is clear. Late in the winter the alevins' wriggling is sufficiently directed that they move upwards, not randomly in the gravel, and eventually they emerge in enormous numbers over a period of a few days to start their free swimming existence.

The next stage for cohos and chinooks clearly involves habitat maintenance. There is considerable survival value to them in main-

taining a feeding station at a point where much food will drift by.
Such underwater stations are usually constant in position relative to
visually obvious underwater structures such as boulders and vegetation,
and even to derived eddy patterns generating points of low current
velocity in which a swimming fish can coast with an energy saving,
while being in close proximity to a food-providing current. The best
feeding stations are commonly occupied by the largest or the most
aggressive individuals; aggressive in the sense that they will attack
and nip an intruder of their own or similar species. Unlike many other
animals though, the young salmon occupy their territory for only short
periods of time possibly as little as a few days. The fish change
station as they grow and develop the strength to maintain a position in
faster water where there is more food, but also strength to avoid fiercer
predators from which they must escape. They are also subject to displacement as river flows change and may sweep them away, or drop to
levels that a previously good station can no longer support an active and
voracious feeder.

This habitat maintenance by territoriality is lost when the cohos
and chinooks make their next change to the open water environment of
lakes, an environment where they have been preceded by sockeyes.
This is similar, in some ways, to the estuarine environment which
received the pink and chum fry. In open still water there is no competitive advantage to a good feeding station, and the food, though
abundant, must be sought out with the predator taking the initiative.
However, the risk of predation to small fish is considerable in open
water, and the social behaviour of schooling, through its widespread
appearance in such fish, is believed to be of some advantage in confusing predators. Certainly it is not difficult to believe that a visually
hunting predator will have a more difficult time following its conventional tactics of holding a visual fix on its prey if there are thousands

milling closely together and liable to explode out of their school when attacked.

There appear to be some habitat-maintaining behaviours in operation in open water, at least in lakes, since juvenile sockeye are reported as keeping within particular lake basins, and schools of lake juveniles can be seen escaping from the river-generated currents which could drift them out of their lakes in advance of the right time to make the next habitat change.

This next habitat shift is the one that takes the freshwater juveniles down to the sea in the form of smolts. On their way, they may pass along the length of one or more lakes, and they do so in very directed and speedy manner.[9] They have a directional sense which serves to take their schools along the lake out of contact with the shoreline, even if it is irregularly shaped. What is more, the directional sense is time-compensated so that the shifts in directional trends while moving through the open water of the lakes coincide with shifts in the axis of the lake. In other words salmon appear to have a biological clock within their bodies, as one might anticipate since habitat changes have been repeatedly related to the seasons. A time sensitivity appears to be a fundamental biological property present in most organisms. It manifests itself in many scales from seasonal through diel cycles and serves many biological functions.

These apparently inherited directional tendencies and their time-compensated changes are significant in management for their importance in determining stocks for transplantation purposes, whether to open up new spawning areas or to regenerate the old and devastated. If they are real and innate phenomena, then transplanted stocks must be chosen for their directional sense which should correspond to the long axes of any lakes that they will need to pass on migration.

Once down to the sea in the nearshore waters, schooling remains the predominant social behaviour, as opposed to territoriality. However, information from the high seas fisheries suggests that growing salmon there are not strongly schooled as they feed and wander.

In the high seas, a new habitat maintenance pattern must be operating. The salmon maintain themselves within certain geographical limits, remaining essentially within the North Pacific Subarctic oceanographic domain. For some reason few overlap with tuna to the south in the warmer and more saline sub-tropical domain and few stocks inhabit the colder and less saline waters of the Arctic ocean. Apparently they have some sensitivity to the environment on a geographic scale, or else drift forces serve to keep them within their known bounds. Drift probably has some influence since there are known major ocean gyrals roughly corresponding with the wanderings of particular stocks; on the other hand the known patterns of movement suggest some orientation by the fish to directional cues from the environment. The mechanism seems to be at an indirect level in the sea, affecting the direction of food-gathering wandering only statistically, rather than by the strongly oriented movements which the salmon are capable of when in schools in rivers and lakes. These extensive wanderings, however directed, are the cause for the international problems of salmon conservation which are now taxing the ingenuity and patience of management charged with national fishery considerations.

The return home to their spawning ground appears to be initiated by the salmon's annually cycling clock initiating more directed swimming towards the coast as the salmon arrive in the spring of the year at the general offshore point of their eventual landfall. Less is known concerning this phase than any other, although it is postulated from fishing practices that the fish may on occasions school up intensively en route to the coast,or at other times,not until after they arrive there. Profitable seining is obviously dependent on the size of such schools, where they can be found, and the routes they will follow. In 1958, there was considerable consternation amongst management and United States fishermen when unusually warm oceanographic conditions coincided with Fraser sockeye stocks making their landfalls from the ocean far to the north of usual locations and traversing the northern Queen Charlotte Strait between Vancouver Island and the mainland to the Fraser River, rather than the international waters of the southern Strait of Juan de Fuca. For the individual seiner there is a premium on foresight in predicting where the landfall of the major runs will be and when, and the best seiners mix intuition and private record keeping with a good deal of success.

The 1958 Fraser sockeye migrations are a good illustration of the complexity of the biological problems underlying habitat changes. Whatever sensitivities, or mixture and sequence of sensitivities, are involved, there must be some capability of adjustment to different environmental requirements from generation to generation. Postulated mechanisms for oceanic guidance range for example from cues in the sky such as responses to the plane of polarisation of light to minute electropotentials between sheering currents. The complexity of the life cycle however probably requires considerable redundancy in sensitivities at any one time so that many mechanisms can work as alternatives or in sequence as needed.

From the estuary the adult salmon move upriver by steady swimming in schools interrupted by the needs to escape from the occasional predator and to pass turbulent, fast-flowing, even falling, water.[10] The strategy adopted appears to be seeking as great a depth as possible, subject to finding currents of sufficiently low velocity that energy-conserving steady swimming, as opposed to fatigue-inducing dart

PLATE 7
Coho Fry in Natural Conditions

D.V. Ellis Photo

swimming is effective. In other words, the upriver migrants have adopted the strategy of the marathon runner rather than the sprinter. Depth-seeking on migration is, of course, a protection against predation which in rivers comes largely from surface feeding mammals: bears and humans. However, the greatest river depth may often contain currents so fast that they exceed the ability of salmon to make progress against them without running the risk of oxygen debt. Under these conditions the salmon must balance protection and migration, and so in the Fraser and a few other rivers thousands even millions of salmon will follow each other upstream just off the banks, where eddies break up the generally strong currents of the main flow.

Studies on these upriver migrations have demonstrated yet another manifestation of varying activity in salmon. The migrations are often interrupted by periods of low or different activity. They may stop either regularly at certain times of day, commonly in the afternoons or at night-time, and the fish hold motionless or almost so in river pools. Active migration in estuaries can give way to milling behaviour which provides ideal seining conditions. These various breaks in migration and their causes must be understood by management since they obviously influence fishability.

Finally, after the river ascent, the schooled, sexually mature adults move onto the spawning grounds. There they revert to the territorial way of life as females seek and find suitably oxygenated gravel of the right mechanical type, and the males compete by aggression and threat displays to establish a dominant role in the hours-long ritual movements leading to mating. On the spawning grounds the salmon have to abandon their previous behaviour as predatory hunters, only occasionally banding together into schools, to adopt a more direct one-to-one mutually sequencing social behaviour which will ensure fertilisation of eggs and their placement in the right habitat for the next generation of the stock.

Maintaining and changing habitats has been a long and complicated section of this ethogram but rightly so since the complexities of changing habitat generate many problems for salmon management. It would be very convenient if salmon were like their relatives the trout and simply moved annually from stream to lake and back again. But they are not, and, as a result the movement sequences of each stock must be unravelled for successful management. Understanding must be based on homing,[11] and in this context the general subject of animal behaviour provides much information of value to support management. Homing is a very common animal phenomenon, particularly amongst predators where there is a premium on learning good hunting stations. Commonly homing occurs only over the short distances of a home range, but it is not difficult to imagine how homing, once established in the salmonids as a basic stream feeding and spawning tactic provided a return mechanism from more and more distant migrations, eventually permitting the stocks to draw for much of their lifetime upon the enormous energy resources of the high seas. It must be accepted that several environmental sensitivities were refined to extraordinary levels over evolutionary time, and this accumulation of sensitivities operating together, alternatively or in sequence, now functions to return the salmon to their distant, isolated and rare spawning grounds. Without homing there would be no salmon.

Added to homing as a factor in evolution of the group must be schooling, since a species migrating in socially-responding groups, each individual of which can respond to both social and physical-chemical orientating cues, would appear to improve its capability for directedness due to the complementing of environmental by social responses.

51

Caring for the Body

Salmon, like other animals, engage in actions which to our
human interpretation look as though they are functional in caring for
the body. For example they cough, they yawn, they will even rub
themselves against a solid object. This should not be surprising since
almost all fish, birds, mammals and other complex animals do the same.
It can readily be accepted that these actions serve the same mechanical
functions in these animals as they do for us, without believing that
the animals must also feel the discomfort or be as subjectively involved
as humans are in the same circumstances.

Itch-rubbing, utilising a tree or other solid object, is common
amongst birds and mammals. Fish also often rub themselves against
aquarium or stream bed especially when infected. Itch-relief under
these circumstances is quite believable. Coughing serves the function
for humans of removing disturbing stimuli in the upper respiratory
tract. Mammals, birds and fish often cough, the latter by violent
movements of throat and gill covers. Salmon can be seen to cough in
this way, and even to shake their heads spasmodically in a manner
similar to human sneezing. Since coughs and sneezes often occur when
drift matter is obvious in the water, it is reasonable to conclude that
they serve the same function in fish as in people. Yawning in humans
flushes out lungs with air, and in salmon can be seen to coincide with
a violent jet of water squirted out under the gill covers.

From these comments it can be seen that caring for the body
encompasses a range of body actions serving to remove disturbing
stimuli . They have been called comfort movements, which is a useful
group term. However, there are some very unusual features of such
comfort movements. Quite often they occur out of their normal context under conditions when it is difficult to believe that they are

52

serving their normal function. A body of theory about such non-functional activities has been developed by the school of ethology which can perhaps explain some of the peculiar and controversial activities of salmon. The theory revolves around the two terms, vacuum and displacement activities.

Vacuum activity is the term given to an action which occurs in more or less the appropriate context but without the normal external stimuli. It is as though the animal were internally motivated to perform an action to such an extent that it is performed even though not really appropriate at the time.

Displacement activity is the term given to an action when it appears to be clearly out of context, but when the situation simultaneously calls for two or more actions which are incompatible one with another. An attack by a male on another while courting the female is an example. In such cases rather than make a choice the animal appears to break into a third, irrelevant activity such as becoming stationary and exaggerating the fin actions needed to maintain balance and position in the flowing water. This third, irrelevant action is often exaggerated or stilted compared to the action in its proper context and appears to have taken on a signal value, such as a threatening fin-display, which signals to competing male "I will attack if you come closer".

There is much evidence in the literature describing animal behaviour that such postures are functional as signal displays, regardless whether the displacement or vacuum theories of the ethologists are correct or not. The point here is to explore whether such apparently irrelevant actions or ritualised displays occur in salmon, and are meaningful to management practices. The behaviour literature leaves no doubt [12] that signal displays occur in these fish during territorial defense and spawning, and serve the function of social communication between individual fish. There is no doubt also that salmon engage in a number of apparently useless actions, or actions the function of which fishermen have argued about for years.

Salmon leaping in open water is perhaps the most obvious of the controversial actions. No one argues that salmon leaping at falling water is not functional and the energy benefits have been well described.[13] However salmon also leap at sea, in estuaries, in river pools, and in lakes at the point of entry from rivers and the point of exit to spawning streams. Commonly it is believed that this shakes the roe loose, or removes parasites. Perhaps it does, but under displacement theory, salmon leaping in open water can also be an irrelevant action triggered due to the simultaneous conflict between stimuli releasing migration and inhibiting it.

The point of developing this theme is not so much to discuss the hypothesised explanations for open-water leaping, but rather to stress the implicit warning that where irrelevant actions are numerous along the route of a migrating stock, there may be a biological problem which could be resolved by appropriate recognition and management action. As so many of the irrelevant actions relate to care of the body, and the alternative of displacement theory indicates stressful situations, either postulate means that it is good management to investigate the causes of any massed or intensive inappropriate actions.

Resting and Waiting

Salmon like any other animals engage in periods of inactivity. They can often be seen by above-surface observer or a scuba diver remaining quietly in position in pools or eddies. It is easy to separate such resting body action from the alert station-holding of a feeding juvenile or spawning fish. Nevertheless we must be careful in terming

such inactivity as rest, since inactivity is relative, and the inactive
periods come at various stages in the life cycle and occur for differing
durations of time.

There can be little doubt, for example, that maintaining
stations in an eddy of a falls or rapids is often recovery from fatigue,
in the way that a sprinter needs recovery after a race. In addition,
short pauses by an upriver migrant as it enters a new, restricted river
or fishway pool are similar to the cautious scrutiny that people take on
entry to new and alarming situations. However, migrating salmon often
spend several hours a day in a particular river pool, and each day at
a certain time, often early afternoon, the pool will fill up with a new
batch of migrants, as though the stock is on a 24-hour migration-rest
cycle. This type of inactivity is the closest to what we might recognise as sleep, even though it may occur during daylight hours rather
than at night. It should be noted that many birds commonly rest in this
way during afternoon as well as at night, and are most active from
dawn through the morning, and secondarily in late afternoon to dusk.

There is a longer inactivity period assumed by salmon stocks
which hold up in lakes or estuaries for periods of days or weeks before
entering spawning streams or their home river respectively. These are
actually periods of relative inactivity rather than rest, since the fish
may spend considerable time daily cruising the lake or estuary, leaping
at surface as they go, often following an obvious 24-hour cycle. Such
periods of inactivity cannot be fatigue, caution or sleep as we know it.
These breaks in migration are more likely to be programmed waiting
periods; required either after a passage which physically can be made
only at a certain part of the season, or prior to making a physiological
adjustment, such as the osmotic control capability required for entry
to rivers from the sea. Such long waiting periods are features of considerable interest to management and to fishermen, since they can hold

PLATE 8

fishable stocks in accessible places (when conservation is required), or conversely hold the fish in inaccessible places when fishing is needed to reduce escapements.

Once again the message is clear. The capacity for waiting and resting is specific to particular stocks. It influences management practice and may need identification and consideration in whatever management decisions are made for any stock.

Perpetuating the Species

The chief problem facing salmon in perpetuating the species is that the far-ranging males and females must come together in the right habitat at the right time, when on a geographical scale there are very considerable constraints on what is the right habitat and the right time. These constraints are so great (such as stream gravel suitability and water quality, and time of year with its influence on many environmental parameters) that they are met only in rare isolated stream sections for a few weeks in the fall or early winter of each year.

In biological terms a male and a female, of what is a fairly large species of fish, must simultaneously bring their small vents together at the bottom of a pit dug in the gravel by the female, and there eject their eggs and sperm synchronously so that fertilisation is achieved within the short life-time of the sperm. The actions must be sufficiently well timed and placed that the eggs gently drop down between the stones and are covered by the female before waiting trout, gulls and other predators eat too many. The process involves good judgement, both hydrodynamic and in timing, since the redd that the female salmon digs to a certain concavity facilitates adpression of the eggs to the interface rather than permitting them to be flushed away downstream. In addition the female must quickly cover the eggs by

57

gently flipping small stones over them in a tail-flicking action similar to, but gentler than, the violent digging beats that she had employed just a few minutes before. As in so much of the salmon's life a sensitivity for time and a sequence of activities is in operation.

Spawning is perhaps the stage of the life cycle most sensitive to disruption since the physical-chemical and social requirements are most constraining at this time. Management meets the concerns in various ways in which development of artificial spawning systems (streams or hatcheries), improvement of existing spawning grounds, protection from incompatible developments, and escapement of stock from the fishery are all critical. For the latter, the escapement must be from the mid-point of the run, to a maximum number and no more, otherwise repeated spawning on constrained beds by less productive late arrivals digs out the earlier laid better stock. Of course such mid-point stock may also be premium fish from the industry point of view. With mixed stocks entering a fishery, as can occur in the Fraser and Skeena, considerable complications arise in judging escapements, and there is risk of overfishing, even eliminating, smaller runs which enter the fishery simultaneously with the major stocks. Those small runs may be important to particular groups of fishermen.

ACHILLES HEEL

Fishing technology relies on a knowledge of fish behaviour, which is exploited for human purposes. There are two main exploitable weaknesses shown by the fish in their sensitivities. They can be duped by a false lure which attracts them to a hook, and they can be insufficiently responsive to a dangerous, human-made situation so that they do not escape in time.

Our Native Indians traditionally exploited these weaknesses with weirs, traps, and simple bone hooks on cedar lines. From these devices and western technology have sprung the existing seines, gill nets, the fishing wheel and an enormous variety of hook-and-lures.[14]

The hook-and-lure type gears of commercial troller and sports fishermen have as an objective provoking the salmon to bite and get hooked. The lures simulate food, and are dependent on the level of the salmon's motivation to eat. They cannot be used in such a way that they scare the fish, either through moving unnaturally or the smell of aversive chemicals. Surprisingly there seems to be little systematic research into the effectiveness of lures. This may be due to the intractability of the problem since salmon responses to food and lures can vary with the species, with time of year, with time of day, with satiation from previous feeding, and with many other less obvious variables. It has been shown for instance that identical lures used by skilled fishermen under strict instructions still gave variable results between individuals.[15]

Purse seines and the now disused fishing traps have certain points in common, enough to group them both under the heading trap-type gears. Both rely on a social behaviour pattern, that of schooling. In the context of a narrow river channel, "following" is a more descriptive term, but the behaviour pattern is the same: the response of many fish to perform the same action in a group or in sequence. Purse seines are operated by the fisherman locating a large school of salmon and setting his net around it so that the fish are captured by closing the bottom of the net by the purse-strings. Implicit in this operation is that the seiner is not attracting the fish himself (but perhaps this may be a future technological development) but has located a naturally occurring and tight school (Fish intensely responding one to another) and is able to surround

PLATE 9
Massed Gill Netters

it without provoking escape behaviour. Implicit also in the use of purse seines is that a milling school will be easier to surround than one that is actively migrating. The shoreline fish traps in contrast relied on large moving schools and directed them by deflectors through a narrow door into a large trap from which they could be brailed out. The point in common between seine and trap is that they rely on the social behaviour of salmon to stay close to one another or to follow, and must be designed and operated so as not to interfere with this social behaviour pattern by provoking the opposed self-protective behaviour of escape.

The remaining gear in use today, the gill-net, can be character-ized as an enmeshing-type gear. Fish attempt to pass through the light-weight net but get caught by their gill covers as they push their heads through the meshes but cannot pass completely. As with trap-type gear, gill nets must obviously not generate direct escape responses away from the net prior to enmeshment, but there are a number of un-knowns about the extent to which other behaviours affect catchability. It is possible that schooling, or mass escape after some of the fish of a school have become enmeshed, could facilitate enmeshment of large numbers. It is believed that detection of gill net threads may be diff-icult for the salmon either visually or by touch, and that the initial response to slight restraints to swimming caused by the mesh is a thrust forward rather than a withdrawal. If so, the lighter, stronger and less visible the thread the better. Thus nylon nets are more effective than linen. On the other hand, schooling behaviour may only be significant to the gill netter insofar as it concentrates fish along routes which can be predicted or detected by a good fisherman. Salmon behaviour is so variable that perhaps we should consider the gill-net as the general purpose gear which is not dependent on, although it will obviously ben-efit from, intensive activity. It should be noted, however, that a gill net fishery can be of such magnitude in a confined space (such as the mouth of the Skeena River) that it effectively acts as an enormous, ever changing, multi-walled floating trap.[16] In such cases it is dependent as with other trap-type gears on intense activity of the fish, such as mass entry to the estuary from the sea.

The significant behaviour patterns of the salmon for fishing can therefore be seen as feeding, schooling, activity level and escape responses. In general the last is to be minimised in the early stages of gear-fish interaction both by good design and operation. The other behaviours are important in that, when occurring intensely, the salmon become vulnerable to various gears. Perhaps the next technological developments will be to artificially induce intense activity in manners exemplified by the use of attractant lights at night and other forms of herding fish. Such developments are in hand and obviously need controlling as they progress.

CONCLUSIONS FOR MANAGEMENT

The fishability of salmon is the composite result of their varying activities in juxtaposition with fishing gear. The fishery manager needs to appreciate the behavioural complexities of the situation and his appreciation must encompass the varying responses of different stocks in apparently similar situations.

It is unreasonable to expect single managers to cope with this total complexity, at least at the levels of international, national and even regional decision-making. Here it is imperative that decision-making be the result of team considerations, with a corps of biologists having sufficient involvement so that they can ensure that management is based on good bioscience. This is nowadays taken to be self-evident; but it may not be so obvious that such a corps of biologists should include those with professional expertise in animal behaviour. This is

62

PLATE 10
The Last of the Traps: Sooke

B.C. Government Photo

particularly necessary during a management period when a philosophy of systems analysis, in which salmon tend to be regarded as statistically predictable automata, rather than living, individually varying animals, is being emphasised.

REFERENCES

1. This chapter was written while the author was on sabbatical leave from the University of Victoria. It condenses original data and other information made available through employment and contract research at the Biological Station, Nanaimo, of Environment Canada, over a period of almost 20 years since 1957. I wish to express my appreciation for the co-operation of many scientists from Environment Canada at Nanaimo and elsewhere. In particular I must acknowledge my working association over many years with J.R. Brett and C. Groot.

2. It is not practical to reference all the significant biological studies and monographs on salmon, but the following can be taken as a means of entering the literature: HART, J.L. Pacific Fishes of Canada. Fisheries Research Board of Canada Bulletin No. 180, 1973. 740 pp. For sockeye salmon there is a substantial monograph: FOERSTER, R.E. The Sockeye Salmon. Fisheries Research Board of Canada Bulletin No 162, 1968. 422 pp. An authoritative popular book is: NETBOY, A. The Salmon. Their Fight for Survival. Boston: Houghton Mifflin 1974. 613 pp. For specifically behaviour studies see the most recent of a long series of papers: HOAR, W.S. "Smolt Transformation: Evolution, Behaviour and Physiology", Journal of the Fisheries Research Board of Canada 33, 1976, pp. 1234 - 1252.

3. Introductions to Ethology are given in: HINDE, R.A. Animal Behaviour. A Synthesis of Ethology and Comparative Psychology. New York: McGraw-Hill, 1970. 876 pp. EIBIL-EIBESFELDT, I. Ethology. The Biology of Behaviour. New York. 1970. 530 pp.

4. The five species of Pacific salmon in North America are: the pink salmon Oncorhynchus gorbuscha, the chum Oncorhynchus keta, the coho Oncorhynchus kisutch, the sockeye Oncorhynchus nerka, and the spring (or chinook) Oncorhynchus tshawytscha.

5. A discussion of behavioural corollaries to predation as a feeding strategy is presented in WATT, K.E.F. Ecology and Resource Management: New York: McGraw-Hill, 1968 450 pp. HOLLING, C.S. "The Functional Response of Invertebrate Predators to Prey Density", Memoirs of the Entomological Society of Canada 48, 1966. 88 pp.

6. For schooling as a behaviour the following provides an introduction: KEENLEYSIDE, M.M.H. Some Aspects of the Schooling of Fish. Behaviour 8(2-3), 1955. pp. 183 -248

7. Animal learning is an enormous topic in its own right, to which reference 3 provides an introduction.

8. Territory is taken in this chapter to mean defended space as opposed to home range, which is the space over which an animal will range, but does not defend against a conspecific.

9. GROOT, C. On the Orientation of Young Sockeye Salmon (Oncorhynchus nerka)during their seaward migration out of Lakes. Leiden: E.J. Brill, 1965, 198 pp.

10. ELLIS, D.V. A Survey of the Behaviour of Salmon on Spawning Migration through a large River System. Fisheries Research Board of Canada Technical Report No. 876, 1966. 32 pp.

11. "Homing" means returning to a place formerly occupied instead of going to other equally probable places. GERKIN, S.D. "Evidence for the Concept of Home Range and Territory in Stream Fishes", Ecology. 34, 1953. pp. 347-365. But see also for a critique of the concepts: HARDEN JONES, F.R. Fish Migration. London: Arnold, 1968. 325 pp.

12. The social behaviour and signal displays of Pacific salmon are similar to those in Atlantic salmon, trout and char, which have been well reviewed in various publications. See for example JONES, J.W. The Salmon. London: Collins 1959. 192 pp. Similar but largely unpublished studies on Pacific salmon have been made at the Nanaimo Biological Station by a number of scientists and particularly C. Groot.

13. STUART, T.A. The Leaping Behaviour of Salmon and Trout at Falls and Obstructions. Scottish Home Department Freshwater and Salmon Fisheries Research No 28. 1962. 42 pp.

14. See for example McKERVILL, H. The Salmon People. Sidney: Gray, 1967.

15. ARGUE, A.W. A Study of Factors Affecting Exploitation of Pacific Salmon in the Canadian Gantlet Fishery of Juan de Fuca Strait University of British Columbia, M.Sc. thesis 1970. 259 pp.

16. TODD, I.S. The Selective Action of Gillnets on Sockeye (Oncorhynchus nerka) and Pink Salmon (O. gorbuscha) stocks of the Skeena River System, British Columbia. University of British Columbia. M.Sc. thesis 1969. 141 pp.

CHAPTER 3

CHANGING
MANAGEMENT OBJECTIVES [1]

Ray Hilborn

and

Randall M. Peterman

Environment Canada
and
Institute of Animal Resource Ecology
University of British Columbia

INTRODUCTION

The history of salmon management illustrates the use of a variety of management objectives ranging from simply catching the most fish commercially, to attempting to satisfy the Indian, sports and a number of differing commercial demands simultaneously. To some extent, the nature of each particular management objective has dictated what kind of information was collected, how those data were used to estimate "best" exploitation patterns, and how the harvesting operations were regulated. Whether recognized explicitly or only implicitly, most salmon management agencies and their associated research branches have operated with a similar underlying conceptual framework in mind. This framework, modified from one formalized by Carl J. Walters,[2] is shown in Figure 1,3.

Figure 1,3 illustrates that there is a natural fish system which has a large number of important characteristics (age, size and spatial distribution, vulnerability to fishing gear, sex ratio, reproductive potential, total population size, etc.). However, man's sampling techniques can only measure a subset of the natural system's character-

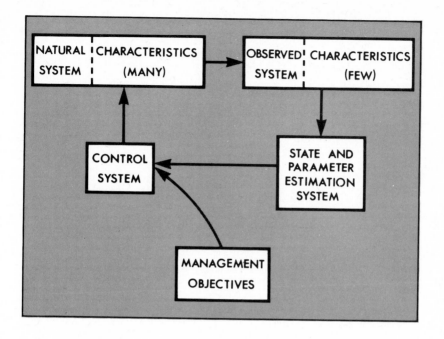

FIGURE 1,3. Conceptual Framework for Management

istics. It is this resulting "observed system," and not the "natural system," which is used in conjunction with various methods of analysis to determine the present state and parameter values of the "natural system" and to predict how it will respond to different management actions (for example, harvest rates). These methods of analysis, which constitute a parameter estimation system, range from trial and error management manipulations to detailed formal mathematical analyses where the biases of sampling methods are taken into account.

The results of the parameter estimation procedure are analyzed in the context of stated management objectives in order to choose the "best" control action to take. For example, should effort or catch be regulated, how much, and where and when should harvesting activities take place? This control system then acts upon the natural system, which in turn affects what is observed.

The first half of this chapter illustrates how management objectives have evolved along with management practices and data analysis techniques. The second half deals with techniques for handling the problems created by today's complex management objectives.

HISTORICAL GOALS
OF SALMON MANAGEMENT

Over 50 percent of the salmon caught in British Columbia come from two major river systems, the Fraser River and the Skeena River. The Fraser has historically supported runs between 2 and 20 million[3] fish each year, while the Skeena has had runs of 1 to 4 million fish.[4] The salmon runs of both rivers have supported native Indian harvests for a few thousand years and commercial harvest since the late 1800s, and they have been regulated by the Federal Government since before 1890. The Skeena River is still regulated by the Federal Government, while the Fraser has been regulated jointly by the Federal Government and the International Pacific Salmon Fisheries Commission (IPSFC) since 1946. There are now three major users of the salmon stocks, the commercial fishermen, the sports fishermen and the native Indians. Pinks, sockeye and chums are harvested almost exclusively by the commercial fishery. Sports fishermen catch mainly coho and chinook, while Indians take small numbers of several species.

It is difficult to determine what the historical goals of management have been, just as it is difficult to determine exactly what current goals are; there has been little documentation of management objectives or the decision-making process. There may be occasional statements such as "...our fishermen should be permitted to take only that portion of the run which is in excess of the number necessary to the perpetuation of the species,"[5] but there may be a large discrepancy between a stated objective and the objective as revealed by management practice. We have had little choice but to look at the regulations that have been in effect, in order to infer the management objectives. We may have mis-interpreted the real objectives because management regulations have resulted from a complex set of considerations. We also wish to review the scientific basis that has been the theoretical underpinning of management practice. There has always been, in theory at least, a very direct connection between the researchers and the management agencies, since the Fisheries Research Board, and more recently the IPSFC, have been the major research agencies.

The Early Years

Anadromous fishes are unique because it is possible to get direct to near-direct estimates of the breeding population. Declining populations led to the very early recognition by salmon managers that overharvesting was possible. In contrast, overexploitation of marine demersal and pelagic fisheries was not recognized as a potential problem until the North Sea catches increased dramatically after World War 1. The realization that the spawning stock of a given year produces the run of the next generation has been the basis for management of salmon stocks since at least 1913.[6] Also it has been recognized at least since 1909 that a sufficient number of spawning adults must be allowed to pass through the fishery,[7] and the management problem has been to determine what constitutes sufficient and to allow that escapement.

Regulations to limit catch have been in effect since 1882 for the Fraser River[8] and 1877 for the Skeena.[9] These regulations have taken three forms: limits on fishing time, fishing location, and fishing gear. Today these are still the dominant forms of regulation.

Management on the Fraser River was confounded in the first half of the 1900's by the occurrence of the Hell's Gate slide in 1913. The dramatic decline of the fishery after that slide has been attributed solely to the mechanical blockage of the river, and the overriding concern of management agencies from 1914 until the construction of the Hell's Gate fish passages in 1941 was the elimination of the obstruction.[10] While the idea probably occurred to many people, there is little documentation to show that consideration was given to the possibility of over-exploitation on the Fraser before 1941. After that year, the objective revealed by management practice seems to have been to allow increased escapements while providing an acceptable commercial catch. The Skeena River also showed a decline in the abundance of salmon during the first half of the century, but this was not as dramatic as that of the Fraser River, and it has long been considered that this decline was due to overharvesting.[11] Indeed, the recognition of overharvesting occurred long before management practice was modified to compensate for it. In the absence of a scientific justification to determine a sufficient level of escapement from the fishery, the Fraser and Skeena management agencies appear to have been giving more weight to commercial catch than to stock rehabilitation.

Lacking a quantitative measure of desired escapement, the primary yardstick available to managers from 1920 to 1950 was the estimated number of spawners in periods of former abundance. However, total runs in 1920-1950 were frequently less than the escapement in former times. But with several thousand fishermen depending upon the fishery for a livelihood, the managers were not prepared to shut down the fishery for the entire season. To further confuse the situation, there was a great uncertainty about the production potential of the stocks. At what level of spawners would they be most productive, and how much

B.C. Archives Photo

of the original spawning grounds had been destroyed by blockages, logging, and other environmental deterioration? In summary, the 1920-1950 period can be characterized by a great uncertainty about sufficient escapement, and by important political constraints which required a sufficient harvest for the commercial fishermen. The objective appears to have been a compromise between pressure applied by fishermen for large catches and the biologists' desire for large escapements.

Maximum Sustained Yield and Quantitative Models

The 1950's brought in the era of extensive use of mathematical models for salmon management.[12] These models permit a determination of specific desired escapement levels. From the stock-recruitment model proposed by Ricker,[13] one can calculate the level of escapement that will produce the maximum sustained yield (MSY). Figure 2,3 shows a stock-recruitment curve for Skeena River sockeye data, from Shepard and Withler.[14] Ricker has shown that the MSY can be achieved by holding the escapement constant at the number of spawners where the production curve is the greatest distance from the 45 degree line. The catch that can be expected for any level of escapement is the difference in height between the 45 degree line and the production curve.

In the context of the real world/observation system/control system diagram presented earlier in this chapter, the Ricker model formed the basis of the parameter estimation system, and determining from this curve the maximum difference between the 45 degree line and the production curve formed part of the control system.

Unfortunately, there were a number of problems left unresolved. Fitting of the Ricker curve to the data was not straightforward. In fact, a Ricker production function accounts for only a small proportion of the variability in the data as shown in Figure 2,3.[15] Arguments have been

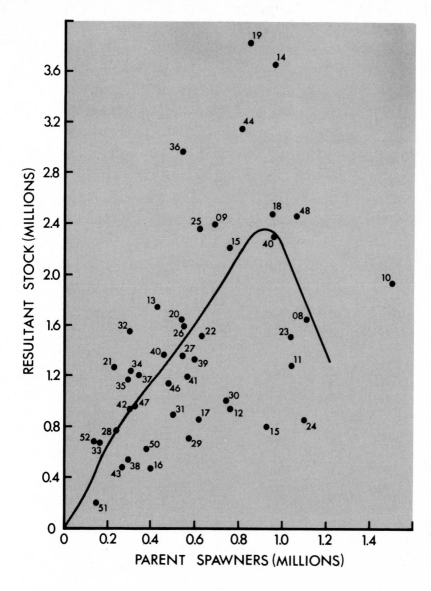

FIGURE 2,3. Skeena River Sockeye Stock-Recruitment Curve

carried on in the literature over how to fit the curve, and which data to include.[16] Many argue that the old data are not relevant to current management,[17] because many conditions have changed through selection, environmental deterioration, and extinction of substocks.

At the same time the question of what constituted the basic stock unit was still unanswered. If there were only one stock being harvested at any given time, there would be no difficulty in achieving desired escapement. However, it is well recognized that both the Fraser and Skeena River sockeye runs are made up of many substocks which have overlapping run timings and different sustainable harvest rates.[18] The management agencies have attempted to harvest the substocks as separately as their run timings will permit.

In addition, there are cases where run timings of different species overlap and such species cannot all be harvested at MSY rates. This has led to the unfortunate situation where, especially on the Skeena River, the commercial harvest of sockeye and pink salmon has been established while the chinook and steelhead populations have continued to decline. This has affected the users of these different species in opposite ways.

Soon after his stock and recruitment paper, Ricker discussed what has proved to be another very serious problem in using his model as a basis for management.[19] The problem is that for a given escapement the resultant run will have a mean and a variance, and that some years will produce very few adults. As Ricker pointed out "...large fluctuations in catch and (sometimes) complete closures of fishing are actually a necessary condition for obtaining maximum average yield from our salmon fisheries."[20] If the management agencies had strictly adhered to the concept of maximum sustained yield, as many fisheries scientists had hoped, fishing would have been completely stopped in certain years.

76

By the end of the 1950's the scientists had quantitative techniques to determine, in principle, desired escapements. The management agencies were aware of this work but faced a very serious problem; the desired escapement levels were usually much larger than they could permit without near-complete cessation of fishing for several years. The agencies were faced with the typical fisheries management problem, trading off between immediate short term yield, and expected long term returns. The overriding concern of the agencies appears to have been provision of a reasonable catch for the commercial fishing fleet in the short term. For example, in 1960 the Skeena Salmon Management Commmittee decided to allow more catch than was desirable on the basis of MSY, because of the poor recent commercial harvests.[21]

The data points in Figure 3,3 show the harvest rate as a function of run size from the Skeena River sockeye for the years 1956-1974. The optimum escapement is about 750,000 spawners for MSY. The curve labelled 'MAX H' represents a fixed escapement, MSY policy, drawn as harvest rate as a function of run size. The curve labelled MIN (H - 0.6) represents a constant catch of 600,000. It can be seen that in most years the harvest was higher than optimal, but that recently (1967-1974), the harvest rates have been very close to optimal by fixed escapement standards. Walters[22] has interpreted this to indicate that in the last 5 - 8 years the efficiency of the regulation has improved so that the management agency is now operating in practice and in theory on a fixed escapement, maximum sustained yield basis. We agree that this appears to be the case, but there has not been a run of less than 1 million since 1966, and it is in such low run years that there is strong pressure to increase harvest and decrease escapement.

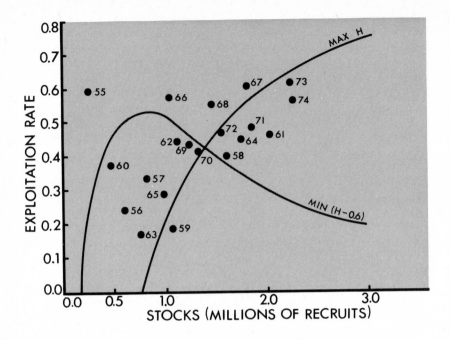

FIGURE 3,3. Harvest Rate Plotted Against Run Size for Two Objectives, Maximum Systained Yield (Max H) and Constant Catch of 600,000 (H - .6)   Redrawn from Walters.[22]

Economic Considerations

Once the maximum sustained yield concept had become firmly entrenched as a biological basis for management, the economists were quick to point out its shortcomings.[23] Gordon[24] and others noted that from an economic viewpoint, maximum sustained biological yield is rarely optimal and Crutchfield and Pontecorvo[25] suggest that in the absence of a complex societal goal the fishery should be managed to maximize economic yield. The first chapter in this book, written by Crutchfield discusses this topic in more detail.

Summary of Past Goals

Very early in the history of salmon management, the goal was
to satisfy commercial fishing demand as much as possible. Then, as it
became generally understood that a certain unspecified escapement was
needed to perpetuate a stock, managers attempted to regulate the
commercial fishery. Conflicts arose between biologists who wanted
large escapements and fishermen who wanted large catches. When
mathematical models showed how to determine the escapement required
for MSY, managers had a more tangible basis for decision-making.
However, the pressures of various fishing interests continued to play an
important role, even though those interests could not be well-quantified.
It is ironic that just as the agencies are beginning to achieve MSY (on
the Skeena sockeye at least), the inadequacies of this theory are becoming widely recognized. It now seems likely that this objective will
be replaced by more explicit complex goals.[26]   In the next few sections,
we will discuss recent management objectives and methods for handling
some issues raised by these new goals.

RECENT MANAGEMENT OBJECTIVES

Although the point is still vigorously debated, more fisheries
managers and researchers are recognizing that the needs of various interest groups ranging from sports and Indian fishermen to commercial
processors must be considered, and that a wide variety of management
options must be contemplated.[27]   A simple example will illustrate how
the MSY concept is inadequate in the context of these complications.
A sockeye stock which should be exploited at a high rate in order to
achieve MSY may overlap in run timing with a steelhead stock which
cannot sustain large catches. A key question asks how much the commercial sockeye catch should be reduced in order to keep the steelhead

PLATE 12
The Too Efficient Salmon Wheel

B.C. Archives Pho

80

stock and its resultant sports catch at a reasonable level. The MSY concept provides no basis for a manager to formally evaluate such a trade-off. Furthermore, such a theory does not help to resolve the conflict between short-term goals of satisfying demand and long-term goals of conserving fish. Yet such conflicts are often at the heart of many management problems.

Thus, the existence of more complex objectives which include social, economic, and biological components makes the fisheries manager's job more difficult. There are two critical issues raised, (1) how to formally express such complex objectives, and (2) how to measure the performance of management options on the basis of such objectives.[28]

Problems Created by Complex Objectives

In recent years, computer simulation models have demonstrated the capability of handling many complexities in natural systems. Examples and useful keys to this extensive literature are given by Jeffers,[29] Patten,[30] Watt[31] and Wiegert.[32] In addition to handling natural system complexities, a large number of social and economic considerations can be added to biological system models. The only limitation of modeling in this context comes from our conceptual understandings of these non-biological parts of the system and how they can be quantified.

However, simulation models are only a partial solution to the problem of complex management objectives. Even with models, and perhaps because of them, the manager is confronted with a large array of indicators for each management option tested. This large number of indicators forces the decision-maker to do some relative importance ranking of the components of his objective. It might be relatively simple to state, for example, that maximizing commercial catch is twice as important as maximizing sports catch; however, there are two problems. First, the value of any indicator is not linearly related to the level of that indicator; for example, there are limits to how many fish commercial boats can handle in a season. Second, the weightings on different indicators are not independent. For example, more emphasis might be put on the maximization of sockeye commercial catch if it turned out that the sports demand for coho were saturated under present conditions. An additional point is that each indicator fluctuates over time. This time variation issue is important because one management option might result in a stable catch over time and another option might give a highly variable catch but with the same mean. Which option is better?

Given these problems of time variation and non-linear, non-independent weightings for different indicators, how can a decision-maker's complex objective be quantitatively described? Some of these issues were recognized but no solutions were offered at the recent symposium on optimum sustained yield.[33] However, some powerful recently-developed techniques are now available.

Possible Solutions

Quantifying Objectives

Multiattribute utility analysis is a decision-theoretic tool that has recently been used to analyze some problems of salmon management.[34] Here we will briefly discuss how this technique can be used to resolve some of the problems posed above; it is a method for quantifying complex objectives.

Utility analysis is used to determine an individual's utility function (a quantitative description of his preferences). It is assumed that utility functions of individuals reflect the social and political climate in which decisions are made, and that there are differences in preferences and value judgments between individuals.

Consider a river that produces one type of salmon; a manager has a number of tools at his disposal that can yield a total catch of between zero and 1 million fish. We wish first to determine how 'satisfied' the manager will be with each level of catch. Let us arbitrarily scale 'satisfaction' (or utility) to be zero at the lowest level of catch and one at the highest level. If adding 1000 fish to the catch when the catch is low is of equal value to the manager as adding 1000 fish to the catch when the catch is high, then the manager's utility function is a straight line, as in function A of Figure 4,3. In this diagram curve A gives an equal value to each additional fish; curve B values additional fish more at low catches than at high catches. Curve A represents the implicit assumption of the maximum sustained yield concept. However, it seems unlikely that curve A represents any real manager's utility function. Unless there are a large number of alternative fishing areas, the manager would probably be very averse to a year of zero catch. This has been demonstrated by the fact that even in the poorest of run years, some catch has always been allowed on the Fraser and Skeena Rivers. Thus a more plausible utility function for a fisheries manager would be depicted by curve B in Figure 4,3. Increasing the catch from zero to 100,000 increases the manager's utility much more than increasing the catch from 900,000 to 1 million.

If the manager were considering two indicators of performance, then multiattribute utility analysis could combine these two into a single aggregate function. A simple example might involve a river that yielded a commercial catch and a recreational catch. Using multiattribute utility analysis, the utility functions for the two indicators could be derived separately. The second step would be to determine the trade-offs between the two indicators. The essence of the technique is that once both indicators are scaled in their own utility units, it is possible to determine how much of one utility unit would be traded for a fixed amount of the other type of unit. The utility function determines

83

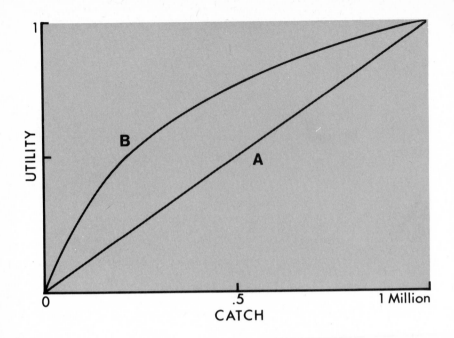

FIGURE 4,3. Utility Functions

a currency of exchange for raw indicators, such as sports or commercial catch. This type of analysis can be extended to a large number of indicators, but it is usually found that an individual only considers about five or six different factors.

We do not propose that the use of multiattribute utility analysis can solve the problems of complex objectives in salmon management, but it does appear to provide a very useful method for quantitatively describing objective functions of individuals involved in fisheries management, for visualizing trade-offs between different objectives, and for stimulating discussion on differences in value judgments.

PLATE 13
Fraser River Cannery

B.C. Archives Photo

After the objective has been quantitatively described, a way is needed to evaluate it for a variety of options in order to obtain a set of "optimal" management actions. Formal optimization techniques constitute one set of evaluation methods.[35] Walters[36] and Hilborn[37] have derived management guidelines in terms of state-dependent harvest rules through use of dynamic programming (Figure 3,3). The major drawback of most optimization methods is that they either require a linear system (for linear programming) or a very simple one (for dynamic programming). What can be done with the latter technique is to use a simplified analog of a more complex model to derive optimal solutions, and then to test the validity of these solutions with the large model.[38]

A second approach to determining optimal management acts is through less formal, more heurisitic devices such as nomograms.[39] Here, a complex system model is run under a series of management regimes and various social, economic and biological indicators are evaluated. The time series of these indicators are compressed into averages, maxima, minima, variances, or whatever other indices are appropriate. Contours of the values of these indicators are plotted for each enhancement (see Figure 5,3). Figure 5,3 on the following page shows a nomogram for one example indicator, minimum annual pink Salmon catch.

Optimal management actions can be determined with nomograms through a series of simple steps. A weighted summation of a group of indicator surfaces can be performed, where the weights are the relative importance values given to thos indicators. This summation could be

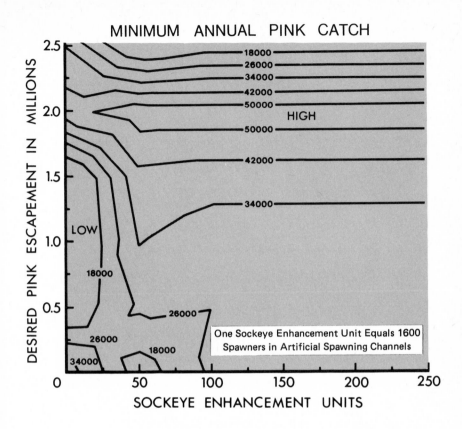

FIGURE 5,3. A Nomogram Showing Values of One Indicator, Minimum Annual Pink Salmon Catch, as Pink Escapement and Amount of Sockeye Enhancement are Varied. One Sockeye Enhancement Unit Equals 1,600 Spawners in Artificial Spawning Channels. Redrawn from Peterman (1975)[39]

done using mathematical weightings and summings or by overlaying sets of shaded transparencies, where shading is equivalent to weighting.[40]

However, any method for handling complex objectives and numerous options should be easily understandable to managers to ensure that the approach is useful. In this context, nomograms have several characteristics which make them effective devices for bridging the credibility gap between modellers and managers.

1. A large amount of information is compressed into an easily understood format.

2. The user can "experiment" with alternative management options, without having to use a computer.

3. Unavoidable trade-offs between indicators become evident by examining shapes of indicator surfaces.

4. A user can determine the best combination of management actions that will achieve his own objective.

5. Constraints imposed by factors not included in the model can easily be added by blocking out areas on certain indicator surfaces which are unacceptable.

Both this nomogram technique[41] and formal optimization procedures [42,43] have recently been applied to salmon management problems. However, the results of these studies do not provide magical solutions to salmon management problems. Instead, they help to identify areas of the "control system" which are worthy of further study and to compare different management actions given different objectives.

Uncertainties Affect Choice of Management Actions

As we have described, there are several formal methods available for coping with the special problems of complex management objectives. However, these approaches are not sufficient in themselves, because no matter how much research effort is put into understanding the natural system and identifying preferences or objectives, managers will always be faced with large areas of unknowns. How should the "optimal" set of actions which were derived from the nomograms, formal optimization, or other techniques be modified in order to account for these uncertainties? We suggest six criteria or areas of analysis which should become part of the process of evaluation of management options:

1.   A policy failure analysis needs to be performed for each option. The probability of some policy or act not working may be very small (for example, disease sweeping through a hatchery), but the costs associated with such a rare event may be very high. Different management actions will have different probabilities of failure and different costs of failure; both should be evaluated and the options compared.[44]

2.   The objectives which managers are trying to achieve will most likely change after some period of time; witness the rapid shift in emphasis to the environmentalist's viewpoint in recent years. Therefore, the sensitivity of any management option to changes in objectives should be assessed. Options which would be least sensitive would be those which were on a relatively flat region of the objective function surface (instead of on a peak with steep surrounding slopes).

3.   Some consideration must be given to the effect any particular set of management actions will have on the ability of the natural system to successfully cope with natural or man-induced perturbations which might occur. This resilience concept[45] is of utmost importance because it has been shown[46] that the harvesting efforts themselves tend to reduce the ability of the system to respond to perturbations and that maximum sustained yield harvest rates put the system near its limits of response, thereby increasing the probability that any disturbance will have disastrous consequences.

4.   Despite recent attempts to control development of the salmon fishing fleet by license limitation, the fleet's catching power continues to increase dramatically.[47] This trend increases the possibility that deviations from desired exploitation rates could result in stock depletion and enormous economic, social, and biological costs. Such costs would

depend upon the management option in effect (for example, gear composition of fleet, number of open fishing days) and therefore, this type of sensitivity analysis to control errors should become an integral part of policy evaluation.

5.   Fishing pressure undoubtedly causes changes in the characteristics of the natural system by selectively removing certain genetic types or changing the competitive balance between species. How sensitive is the "optimal" policy to this evolution in the natural system? This sensitivity can be assessed, for example, by making different assumptions about stock reproduction parameters and by evaluating each management option for each assumption.

6.   Finally, because the system is continually changing, there should be some value attached to gaining information about how the system is changing. A formal approach to this area has been made by Walters and Hilborn.[48] In their example, some advantage is given to management options which deliberately vary escapement over wide ranges, instead of stabilizing it. This fluctuation in spawners permits the acquisition of recruitment data over wider ranges of escapements than would have been possible with stabilized escapement. These wider-ranging data would be more useful in detecting changes in recruitment curves due to loss of substocks, for example.

The above six topics should be added to the classical "objective function" approach to formal evaluation of management options. This new approach will not eliminate uncertainties faced by managers, but at least the proposed management policies will be more thoroughly explored prior to their implementation. Walters' chapter later in this book presents a framework for inclusion in formal policy analysis of some of the foregoing points on uncertainty.

90

PLATE 14
Brailing out a Seine

B.C. Government Photo

PROSPECTS FOR THE FUTURE

Current trends indicate that in the future fisheries managers will consider social, economic, and biological criteria in more explicit, quantitative ways when evaluating management options. Furthermore, the present intensity of harvest and the rapid increase in catching power of fishing fleets means that trial-and-error management will no longer be acceptable - costs of errors will be too high. Therefore, explicit consideration of sources of uncertainty and error will become the rule, rather than the exception. The complexity of the resulting decision-making process will be far beyond the intuitive abilities of most managers. Application of computer models, as described here and in Walters' chapter, provides a useful way of handling this complexity. However, it should be emphasized that such models should only be used as a supplement to, not a replacement for, the normal decision-making process. In fact, computer analyses of management options would be totally misleading unless they were combined with the judgment and intuition of experienced managers.[49]

The use of computer models in evaluation of management options requires a more quantitative description of objectives than is the usual practice. The technique of utility analysis described earlier provides a framework to do this, and it also serves as a valuable means of identification of areas of conflict between different interest groups. However, as a result, decision makers will also have to make explicit the kinds of trade-offs they are willing to make (for example, how much less commercial catch they would tolerate for a given increase in sport catch.)

It is doubtful that in the foreseeable future each salmon stock or species will be managed with all of the above social, economic, biological and sources -of-uncertainty criteria in mind. Instead, it is more likely that particular stocks will be managed by considering only subsets of these varied criteria. For instance, as long as there were other salmon stocks around to satisfy some sources of demand, the risk might be taken to enhance a stock which had a low probability of successful enhancement, but which had huge payoffs if the enhancement worked.

Another trend which is just beginning to emerge in salmon management is the recognition that an observational model is needed, a model which relates what is observed to the natural system, and which accounts for sampling biases. This will help the parameter estimation system of Figure 1,3 to yield results closer to the "true" parameter values. This notion applies to other fisheries as well.

The existence of the more sophisticated tools for policy evaluation such as utility analysis, systems analysis, and simulation does not eliminate the need for documentation of the steps in decision-making as they are made. We can only learn from our past mistakes and improve fisheries management in the future if we understand how and why decisions were made.

Quantitative approaches to definition of objectives and evaluation of management options are probably here to stay; it is only a question of how rapidly such techniques will become widely used. These approaches, judiciously combined with intuition and experience, will enable fisheries managers to make more responsible and comprehensive decisions. However, it is essential that researchers become involved with managers in development of such management programmes, otherwise the techniques that evolve will be largely irrelevant exercises.

REFERENCES

1. Parts of this study have been supported by Environment Canada and the International Institute for Applied Systems Analysis, Laxenburg, Austria. The order of the authors was decided by a coin toss. We gratefully acknowledge P.A. Larkin for his extensive comments on a draft.

2. Personal communication, Carl J. Walters, Institute of Resource Ecology, University of British Columbia, Vancouver, B.C. , Canada, February, 1976.

3. WARD, F.J. and LARKIN, P.A. "Cyclic dominance in Adams River sockeye salmon." International Pacific Salmon Fisheries Commission, Progress Report No. 11, 1964, p. 116.

4. MILNE. D.J., "The Skeena River salmon fishery, with special reference to sockeye salmon." J. Fish. Res. Board Canada, 12., 1955. pp. 451-485.

5. BABCOCK, J.P. Report of the Commissioner of Fisheries of British Columbia. 1902, 1909, 1913.

6. Ibid.

7. Ibid.

8. ROUNSEFELL. GEORGE A. and KELEZ, G.B. "The Salmon and salmon fisheries of Swiftsure Bank, Puget Sound and the Fraser River. " U.S. Department of Commerce, Bureau of Fisheries Bulletin No. 27, 1938.

9. MILNE, D.J. op.cit.

10. THOMPSON, WILLIAM F. "Effect of obstruction at Hell's Gate on the sockeye salmon of the Fraser River." International Pacific Salmon Fisheries Commission Bulletin No. 1, 1945, p. 175.

11. MILNE, D.J., op. cit.

12. RICKER, W.E. "Stock and recruitment." J. Fish Res. Board Canada. No. 11. 1954. pp. 559-623.

13.   Ibid.

14.   SHEPARD, M.P. and WITHLER, F.C. "Spawning stock size and resultant production for Skeena sockeye." J. Fish. Res. Board Canada, 15, 1959, pp. 1007-1025.

15.   SHEPARD, M.P. and WITHLER, F.C. op.cit.

16.   TANAKA, S. "Studies of the question of reproduction of salmon stocks." INPFC Bulletin No. 9, 1962. pp. 85-90.

17.   RICKER, W.E. and SMITH, H.D. "A revised interpretation of the history of the Skeena River sockeye salmon (Oncorhyncus nerka)." J. Fish. Res. Board Canada, 32, 1975. pp. 1369 - 1381.

18.   LARKIN, P.A. and MCDONALD, J.G. "Factors in the population biology of the sockeye salmon of the Skeena River," J. Anim. Ecol., 37, 1968. pp. 229-258.

19.   RICKER, W.E. "Maximum sustained yields from fluctuating environments and mixed stocks." J. Fish. Res. Board Canada, 15, 1958. pp. 991-1006.

20.   Ibid.

21.   Skeena Salmon Management Committee. Annual Report. 1960.

22.   WALTERS, C.J. "Optimal harvest strategies for salmon in relation to environmental variability and uncertainty about production parameters." J. Fish. Res. Board Canada, 32, 1975. pp. 1777-1784.

23.   GORDON, S. "Economic theory of a common property resource: the fishery." J. Polit. Econ., 62, 1954. pp. 124-142.

24.   Ibid.

25.   CRUTCHFIELD, JAMES A. and PONTECORVO, GIULIO. The Pacific Salmon Fisheries. A Study of Irrational Conservation. John Hopkins Press. 1969.

26. ROEDEL, P.M. (ed). Optimum Sustained Yield as a Concept in Fisheries Management. Spec. Publ. No. 9, Amer. Fisheries Soc. Wash. D.C. 1975.

27. Ibid.

28. POWERS J.E., LACKEY, R.T. and ZUBOY, J.R. "Decision making in recreational fisheries management: an analysis." Trans. Amer. Fish. Soc., 104, 1975. pp. 630-634.

29. JEFFERS, J.N.R. (ed). Mathematical Models in Ecology. Oxford: Blackwell Sci. Publ., 1972.

30. PATTEN, B.C. (ed) Systems Analysis and Simulation in Ecology. New York: Academic Press, Vol.1, 1971, Vol.2, 1972, Vol. 3, 1975.

31. WATT, K.E.F. Ecology and Resource Management. New York: McGraw-Hill Book Company, 1968.

32. WIEGERT, R.G. "Simulation models of ecosystems." Ann. Rev. Ecol. Syst., 6. 1975. pp. 311-338.

33. ROEDEL, P.M. (ed). op. cit.

34. KEENEY, R.L. "A utility function for examining policy affecting salmon in the Skeena River." J. Fish. Res. Board Canada, in press, 1977. See also HILBORN, R. and WALTERS,C.J. "Differing goals of salmon management on the Skeena River." J. Fish. Res. Board, Canada, in press, 1977.

35. WATT, K.E.F. op. cit.

36. WALTERS, C.J. op. cit.

37. HILBORN, R. "Optimal exploitation of multiple stocks by a common fishery: a new methodology," J. Fish. Res. Board Canada, 33, No. 1, 1976. pp. 1-5.

38. HOLLING, C.S., DANTZIG, G.B., BASKERVILLE, G., JONES, D.D., and CLARK, W.C. "A case study of forest ecosystem/pest management." Proc. Canad. Conf. Applied Systems Analysis, in press, 1976.

39. PETERMAN, R.M. "New techniques for policy evaluation in ecological systems: methodology for a case study of Pacific salmon fisheries." J. Fish. Res. Board Canada, 32, No. 11, 1975. pp. 2179-2188. See also PETERMAN, R.M. "Graphical evaluation of environmental management options: examples from a forest-insect pest system," Ecol. Modelling, in press, 1977.

40. PETERMAN, R.M., 1975(a), op. cit.

41. Ibid.

42. See WALTERS C.J. op.cit.; HILBORN, R. (1976) op.cit;

43. LORD, G.D. "Characterization of the optimum data acquisition and management of a salmon fishery as a stochastic dynamic program." Fish. Bull., 71, No. 4. 1973. pp. 1029-1037. See also WALTERS, C.J. and HILBORN, R. "Adaptive control of fishing systems." J. Fish. Res. Board Canada, 33, No. 1.(1976), pp. 145-159.

44. HOLLING, C.S. and CLARK, W.C. "Notes towards a science of ecological management."in VAN DOBBEN, W.H. and LOWE-McCONNEL, R.H. (eds), Unifying Concepts in Ecology. The Hague: Dr. W. Junk, B.V. Publ. 1975. See also PETERMAN, R.M. "Ocean effects in salmon." Prog. Rep. PR-3, Institute of Resource Ecology, University of British Columbia, Vancouver, B.C., Canada. 1975b. 37pp.

45. HOLLING, C.S. "Resilience and stability of ecological systems." Ann. Rev. Ecol. Syst., Vol. 4, pp. 1-23. Palo Alto: Annual Review Inc. 1973.

46. PETERMAN, R.M. "A simple mechanism which causes collapsing stability regions in commercial fisheries," W-8, Institute of Resource Ecology, University of British Columbia, Vancouver, B.C., Canada. 1976. 38 pp.

47. LOFTUS. K.H. "Science for Canada's fisheries rehabilitation needs." J. Fish. Res. Board Canada, 33, No.8, 1976. pp. 1822-1857.

48. WALTERS, C.J. and HILBORN, R. op.cit.

49.   WALTERS, C.J. and BUNNELL, F. "A computer management game of land use in British Columbia." J. Wildlife Mgmt., 35, No. 4. (1971). pp. 644-657. See also DRUCKER, P.F. Technology, Management and Society. New York: Harper and Row, 1970.

PLATE 15
The Moment of Truth

B.C. Government Photo

99

PRACTICAL MANAGEMENT

"...if each excludes the other, one will always
be cold and one will always have
poor fishing. "

"...the history of the Department of Fisheries
in managing and protecting the salmon
resources of British Columbia has
been an impressive one."

"...the objective now is to achieve socio-economic
goals on a sustained basis through
wise use of the resource."

"A question arises as to whether those who left
the industry are better or worse off
than before they left it."

"...limited entry means...social and economic
change with all the consequences, bad and
good, that such change provokes."

B.C. Government Photo

101

PLATE 17

CHAPTER 4

NEW APPROACHES TO
CANADIAN RECREATIONAL FISHERIES

P.A. Meyer

Department of Fisheries and the Environment

THE RECREATORS

Salmon sport fishermen and, more broadly, recreators, hold the widest constituency of any of the referent groups associated with Pacific salmon. The boy with the fishing pole on a dock, the man sitting quietly mooching in a coastal inlet, the fisherman standing hip-deep in a fast-flowing stream, or the one of thousands watching the salmon spawn at Adams River are all salmon recreators. Even those now too old to actively participate as recreators again and again stress the importance of the opportunities offered by Pacific salmon.

At present, British Columbia's sport fishermen are predominantly male. Women have traditionally not been involved in sport fishing to an appreciable extent, and are only now beginning to participate in greater numbers. Within the broader recreational category perhaps best captured by the term "viewing", they have participated more fully, this latter pursuit tending to be more family or group oriented in nature.

Salmon recreation depends on distribution of population, location of opportunities, and access. In British Columbia population is concentrated in the Lower Mainland and on southern Vancouver Island. Access to the north and the east is difficult and although salmon recreational opportunities are available across the Province, it is not surprising that the heaviest recreational pressures take place in the Lower

Mainland/Fraser Valley; on Vancouver Island; and in the Gulf of Georgia and eastern Juan de Fuca Strait. From these centres demand radiates to more distant recreational areas, where those willing to travel further distances for a salmon recreating opportunity of special importance to them are more prevalent. Others, satisfied by some alternative experience closer to their home, are "selected out" of those more distant sites.

The salmon sport fisherman is often assumed a "meat" fisherman, or, alternatively, an elitist whirling handmade flies on his light-weight line in intricate patterns prior to casting for the elusive steelhead. Both images are true for some fishermen, but are insensitive to the broader range of satisfactions provided by the sport fishing experience. Sport fishermen have been further categorized by the primary species they sought, so that they were referred to as "steelheaders", "coho fishermen", "trout fishermen", and so on. Again, this categorization is true for many. The avid fisherman does consider the species he will seek and the type of gear or technique required to be successful. On the other hand, it is becoming increasingly apparent that these different "groups" of fishermen share great commonalities in their particular sporting pursuits.

The non-consumptive salmon recreator has generally been "noted in passing". Only at such places as the Adams River and Weaver Creek spawning channel, the Big Qualicum project and Capilano Hatchery, have their recreational pursuits been emphasized. Yet, with the increasing concern for natural environments, it is becoming evident that much of the recreational public at large may not feel that they have to consume the salmon resource in order to draw satisfaction from the opportunities its existence affords.

PLATE 18
Carrying Capacity?

Victoria Press Photo by J. Ryan

RECREATIONAL NEEDS

The sport fisherman had traditionally been considered by many to be only "after fish". This single purpose approach has been steadily eroded of late. In 1974, for example, Bryan[1], in a study in tidal waters, identified more than thirteen motivations associated with sport fishing. (See Table 1,4). His findings should not be taken to conclude that sport fish abundance is unimportant. Sport fishermen do want more fish[2], and catch per unit of effort adjacent to urban areas is relatively poor.[3] A proper response to the recreational needs of sport fishermen will thus involve protection and enhancement of sport fish stocks, but equally important, attention to a broader range of satisfactions. Bryan concludes:

> The pressing demands of civilization are acting
> to both reduce the supply of the characteristics
> of a natural environment close to population
> centres while, at the same time, increasing the
> demand for these characteristics. Sport fishing
> represents an ideal outlet for the frustrations of
> modern living in that it produces multiple benefits
> with few social costs.[4]

THE VALUE OF RECREATION

All too often in our modern society the words "value" and "dollar" are treated synonymously. In point of fact, dollars may have very little to say about the satisfaction derived from many salmon-related recreational pursuits. A strike on the line in the solitude of a breaking dawn, the closeness of a shared experience with wife, child or friend, are often described as "priceless". The degree to which such opportunities impact directly upon the health and peace of mind of British Columbians, particularly those in urban areas, is only now being studied.

TABLE 1,4

SPORT FISHERMEN MOTIVATIONS
TIDAL AREA OF
GULF OF GEORGIA

Motivation	Primary Motive Percentage
To be outdoors	21.4
To take it easy and get rid of tension	28.2
To eat fresh fish	3.1
Change from working pressures	7.6
The experience of a catch	4.4
To take family and/or friends out	11.3
Change from home pressures	1.9
To do something different	5.5
Solitude	4.7
Good fishing available	2.3
Fair fishing available	2.7
To enjoy the scenery	0.4
Travelling to and from the fishing area	0.5
Other	6.0
	100.0

Yet, in a world of complex choices, dollars are often used as a yardstick of a commodity's value. It is, therefore, pertinent to consider recreational value in the dollar sense, and the means available for its assessment.

Residents of the Province traditionally have considered salmon as a common property resource accessed free, or at nominal cost. Many of them consider it a birthright. Such a practice raises the joint questions of value for the resource and payment for benefits received.

Salmon recreational benefits can, of course, be manipulated, primarily by management of fish production or harvesting and improvement of accessing opportunities. Direct beneficiaries of any such improvements should at least bear this cost, including an appropriate return on the monies expended. A "qualifying" question thus concerns the price direct beneficiaries are willing to pay, relative to the costs associated with the beneficial manipulation intended. With regards to negative trade-offs involving salmon recreational resources in the public domain, the relevant question is not what would the recreational beneficiary be willing to pay, but what price would the recreator accept to forego the benefits generated from investments in the recreational stock, made by himself and his forebearers, either in money or in kind. Estimation of such values can only be approximate. On the Fraser River a recent study[5] evaluated the recreational salmon resource within the context of public expenditures on local community services. Updating those results, and extrapolating coastwide, an annual value of $550 million was associated with both salmon recreational activities and stock preservation values by residents of British Columbia. It is this value that must be confronted when contemplating irreversible damage to salmon stocks and/or habitat. Market values associated with salmon recreation activities are also substantial. A recent study[6] estimated the value of the current recreational boating fleet in coastal British Columbia

108

PLATE 19
Salmon Barbecue at All Sooke Day

to be $450 million and that expenditure on replacement and repair of
recreational boats, together with boating equipment, likely reaches
$100 million annually. Eighty-six percent of these boaters indicated
sport fishing to be a major motivation for recreational boat use.[7]

THE QUALITY OF THE
RECREATIONAL EXPERIENCE

The salmon recreator's search for a variety of experiences will
lead him to focus on different aspects of his activity. While "value" or
"satisfaction" may record aggregative changes in recreational quality,
it will do little to explain them. Unquestionably, the number of salmon
available to each recreator will be an important aspect of the quality
of his experience. For instance, salt water anglers on the West and
Northwest coasts of Vancouver Island are estimated to take between
four and five times as many fish at constant effort than sport fishermen in
the Gulf of Georgia[8] and Eastern Juan de Fuca Strait. A significant
quality differential is obvious from such information.

As shown in Table 1,4, quality has other important parameters,
particularly those affecting "taking it easy", "getting rid of tension",
and "being outdoors". Three aspects often considered important to these
objectives are pace of activity, density of persons, and the sensory
aspects of the outdoors themselves. It is not likely that the optimal
characteristics for satisfaction in these areas are uni-directional. Research to date suggests that man seeks neither to recreate totally in an
up-tempo setting, nor totally in a passive setting, neither total solitude
nor continuous crowding, neither totally a pristine wilderness nor a fair
grounds or football game. Rather, it might be argued that recreation
is simply part of man's life fabric, providing a variety of satisfactions

110

in concert with those stemming from other areas of his existence. If
this is so, the satisfactions stemming from salmon-related recreation must
be gauged in this context, as must its "replaceability" by other recreational pursuits.

SUBSTITUTABILITY

Assessment of replaceability in recreation, or as it is more usually termed, "substitutability", has traditionally focussed on activities,
participation, and sites, or in the case of economics, on price-quantity
interrelationships. A recent study suggests that focus on "satisfactions"
rather than activities may significantly alter results.[9] In this piloting
endeavour, 475 activity responses were factor analyzed on the basis of
the satisfactions they generated, and the resulting groupings cross-
checked by direct questioning on activity substitutability. Sport fishing
was found to generate similar satisfactions to backpacking, hiking,
driving for pleasure, bicycling, motor boating, skiing and camping, but,
interestingly, different satisfactions than such pursuits as water skiing,
often posed as substitutes in multiple use controversies. The activities
identified as similar to salmon derived recreation have been characterized by Phillips as "escapes to the country". In this context it seems
that the "country" is becoming increasingly pressured, and less and less
of an "escape", hence "substitutability" paradigms must be undergoing
changes.

A major fallacy associated with much of the empirical consideration of substitutability to date concerns the assumption that if two
activity options generate similar satisfactions, one can be abandoned
in favour of the other. In fact, if two activities are considered close
substitutes, destruction of the opportunity for pursuit of one reduces the
amount of satisfaction that can be generated, regardless of whether the
other activity is substituted or not. If it is not, those denied the right

111

to, say, sport fish, lose all satisfactions previously derived. If the sport fishermen substitute other activities or areas, crowding increases, and quality will likely decline.

CROWDING

Several studies [10] have indicated that crowding not only reduces the enjoyment persons derive from recreation, but that recreators actually have a threshold level beyond which they will not incur further crowding. [11] The impact of such crowding can be generalized in Figure 1,4.

Utilizing only "average curves" for ease of exposition, let AR equal the amount of recreation demanded at each of a series of possible prices, and AVC the costs incurred in supplying that recreation. Also assume an original pricing position where average variable cost equals average revenue. At this point, price is P_1 and quantity equals Q_1. Now let us consider the effect of an influx in salmon recreators. On the supply side, as a result of increased crowding, all recreators will incur a social cost. This cost, while not monetized, is nevertheless incurred and would have the effect of shifting AVC to AVC^1. On the demand side, the effect of more recreators at site will be to increase the number of persons who will take any given recreational product at each of a series of possible prices – hence AR will shift to the right to AR^1. This will establish a new equilibrium quantity, Q_2, and a new equilibrium price (including social costs) P_2. It will also disenfranchise a group of users equal to Q_3-Q_2, who would have participated at P_1, but will not at P_2. It can be generalized, that those excluded will be persons who are the most sensitive to crowding (they incur the highest social costs), and, in the event that a user fee is involved, those least able to afford the fee. The resulting equilibrium at the original site

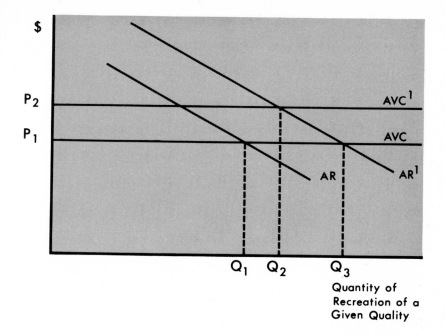

FIGURE 1,4.   The Impact of Crowding on Recreation

is "optimal". However, a single site optimum does not indicate regional optimization, and the search of disenfranchised recreationalists
for "less crowded" recreation, and the costs they incur as they are
forced farther afield in that search, are at the heart of the recreation-
crowding controversy in British Columbia today.

A QUESTION OF OWNERSHIP

As recreational pressure on the salmon resource increases in
British Columbia, the question of ownership by "which group" of recreators will likewise become more controversial. Traditionally, each
group of sportsmen has tended to view the salmon as "their fish", attempting to demand special consideration over outsiders, or to exclude them

altogether. This tendency is most noticeable geographically, with "locals" sometimes resenting "non locals", British Columbians, non-British Columbians, and so on. Certainly, when one considers costs borne by local residents, and particularly the costs associated with alternative developmental opportunities foregone to maintain a salmon habitat, a case exists for a differential system of charges assessing non-local users more stiffly. However, massive discrimination by one localized user group against "non-residents" is unlikely to be in the common interest, or in the interest of the particular local recreational user group.

Firstly, the salmon is not localized. In British Columbia, in its normal route from river to sea and return, it is sometimes accessible to the residents of more than one area and to more than one country. If each "localized" jurisdiction pursues a programme of maximized local interest, without regard to non-local affected parties, the result will be decimation of the commonly held salmon stock and a loss of benefits to all.

Secondly, even where stocks are not commonly held, there may be real advantages to an avoidance of escalating isolationism between different jurisdictions. It has long been recognized that where two countries or regions possess a relative comparative advantage, each in a product sought by the other, that it is to the benefit of each to concentrate on the product it produces best, and for them to trade. The same "trading" principles can be applied to recreation. If residents of a cooler climate, possessive of viable recreational salmon resources, like to recreate south in winter, and residents of that warmer clime with a poorer recreational salmon resource like to come north to fish, and if each excludes residents of the other, one will always be cold and one will always have poor fishing. These considerations apply broadly to urban versus rural areas, to north versus south, to the Gulf of Georgia versus Puget Sound, and so on. It should be emphasised that such advantages in trade depend upon maintenance of comparative advantages in the product to be traded, in this case a viable salmon resource. This will require maintenance of a viable sport fishery in terms of fish stocks accessibility, and the natural recreational setting upon which said viability depends. As recreational pressures mount, quality requirements will inevitably dictate a system for equitable apportionment of opportunity and use charges between local and non-local groups. In this apportionment, local residents should hold a preferred place. But the total exclusion of other recreational demanders is unlikely to be in the local self-interest.

Finally, a comment on criterion for allocation of salmon recreation may be appropriate. Some criterion will be circumstantial. Residential proximity to opportunity, knowledge, exposure to sport fishing as a youth, and so on, will undoubtedly affect participation. Other allocation criteria are often more explicitly determined, particularly in the case of a managed approach to accessing. In this case, ability to pay has often provided a focus for selection and, as has been indicated, a consideration of benefits received relative to contribution made is a legitimate part of any allocative system. On the other hand, to the extent that one believes salmon sport fishing to provide healthful opportunities beneficial to society as a whole, allocative systems based upon ability to pay should take special cognizance of those social groupings perhaps unable to do so – the old, the young, and the economically deprived. If this does not happen, the allocative system selected may generate direct recreational benefits for those included, but significant social costs for society as a whole.

SALMON RECREATION AND
THE FUTURE

The salmon recreator in British Columbia will demand a con-
tinuation in the quality of salmon recreational opportunities available
to him. He will seek a maintenance of current sport fishing success, or
perhaps even improvement to levels experienced "when he was a boy."
He will seek a quiet, natural setting in which to relax, escaping the
stresses of an increasingly fast pace society. He will avoid crowding.
He will seek to preserve a legacy to hand down to his child. It is possible he will be successful, but it is not likely, for his numbers will more
than double before the turn of the century. The Pacific Salmonid Enhancement Programme will keep pace with this demand for fifteen to
twenty years. But the marine areas and river valleys of the Province
will not double, and pressures associated with man's other needs will
continue to erode natural opportunities.

It is possible that awareness of man's finite resource base will
bring some eventual slackening in pressure, but this cannot be expected
for some time. In the interim, maintenance of a quality salmon recreational experience will involve both control of that experience, and
denial of developmental alternatives injurious to salmon and their habitat. This more complex, more self-controlled and sometimes more
pressured future will inevitably see changes in the character of the
salmon sportsman. Already, one can observe the rise of non-consumptive recreational pursuits to stand alongside traditional consumptive
ones, and increased awareness of the value of preserving salmon resources in their own right. As this trend continues the interests of the
salmon sportsman merges ever more closely with those of the population
at large. Other changes are in the hands of the sportsman himself, and
those who manage salmon recreational activities. Will they be able to
successfully implement quality controls? Will they be successful in

protecting habitat? Will they continue to introduce children to the joys of sport fishing and salmon viewing? Or, will children grow up without seeing a salmon or knowing what salmon recreation is? Will local resident turn against local resident for the last salmon in the river?

REFERENCES

1. BRYAN, R.C. The Dimensions of a Salt Water Sport Fishing Trip, or What do People Look for in a Fishing Trip Beside Fish? Technical Report Series No. PAC/T-74-1, Environment Canada, Fisheries and Marine Service, Vancouver, 1975.

2. BRYAN, R.C., A Survey of Customer Management Options as they Relate to the Capilano River Sport Fishery, Environment Canada and Department of Recreation and Conservation, Vancouver, 1975; and MEYER, P.A., Perceptions on Recreation and Sport Fisheries of the Chilliwack/Vedder River, Environment Canada and Department of Recreation and Conservation, Vancouver, 1976.

3. HARRISON, M.C., Resident Boating on the West and North-East Coasts of Vancouver Island, PAC/T-75-13, Environment Canada, Fisheries and Marine Service, Vancouver, 1975.

4. BRYAN, R.C. 1975, op.cit.

5. MEYER. P.A.. Recreation and Preservation Values Associated with the Salmon of the Fraser River, Environment Canada, Fisheries and Marine Service, Vancouver, 1975.

6. MEYER, P.A., Marina Policy in the Tidal Area of the Pacific Coast - A Study of the Recreational Responsibilities of the Small Craft Harbours Branch, Environment Canada, Fisheries and Marine Service, Vancouver, 1976.

7. MOS, G.S. and HARRISON, M.C. Resident Boating in Georgia Strait, Environment Canada, Fisheries and Marine Service, Vancouver, 1974.

8. HARRISON, M.C. 1975 Op.cit.

9. PHILLIPS, S.D. Satisfaction and Substitution in Recreation: A Pilot Study, Environment Canada, Vancouver (forthcoming).

10. See, for instance, MEYER, P.A. and BRYAN, R.C., Recreational Crowding and the Prospects for Fish-Related Recreation - Pacific Rim National Park, PAC/T-74-22, Environment Canada, Fisheries and Marine Service, Vancouver, 1974.

11. EVANS, L.K., Human Spacial Behaviour and Associated Psychological Correlates in Public Beach Settings, University of British Columbia (forthcoming dissertation).

PLATE 20
Conflicting Water Use

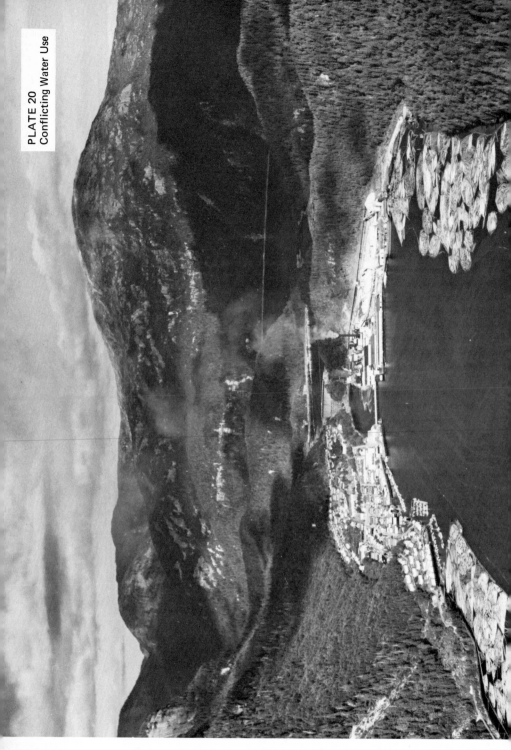

CHAPTER 5

ENVIRONMENTAL FORESIGHT AND SALMON:
NEW CANADIAN DEVELOPMENTS

P. Scott

and

W. Schouwenburg

Environment Canada

INTRODUCTION

Webster defines "foresight" as "an act of looking forward. To many this may conjure up images of fortune tellers, crystal balls and other magical devices. Unfortunately, the environmentalist is not blessed with such wondrous powers and must, instead, rely upon more mundane and practical methods for ensuring that today's actions will not result in tomorrow's ecological disaster.

Environmental foresight associated with salmon can take on many forms. It may involve the establishment of new stocks of salmon, improved licensing procedures or a myriad of other forward thinking activities. In terms of the physical protection of salmon and salmon habitat, the environmental foresight sought by most environmentalists and fisheries officials today is aimed at ensuring that the environmental consequences, including the consequences to salmon, of new development proposals are thoroughly considered and assessed before the developments are approved, and that the recommendations arising out of these assessments are incorporated into the project planning and design.

HISTORICAL REVIEW

Before examining in detail the degree of environmental foresight associated with salmon in effect today, some of its past forms will
be reviewed. How this has helped to protect and preserve British Columbia's salmon resources will also be demonstrated.

There can be little doubt that much of this past concern for
salmon has been due largely to the significance of the fishing industry,
especially the salmon fishing industry, to the economy of British Columbia, and not to any great desire to protect our natural environment.
Over the past several decades, the fishing industry has ranked third in
the economy of British Columbia, directly behind the forestry and mining industries. Fortunately, this economic concern has been supported
by a strong federal Fisheries Act.

The Fisheries Act includes specific sections relating to the
protection of fish from the effects of pollution, dam construction and
water diversions. While much of this legislation was revised and amended in 1932, it dates back to Confederation.[1] The most pertinent
sections of the Fisheries Act relating to protection of fish and their
environment are Sections 20, 28, 33, and 34.

Section 20 of the Fisheries Act stipulates that the owner of a
dam must, if the Minister of Fisheries deems it necessary and in the
public interest;

1. provide fishways of any approved design to permit free
    passage of fish upstream beyond the dam or if this is not
    feasible or that spawning areas are destroyed so that the
    annual return of migrating fish cannot be maintained,
    the owner is required to pay, in whole or in part for the
    construction, operation and maintenance of hatchery
    facilities to ensure the maintenance of the annual re-
    turns of migrating fish.

2.   provide for sufficient quantities of water to be released
      below the dam at all times for the safety of fish and for
      the flooding of spawning grounds to sufficient depths to
      ensure the safety of ova deposited within them.

The above Section provides Canadian fisheries officials with a
great deal of scope in influencing the nature of dam-oriented developments and their resultant effects on migratory species, notably salmon.
In almost all instances, fish passage facilities have been provided on
low head dam structures. In several developments, minimum flow requirements for sustaining migration and spawning were stipulated or
negotiated for by federal fisheries officials. In a few situations, miti-
gative facilities in the form of artificial spawning channels have been
provided in association with dams on rivers. With recent advances in
technology, the use of hatcheries and spawning channels on British
Columbia rivers has become more widespread, not only as a mitigational
measure associated with dams, but also as a means to increase salmon
runs on undammed rivers.

Section 28 of the Fisheries Act stipulates that:

the owner of any ditch, canal or channel constructed
for the purpose of conducting water from any water course
for irrigation, manufacturing, domestic or other purposes
may be required to provide fish screening devices of any
approved design to prevent fish from entering that water
supply.

In British Columbia, it was not until the early 1950's when
biological and engineering expertise was made available to the Department of Fisheries that the technical aspects of this regulation were
addressed in a serious manner. Major industrial water intakes at Kitimat,
Prince Rupert, Prince George, Quesnel, Kamloops, Port Mann and
Sproat Lake illustrate the complexity of the fish screening problem and
the success of the Department of Fisheries in negotiating for their in-

stallation and assisting in their design. Design details and indications of the costs involved in some of these installations have been described by Clay.[2]

Section 33 of the Fisheries Act is Canada's original pollution control legislation in terms of protecting the nations waterways from man-made pollutants. The pertinent clauses of Section 33 state that:

1. substances deleterious to fish must not be released into fish rearing waters or into water courses leading to such waters, and

2. that slash, logs, sawdust and other debris resulting from logging, land clearing or lumber manufacturing cannot be disposed of into fish bearing waters or onto ice over such waters.

With the exception of the logging debris clause, this legislation was not applied to any extent in British Columbia until after the advent of large scale pesticide applications by the forest industry in 1956/57 which resulted in very serious losses of salmon and resident sport fish in several watersheds on Vancouver Island. The gravity of the potential problems resulting from pesticide use encouraged the Department of Fisheries to assign biologists to the pollution control function. This assignment coincided with the commencement of the expansion in the primary and secondary industries that characterized British Columbia's economic development in the late 1950's and early 1960's. Prior to incorporation of the Department of Fisheries into the new Department of the Environment in 1972, the pollution section had grown to include a professional and technical staff of 25. This staff had amassed, with the assistance of members of the International Pacific Salmon Fisheries Commission and the Fisheries Research Board, a truly remarkable record of achievement which has made British Columbia the pace setter in Canada insofar as the application of available pollution control tech-nology was concerned. Among these accomplishments were:

1. Negotiations with Weyerhauser of Canada Ltd., which resulted in Canada's first biological treatment system for Kraft pulpmill effluent at Kamloops (1964). This success was followed by three more at Prince George and one each at Kitimat, Port Alberni and Quesnel.

2. Adjudication of over a thousand pesticide applications over a period of a dozen years without a fish kill.

3. Negotiation of the first total effluent recirculation system for the mining industry in British Columbia (Endako Mines) which was rapidly followed by others on Babine Lake and in the Highland Valley.

4. Justifying and recommending revisions to Sections 33 of the Fisheries Act which provided for the establishment of waste regulations and required potential polluters to formally submit their proposals to the Department prior to commencing construction.

With the creation of the Federal Department of Environment part of the Department of Fisheries' pollution control group was transferred to the newly created Environmental Protection Service, which was assigned the responsibility for administering much of Section 33 of the Fisheries Act.

Section 34 of the Fisheries Act allows for regulations to be made to support the broad tenets of the Act. In British Columbia, two specific regulations that are of importance to the protection of salmon habitat, in particular spawning beds, are the Logging Order and the Gravel Removal Order.[3]

The Logging Order allows for the controls of booming, driving and storage of logs on a number of British Columbia rivers and lakes by either prohibiting these activities or by requiring a permit from the Regional Director of Fisheries setting out conditions under which these activities may take place. Similarly the Gravel Removal Order stipulates that no person can remove or displace gravel from within the

normal high water wetted perimeters of 29 streams, rivers or river systems
without first securing a permit which also specifies the conditions under
which such removal may take place. These two Orders afford a considerable degree of protection for spawning beds in the specific bodies of
water identified in the respective orders. The list of bodies of water
so protected can be expanded if necessary.

One interesting aspect of the work of the Department of Fisheries
that illustrates the past effectiveness of this Department in encouraging
development agencies to recognize the importance of incorporating
fisheries protection measures into their developments plans, is the relationship developed with the forestry industry in British Columbia.
Prior to 1932, Canadian law contained no provision for the protection
of fish and their environment from the influence of logging activities.
After 1932 those involved in logging, lumbering, land clearing and
other related operations were prohibited from putting slash, stumps or
other debris into waters frequented by fish or into the sources of such
waters. Strict enforcement of the "letter of the law" would have effectively stopped all logging operations in the province. This, of course,
was not the intent of the legislation and a degree of judgement had to
be exercised in applying the legislation. Initially, this judgement was
exercised only after that fact; that is, after significant damage was done
to the fisheries resource, charges were laid under the Fisheries Act.
Under these circumstances, the possibility of preventing the damage
before the fact was lost, a lengthy Court case had to be entered into,
and the fisheries resource consistently suffered some degree of loss.
These difficulties were substantially overcome by inter-agency co-operation between federal and provincial fisheries agencies and the B.C.
Forest Service. This co-operation took the form of adding watershed
protection clauses to the operational regulations applied by the Forest
Service as part of their licensing system.

C. Morley Photo

127

Subsequently, in the mid-1960's, the Forest Service arranged to advise fisheries agencies of impending long term logging contracts. The area involved in these logging contracts commonly includes one or more minor watersheds. This procedure permitted early liaisons with logging operators and greatly facilitated discussion and resolution of inter-resource conflicts.

It is not great revelation to say the forester, until recently, was dedicated exclusively to the management of wood. This climate of single-resource orientation has undergone an exceptional improvement. Among the reasons for this welcome change in attitude has been a desire upon the part of the forestry sector to reduce inter-resource conflicts. This desire was probably stimulated by increased communication with fisheries agencies in the process of problem resolution, by increased awareness of the advantages of multiple resource use planning, and by a desire to project a good image to a public who have become increasingly aware of environmental values. This co-operative multiple resource planning attitude has recently undergone a further improvement with the adoption, by the B.C. Forest Service, of a resource folio concept. This is a system in which all resource values of an area are considered by the Forest Service in the long range planning of logging operations for the area.

The relationship developed between the Department of Fisheries and the forestry industry is but one example of many similar relationships that have been developed over the years with other industrial and resource development sectors, including highways, petroleum resources, mining, hydro electric development, agriculture, and many others.

PRESENT SITUATION

As can be seen from the foregoing, the history of the Department of Fisheries in managing and protecting the salmon resources of British Columbia has been an impressive one. Unfortunately, other elements of the province's natural environment without the economic significance as salmon, have not always received the same degree of recognition and protection. In recent years, however, this situation has changed considerably, and today there is developing in the eyes of the public, and from within government agencies, an ever increasing awareness of the importance and fragility of all elements of the natural environment. One of the federal government's first expressions of this new awareness came in 1972 with the creation of the Department of the Environment or Environment Canada. Environment Canada is today comprised of a wide range of resource and environmental protection agencies and incorporates the old Department of Fisheries as the Fisheries and Marine Service.

This increasing concern for the environment in recent years has led to the implementation of a new form of environmental foresight with a number of new procedures and mechanisms for ensuring that all environmental implications of any proposed new development are thoroughly considered and assessed throughout the planning process, and that the development is not approved unless all identified adverse environmental impacts, including any on salmon or their habitat, can be avoided or adequately mitigated. The main federal process for meeting these concerns was adopted by the federal Cabinet in 1973. It is known as the Environmental Assessment and Review Process, and is frequently referred to by the rather ungraceful acronym EARP. EARP, being a federal process, is intended only to apply to projects initiated by the federal government, where federal funds are solicited, or where federal

property is required. At first glance, this may appear to severely restrict the applicability of EARP, but upon closer examination, one finds
that a surprising number of projects, even if they are not initiated by
federal departments, have some federal funding or involve federal lands
and, therefore, are subject to EARP.

How then does EARP work and how does it relate to the protection of the salmon resource? Briefly, EARP is a process intended to
ensure that all federal projects are screened for possible environmental
effects and where potential adverse environmental impacts are identified,
to ensure that an environmental assessment is undertaken and that the
recommendations arising out of the assessment are incorporated into the
project planning and execution. Where the project interacts in any way
with salmon or salmon habitat, the environmental assessment would have
to address itself to any impacts on the salmon resource.

For developments that do not have any federal involvement, a
number of procedures exist for ensuring that the environmental implications of these developments are not ignored. In British Columbia,
one of the main vehicles for managing and protecting the province's
environment is the provincial Environment and Land Use Act. This Act,
which was passed in 1971, established the Environment and Land Use
Committee which is composed of members of the provincial Cabinet.
The main duties of the Committee are to establish and recommend programmes to foster public concern and awareness of the environment, to
minimize the despoilation of the environment occasioned by resource
and land use development, and to report to the Cabinet on matters per-
taining to environment and land use.

The Committee is assisted in its duties by a Secretariat whose
activities include an overview of regional resource management, the
compilation of inventories of land use and land use capabilities, and
the co-ordination of environmental and social impact studies associated

130

PLATE 22
Migration Assist

D.V. Ellis Photo

with major new projects or groups or projects.

The Environmental and Land Use Committee and its Secretariat have been very active in recent years and their activities have, together with the activities associated with the federal Environmental Assessment and Review Process, virtually ensured that all new major developments, or developments with a potentially significant impact on the environment will have to undergo a comprehensive environmental impact evaluation before they are approved.

The requirements for formal environmental impact assessment are normally directed to fairly large developments. Although minor developments or projects may not be required to undergo a formal assessment in all cases, mechanisms do exist to ensure that, in virtually every case, these projects are subjected to an appropriate form of environmental scrutiny. The actual mechanisms for ensuring that these "minor" projects are reviewed for possible environmental effects are many and varied. Probably the most satisfactory such mechanism, and the one that more and more developers and development agencies are adopting, is the voluntary submission of plans to environmental agencies for review prior to the implementation of the project. Through this mechanism, potential impacts can be identified and environmental constraints and mitigational actions incorporated into the project design.

Other than the strictly voluntary route, there are a number of other mechanisms for ensuring that new projects of a minor nature are reviewed for their environmental effects including any impacts on salmon. A few examples of these other mechanisms include:

1. All projects for which an application under the federal Navigable Waters Protection Act is submitted (this includes all projects that in any way impinge upon navigable waters), are referred to Environment Canada for a review.

132

An important part of this review is handled by the Fisheries and Marine Service who assess the impact of the project on the salmon resource.

2. All projects requiring an application to the B.C. Land Management Branch for the use of provincial Crown Land or Crown foreshore are normally referred for comments to a number of environmental agencies, including the Fisheries and Marine Service.

3. All applications for a Pollution Control Permit under the provincial Pollution Control Act, and which may have an impact on the salmon resource, are referred for comments to Environment Canada.

4. All provincial water use applications are forwarded to the Fisheries and Marine Service for comments.

5. All B.C. Department of Highways projects are forwarded for review to a number of environmental agencies, including Environment Canada.

Thanks to these and other similar environmental review mechanisms and to the more formal environmental assessment requirements, there are a very few new projects or activities undertaken today in British Columbia that have not been previously reviewed by Environment Canada for their possible impacts on salmon or salmon habitat. That is not to say that our environmental foresight is perfect or that salmon and salmon habitat are no longer in any danger from industrial or urban encroachments. In reality new projects or activities in, abutting or near bodies of water inhabited by salmon invariably have some effect on the salmon inhabiting these waters. The main purpose of the procedures for reviewing and conducting environmental assessments of new projects and activities is, to first of all identify where negative impacts exist, and then to minimize or mitigate the effects of these impacts. The key of course is that we can normally only hope to minimize or mitigate these impacts and not to entirely eliminate them. Compromises are normally required

and only in extreme cases where significant impacts on salmon are identified, that cannot be reduced or mitigated, would the project or activity
be stopped as a result of these impacts.

In terms of the total salmon resource in British Columbia, small
losses to salmon habitat or a very slight degradation of the water quality
of a salmon stream, can normally be tolerated without significant consequences to the total resource. The concern today of many environmentalists involved with salmon resource protection is directed to the question
of how many of these small losses can be tolerated before they, cumu-
latively, become intolerable. It is difficult to argue that the loss of
say, 1/4 acre of productive salmon habitat in the Fraser River estuary
associated with a new development proposal, will have a significant
effect on the Fraser River salmon run. A succession of such projects,
however, will undoubtedly have a measurable effect.

How then do we determine the cumulative effect of these many
small encroachments on a resource base and how do we set limits to
ensure that these cumulative effects will not significantly damage the
resource base? Studies have been and are being undertaken in a number
of areas to more clearly define the extent and importance of the resources of these areas and from these, attempts are being made to establish
development limits that can be tolerated without seriously endangering
the resource base. From this type of approach, it is hoped that plans
can be established for specific areas that will allow the areas to be developed in such a manner that industrial and urban needs can be met
while at the same time, preserving the area's natural resources, including salmon.

Thanks to the economic importance of salmon to British Columbia's economy and to the strength of the federal Fisheries Act, a form of
environmental foresight, associated with the salmon resource, has existed
in British Columbia for a relatively long time. In recent years, a rising

public awareness of environmental concerns has led to this environmental foresight being extended to cover all areas of the natural environment and has led to the adoption of new procedures and new attitudes so that today environmental assessments and environmental design are becoming an accepted and integral part of the planning and execution of new projects and developments.

Our environmental foresight may not be perfect as yet, but as environmental factors increasingly become accepted as an integral part of the planning and execution of new developments, and as knowledge of our natural environment increases, this environmental foresight will be brought into sharper focus and our Pacific Salmon will be afforded still better protection.

REFERENCES

1. Statutes of Canada 1868 CAP 60, pages 177-193

2. CLAY, C.H., P.Eng., Design of Fish Ways and Other Fish Facilities, Queens Printer, Ottawa, catalogue #FS-31-1961/1.

3. B.C. Logging Order, Canada Gazette, part 2, volume 107, #13, pp. 1513 - 1514, Registration #SOR/73-347, 22 June 1973.
   B.C. Gravel Removal Order, Canada Gazette, part 2, volume 108, #11, pp. 1752 - 1753, Registration #SOR/75-324, 21 May 1974.

CHAPTER 6

ENHANCEMENT TECHNOLOGY:
A POSITIVE STATEMENT

J.R. MacLeod

Environment Canada

THE CASE FOR ENHANCEMENT

In early 1975 the Minister of State for Fisheries the Honourable Romeo LeBlanc, announced a programme to increase the production of Pacific salmonids through the application of enhancement technology. The ten-year, $250-$300 million programme is intended to restore Canada's Pacific Coast salmon stocks to their pre-1900 level of abundance.

Decline in the abundance of salmon has long been noted. The historic potential for commercial production of salmon has been estimated as being of the order of 300 million pounds annually, as compared with with current production of 145 million pounds.[1] The decline began as early as the gold rush days of the mid-1800's and has continued in varying degrees into the present. By the 1920's, the total catch of the five species of Pacific salmon (sockeye, pink, chum, chinook and coho) had declined to 186 million pounds per year. This catch dropped to 164 million pounds in the 1930's, to 155 million in the 1940's and, to 137 million in the 1950's - an all time low.

The post-war industrial boom in British Columbia brought pressure on the productivity of already depressed stocks. Pulp mills, power dams, urban growth and port development decimated watersheds and estuaries used by the salmon. Overfishing, illegal fishing, and lack of management know-how also contributed to the decline in abundance of salmon.

PLATE 23
Modern Enhancemen

The federal government responded to the crisis by substantial increases in conservation, protection and research activities. By the end of the 1960's the decline had been halted and the ten-year average catch had risen to 139 million pounds. This figure has increased slightly during the first half of the 1970's.

Nonetheless, the long-term survival of these fish is in doubt. Gains from improved management have been nullified by losses through environmental damage. It is apparent that unless salmon-bearing waters are made fully productive these waters will continue to be diverted to other uses and the present rate of habitat degradation will continue.

Water and land resources come under provincial jurisdiction to a large extent. Accordingly, since salmon facilities will require extensive use of water and land a federal-provincial agreement is under negotiation. In addition to land and water use rights for salmon facilities, the Province is also being asked to forego benefits from alternate uses of the water and land.

The Province's interest in the programme is substantial. A doubling of current annual salmon production will markedly affect the commercial fishing industry, an important contributor to the provincial economy. Steelhead and other coastal trout, gamefish administered by the Province, use the same habitat as salmon and enhancement of one will affect the other. A large segment of the tourism industry of British Columbia is based on the sports fishery, a prime beneficiary of the enhancement programme.[2]

The rationale of the programme is to apply enhancement technology to create wealth. The programme, by doubling today's annual commercial catch value to $400 million, will produce a rich flow of public benefits.

It will:

1.   Increase employment, earnings and returns on investment in the commercial fishing industry.

2.   Supply the needs of the recreational fishery, a demand presently increasing by six percent annually.

3.   Supply the growing Indian population with salmon for home consumption.

4.   Extend fishing and processing seasons.

5.   Stabilize supply at a higher level of abundance.

6.   Strengthen the economic base of coastal communities.

7.   Improve Canada's balance of payments in commodity trade.

On the assumption that forthcoming international agreements will protect the salmon from overfishing by foreign fleets, Ottawa has launched its scheme to double present salmon stocks. The programme is based on 25 years of research, including development and evaluation of spawning channels, flow control systems, hatcheries and rearing facilities.

A DESCRIPTION

The programme will develop in two phases, the first being the planning-preparation phase, and the second being the construction-operation phase.

During phase 1 (which extends through 1975-76 to the end of fiscal year 1976-77) studies will be directed to conceptive and feasibility planning and, the preparation of major Phase II projects. Construction of a relatively large number of small facilities will be undertaken, with emphasis on restoration of threatened stocks and habitat, stream rehabilitation, obstruction removal, and other forms of environmental engineering. The principle here is that if the fresh-water needs of salmon are

140

looked after, their production can be enhanced since it is in the fresh-water phase of their life cycle that greatest mortality occurs.

Phase II (the period commencing April, 1977) will see the construction of larger facilities coupled with an expanded environmental engineering programme. In the first two years of this phase, building costs will be in the order of $5-$10 million annually, rising to $15-$20 million per year beginning in 1979.

Major construction may be concluded by 1987 and all projects fully 'on stream' by 1992. Evaluation studies will commence in 1977-78 and will continue on a selective basis to at least the end of the century.

Principal among facilities planned for Phase III are spawning channels, hatcheries and fishways. Associated works include incubation boxes, rearing ponds, stream engineering, flow and temperature controls on spawning grounds.

There are several important biological conditions which must be met if the programme is to be successful. The natural system must have sufficient capacity to support the additional fish produced by enhancement. Secondly, enhanced stocks must not adversely affect other stocks in biological interactions such as competition for food or predation. And thirdly, the resulting fisheries which harvest the enhanced stocks must be manageable, that is, they must be capable of harvesting these stocks without over-fishing natural stocks.

From initial conception each project will pass through a progression of phases. This is, from concept through a reconnaissance and feasibility study, to design, to construction, to final operations and follow-up evaluation. Research and development constitutes an integral part of each phase.

The phasing of projects has been staggered to optimize use of personnel; to spread capital costs over a period of time; to permit feed-

141

PLATE 24

142

PLATE 25
. . . . . and Today

B.C. Government Photo

back from projects in more advanced stages of development; and to incorporate results from continuing research.

Ten separate project areas have been identified, involving individual species or combinations of species. They are organized as 'development units' and include: Bella Coola; Skeena; Queen Charlotte
Islands; Kitimat; Nass; Rivers Inlet; Fraser; Johnstone Strait; Strait of
Georgia; and the west coast of Vancouver Island.

The projects are designed to benefit both commercial and recreational fisheries. In the north coast area of British Columbia the emphasis is on increasing native Indian employment, extending the fishing
season and, generally, on expanding the economic base of coastal
communities. While similar objectives hold true for south coast projects,
emphasis is placed on meeting the demands of the very popular recreational fishery in the Strait of Georgia.

The technology on which the programme is based has already
been through experimental and pilot stages in British Columbia. Spawning channels for chum salmon at Big Qualicum River, on Vancouver
Island; for pink salmon at Seton Creek and for sockeye at Weaver Creek,
Pitt River and Gates Creek in the Fraser River system; are providing
benefits each year equal to their original capital costs of construction.[3]

The most ambitious spawning channel project is the $8.5 million
complex at Babine Lake in north-central British Columbia. From an
additional input of 125 million fry into Babine Lake, the Skeena River
commercial fishery each year will harvest an extra one million adult
sockeye worth more than four million dollars to commercial fishermen.[4]

Many streams in British Columbia are under-utilized or not
occupied by Pacific salmon. In the case of pink salmon, with its rigid
two-year life cycle, many important runs occur only in alternate years.
Although traditional transplants have historically failed to restock such

PLATE 26
Planting the Fertilized Eggs

B.C. Government Photo

streams, methods developed in recent years show promise. Research
is continuing.

Other research includes study of the relationship between artificial and natural production of salmon in freshwater streams; factors
limiting the productive capacity of estuarine and marine environments;
the effect of predators on salmonid productivity; and, control of fish
diseases.[5]

CONCLUSION

Although authorities have been aware for some years of the need
for such a programme, it is only recently that the certainty for success
has been established. The productive capacity of the stocks is known;
management methods are now precise; the technical capability is established.

What is emerging concurrent with the development of this programme is a change in resource management attitudes. The emphasis is
shifting from a purely biological to a socio-economic focus. Instead of
managing fish stocks to achieve only stock conservation goals, the objective now is to achieve socio-economic goals on a sustained basis
through wise use of the resource. It's a new challenge for all those
involved with the salmon resource.

REFERENCES

1. Annual summary of British Columbia Catch Statistics 1975.
   D.O.E. Fisheries and Marine Service, February 24, 1976.

2. D.O.E., Fisheries and Marine Service, Unpublished Report.

3. Proposed Programme for Restoration and Extension of the Sockeye
   and Pink Salmon Stocks of the Fraser River: International
   Pacific Salmon Fisheries Commission 1972.

4. D.O.E., Fisheries and Marine Service Unpublished Report.

5. D.O.E., Fisheries and Marine Service Unpublished Report.

CHAPTER 7

HINDSIGHT REVIEWS:
THE B.C. LICENCE PROGRAMME [1]

Bruce Mitchell

University of Waterloo

INTRODUCTION

In September 1968, the federal Minister of Fisheries announced
the first phase of a licensing programme for the British Columbia commercial salmon fishery. A range of comments indicates some of the
feelings subsequently generated by the programme. During the United
Fishermen and Allied Workers Union convention in March 1970, the
Minister was asked to elaborate upon the entire programme. He responded by saying

> We've gone through two phases, both
> of which have been put forth as proposals.
> There has been plenty of playback and we
> have come out with modified proposals.
> That is consultation. It may not be to the
> satisfaction of everyone but it is consul-
> tation.
> Now I don't pretend to know in detail
> what we can do right now or should do
> right now about the use of gear. We'll
> put some proposals forward after talking
> to a lot of people,..., and then back
> will come the criticisms, comments and
> some useful suggestions, and we will work
> out phase three and four together.
> It's the only way we can do it. I don't
> claim to know all about the industry and
> our people in the department don't claim
> to know all about the industry,....I can't
> lay it out in all its detail.[2]

One year later, the Prince Rupert Fishermen's Co-operative Association requested clarification. In its words

> With regard to the entire "license limitation" program, we have repeatedly requested the Minister to put his complete plan from a longer range point of view before the industry. All to no avail; all we get are the bits and pieces of what appears at times to be a somewhat disorganized jigsaw puzzle, seemingly to be rearranged at the dictate of a single person, or at the best, one government. Such is not good enough....[3]

In the same year a Fisheries Service official added a different perspective when commenting that

> ...as a result of the experience in British Columbia it is suggested that it is essential in any plan to move a step at a time, review the results of that step and then move on to the next. Even in the four years that the program has been in effect, it has been found that unanticipated changes have required a re-examination of the original objectives that have been set.[4]

Using different words but expressing similar sentiments, the Manager of the Fisheries Association of B.C. wrote in 1973 that

> The programme was not a finished thing when it was introduced. It hadn't been thought through and many of the ideas were half-baked. But the mistakes haven't been serious ones. It was breaking new ground and it was difficult to know just how to proceed except by trial and error.[5]

And finally the observation of an academic

> In their criteria of "success", program
> planners have yet to account for and justify
> the impact of the program on the distrib-
> ution of prospective benefits among companies,
> fishermen, and the public, and its effect on
> the dynamics of industry control.[6]

With these comments for perspective this study has several objectives. First, the background to, and nature of, the British Columbia salmon licensing programme are outlined. Second, general considerations and principles involved in hindsight reviews are identified. And third, some specific problems in conducting hindsight reviews are examined in context of the licensing programme. In this manner, the investigation extends previous work. Hedlin Menzies, Morehouse, Pearse and Campbell have considered economic implications of the programme.[7] Mitchell has examined the role of communication and consultation during its evolution,[8] while Mitchell and Ross have explored in a preliminary fashion some problems associated with its evaluation.[9]

THE BRITISH COLUMBIA SALMON LICENSING PROGRAMME

The common property aspect of the salmon fishery had resulted in a commercial salmon fishery characterized by too many boats with excessive investment harvesting a relatively stable biomass. Over-crowding and overcapitalization dissipated any economic rent, and led to regulated inefficiences being imposed by the federal government through gear, area and timing controls. The Fisheries Service had documented these inefficiences,[10] and recognized that management beyond traditional controls was needed.

Restricting entry into the commercial fishery was the key to tackling the problem. While the industry was in general agreement

with this ultimate end, sharp differences existed over the means to be
used. Some in the industry favoured licensing of vessels, while others
supported licensing of fishermen. Indeed, this difference over means
stopped implementation of a licensing programme suggested in 1960 by
Sinclair.[11]

In September 1968, two months after taking office, the Fisheries
Minister announced the first phase of a limited entry programme by licensing those vessels which had participated in the fishery during the
previous two seasons. Vessels were licensed into "A" and "B" categories.
The "A" vessels, the most productive and to pay $10 for a licence, were
the only ones which could be improved or replaced. When introducing
the programme the Minister indicated that the programme objectives were
"to increase the earning power of British Columbia salmon fishermen and
to permit more effective management of the salmon resource." He further indicated that by curtailing the size of the fishing fleet, the programme would "...reduce production costs."[12]

The number of vessels has decreased (Table 1,7). Reasons for
the reduction are removal of about 350 boats during the phase 2 Buyback
programme, the lapse of 1,390 vessels due to failure to pass inspection
standards (under phase 3), to pay higher licence fees, to report landings
and "...most importantly, the retirement of small gillnet and troll vessels for replacement by larger seine vessels on a ton-for-ton basis."[13]
During June 1970 it had been stipulated that replacement of "A" category vessels would be only on a ton-for-ton rather than a boat-for-boat
basis. During the early years of the programme it was found that while
the number of boats was decreasing, the tonnage was increasing. If
tonnage may be used as an indicator of fleet harvesting capacity, this
trend meant that productive capacity was increasing rather than declining.
Even more bothersome, given the objectives of reducing production
costs, it was discovered that capitalization increased without a compar-

151

TABLE 1,7

NUMBER OF VESSELS
LICENSED BY CATEGORY

Year	"A" Licence		"B" Licence		Total Licences	
	No.	% Decrease	No.	% Decrease	No.	% Decrease
1966	–	–	–	–	–	–
1967	–	–	–	–	–	–
1968	–	–	–	–	–	–
1969	5869		1062		6931	
		3.88		9.60		4.76
1970	5641		960		6601	
		6.19		-1.56		5.06
1971	5292		975		6267	
		6.76		8.72		7.07
1972	4934		890		5824	
		4.95		22.58		7.64
1973	4690		689		5379	
		2.79		8.27		3.50
1974	4559		632		5191	

(1)   In 1974, vessels not having passed inspection were with-
held for the first time from the final total of licences. If
these vessels subsequently were passed, the 1974 figures
would increase by 79 A vessels and 19 B licences.

(2)   "A" licensed boats must land $20,000 value of fish each
season to maintain their A status. "B" licences expire
after 10 years and cannot be renewed, extended or
changed to A licences. A third "C" category included
boats that are licensed but do not fish for salmon regularly. Their numbers were 1969 (133), 1970 (166),
1971 (339), 1972 (712), 1973 (2,082), 1974 (1,731 or
2,227 if all passed inspection).

Source: HSU, H.S.Y. An analysis of gross returns from commercial
fishing vessels in British Columbia 1971-1974, Technical
Report Series No. PAC/T-76-5, Vancouver, Environment
Canada, Fisheries and Marine Service, Pacific Region,
Special Economic Programmes and Intelligence Branch,
1976, p. 31.

able rise in returns (Table 2,7).

During January 1970, the second phase was started. "B" category vessels were given a 10-year life span, and increased licence fees were described. Since 1971 annual licences for "A" category vessels have been $100 for boats under 30 feet, $200 for boats under 30 feet and less than 15 net tons, and $400 for boats greater than 15 net tons. The increased fees, to be used to buy vessels out of the industry, have generated slightly under $1 million annually.

"A" licence holders who wished to leave the industry could sell their boats to the Buyback Programme. The fishermen would be paid an average of two appraisals plus 5 percent. Vessels purchased by the government would be sold in a public auction on the condition that they could never operate in the British Columbia commercial fishery. While the intent of the licences was to freeze the size of the fleet, the Buyback Programme was designed to accelerate a reduction in its size. The Buyback Programme was discontinued in April 1974 after the purchase of 354 vessels and 7 public auctions (Tables 3,7 and 4,7).

Phase 3 incorporated two aspects. First, in February 1971, special provisions were made for Indian fishermen to pay only $10 annually for an "A" licence but lose the right to offer their boat to the Buyback Programme. The second aspect affected the entire fleet. Early in 1971 the Minister stated that to obtain a licence in 1972 all commercial vessels would have to meet quality standards regarding facilities to protect fish from the sun and weather and from bilge and other contamination. However, the rate of failure was so high in the initial 2,000 vessels inspected (47 percent) that it was impossible to reinspect these vessels plus inspect the other 4,000 boats before th 1972 season started.[14] The 1973 fishing season later was set as the new deadline.

Phase 4 consisted of a review of gear and area regulations, size and composition of fleet, hatcheries and spawning channels, and

TABLE 2,7

AVERAGE GROSS RETURNS, AVERAGE VESSEL VALUE
AND AVERAGE RETURNS ON CAPITAL 1966-1974 (in dollars)

	SINGLE OPERATION			COMBINATION OPERATION		
	Salmon Seine	Salmon Gillnet	Troll and Handline	Salmon Seine	Salmon Gillnet	Troll and Handline
1966						
Return	24,900	3,800	5,100	68,400	6,800	11,000
Vessel Value	31,500	5,100	8,700	56,300	7,900	12,300
Return/Vessel Value	0.79	0.75	0.59	1.21	0.86	0.89
1967						
Return	20,500	3,500	4,300	44,800	6,100	7,000
Vessel Value	33,800	5,100	10,100	60,800	8,800	12,000
Return/Vessel Value	0.61	0.69	0.43	0.74	0.69	0.58
1968						
Return	29,600	4,900	5,100	37,100	8,000	19,400
Vessel Value	41,900	5,600	11,000	43,300	10,100	29,500
Return/Vessel Value	0.71	0.88	0.46	0.86	0.79	0.66
1969						
Return	10,700	3,100	5,200	28,100	6,900	13,200
Vessel Value	46,000	7,100	13,400	59,100	12,500	21,400
Return/Vessel Value	0.23	0.44	0.39	0.48	0.55	0.62
1970						
Return	28,400	4,100	6,800	52,800	8,700	15,800
Vessel Value	45,800	7,400	14,400	62,600	13,600	25,800
Return/Vessel Value	0.62	0.55	0.47	0.84	0.64	0.61
1971						
Return	28,700	4,200	7,900	45,500	8,400	20,600
Vessel Value	48,400	8,200	15,900	53,800	14,500	27,200
Return/Vessel Value	0.59	0.52	0.50	0.85	0.58	0.76
1972						
Return	35,900	5,400	8,800	61,600	11,100	32,600
Vessel Value	45,300	9,100	18,400	61,000	15,400	30,200
Return/Vessel Value	0.79	0.59	0.48	1.01	0.72	1.08
1973						
Return	69,000	11,000	13,500	102,000	18,400	32,100
Vessel Value	57,100	11,600	26,300	79,900	20,900	48,800
Return/Vessel Value	1.21	0.94	0.51	1.28	0.88	0.66
1974						
Return	38,500	8,000	13,500	69,000	13,800	23,400
Vessel Value	105,200	22,200	38,400	147,200	34,900	52,500
Return/Vessel Value	0.37	0.36	0.35	0.47	0.39	0.45

Source: (1) 1966 to 1968 figures calculated from CAMPBELL, B.A. Returns from fishing vessels in British Columbia 1966, 1967 and 1968. Vancouver: Department of Fisheries and Forestry, Pacific Region-Fisheries Service, September 1969, p. 9.

(2) 1969 and 1970 figures calculated from HUNTER, M. An analysis of gross returns from fishing vessels in British Columbia 1969 and 1970. Vancouver: Department of the Environment, Pacific Region, Fisheries Service, October 1971, p. 14.

(3) 1971 to 1974 figures calculated from HSU, op. cit., p. 23.

155

TABLE 3,7

BREAKDOWN OF VESSEL TYPES
PURCHASED IN BUYBACK PROGRAMME

	No. of Vessels	Total Value $'000	Net Tonnage	Value Per Ton $'000	Value Per Vessel $'000
Gillnet	153	1,576	807	2.0	10.3
Troll	126	2,451	1,041	2.4	19.5
Gillnet/ Troll Combination	62	1,212	464	2.6	19.5
Seine	13	609	409	1.5	46.8
	354		2,721	2.1 Overall Average	

TABLE 4,7

REVENUES AND EXPENSES
FOR THE BUYBACK PROGRAMME

Revenues	$'000
Increased licence fees 1970/71 to 1973/74	3,419
Vessel sales and insurance recoveries 1971/72 to 1974/75	2,565
Total gross revenues 1970/71 to 1974/75	5,984

Expenses	
Vessel Purchases	5,965
Administration	150
Total expenses	$6,115
Deficiency of revenue with respect to expenditures	$130*

*This deficiency was covered by licence revenues from the 1974/75 fiscal year.

Source: WILSON, E. "Licence limitation by Buyback, do results justify second round?" Western Fisheries, 90, No. 3 (December 1975), p. 39.

international policy. An advisory committee of individuals representing the government, industry and fishermen was established in 1972 and was asked to report by April 1973. After ten meetings, the Committee submitted its report on April 10, 1973.[15] A majority and a minority report were included. The 15 major recommendations were general, reflecting the wide divergence of interests among committee members. However, the committee specifically did recommend that the Buyback Programme should be continued as a major instrument of fleet reduction. Nevertheless, during the autumn of 1973 the Minister suspended the Buyback Programme effective April 1, 1974. By 1976, the Buyback Committee, composed of representatives from different groups in the industry, had recommended reinstatement of the vessel Buyback Programme. The government has indicated that this recommendation is under consideration.[16] In general, however, the fate of phase 4 is well summarized in the words of a senior Fisheries Service official that "as the Committee was at stalemate, no official action was taken on the fifteen recommendations of the majority report."[17] Thus, unlike the previous phases, the fourth never led to management action. With this background, it is possible to consider how the entire programme might be assessed.

HINDSIGHT REVIEWS:
GENERAL CONSIDERATIONS

Numerous terms have been given to hindsight reviews: expost facto analysis, post-mortem analysis, evaluation, assessment. Regardless of the terms selected, considerable agreement exists concerning their focus. Weiss states that such research "...is concerned with finding out how well action programs work. ...How well do...programs, new and old, succeed in achieving the goals for which they were established?"[18] Caro suggests that evaluative research "...attempts

157

to provide a program administrator with accurate information on the consequences of his actions."[19] Schick develops a distinction between "analysis" and "evaluation".[20] For him, analysis is prospective, concentrating upon planning of future policy and considering proposed alternatives. In contrast, evaluation is retrospective, focussing upon what was accomplished under existing or terminated programs.

Other investigators have provided similar definitions. Wholey et al argue that hindsight study includes

> ...the definition of program objectives, the development of measures of progress toward these objectives, the assessment of what difference public programs actually make, and the projection of what reasonably could be expected if the programs were continued or expanded.
> The essence of evaluation is the comparison of both outcome - what happened that would not have happened in the absence of the program? - and relative effectiveness - what strategies or projects within programs work best?[21]

Suchman probably has provided the most thorough definition. In his now classic work, he defined evaluation as

> ...the determination (whether based on opinions, records, subjective or objective data) of the results (whether desirable or undesirable; transient or permanent; immediate or delayed) attained by some activity (whether a program, or part of a program, ..., an ongoing or one-shot approach) designed to accomplish some valued goal or objective (whether ultimate, intermediate, or immediate, effort or performance, long or short range).[22]

While hindsight reviews concentrate upon determining the relative success of an activity, it should be recognised that there are both different types of and approaches to such studies. Wholey <u>et al</u> suggest four major types may be distinguished: programme impact evaluation, programme strategy evaluation, project evaluation, and project rating.[23] In contrast, Paul categorizes types of study depending upon whether the emphasis is upon effort, effect, or process.[24] These different categories are significant, as the choice of research design and criteria may change depending upon the type of review being conducted.

At least three approaches may be used, none of which are mutually exclusive.[25] One often is labelled as impressionistic, and involves an individual or team asking questions of the director, staff and recipients of a programme. By combining informal interviews with study of reports and other written material, a report is produced within a few weeks or months. If the investigators are skillful, a substantial amount can be accomplished in this manner. On the other hand, opportunities for checking the reliability of judgements are difficult.[26] Furthermore, a frequent emphasis upon present conditions may result in little being ascertained about actual outcomes. A second approach relies upon questionnaires or structured interviews. Although superficially more scientific than the impressionistic approach, the survey results may still be constrained by what individuals are willing to divulge and by a contemporary temporal perspective. The third approach draws upon established standards or criteria. This approach compares programme outcomes against pre-established standards in order to determine relative success. The major shortcoming of this approach of course, is its dependence on valid and reliable standards. When changes to traditional ways of life and occupations are involved, creation of such standards is a formidable task.

What are the general types of questions and procedures associated with hindsight reviews? The traditional form of an evaluation would include the following steps: determine the goals of the

the programme; translate the goals into measurable indicators of goal achievement; collect data on the indicators for those who have been exposed to the programme; collect comparable data on an equivalent group not exposed to the programme; compare the data on programme recipients and the control group relative to goal criteria.[27] In this sense the ideal procedure duplicates conditions of a classical research experiment.

The questions relate to determining the success of the programme and reasons for its effectiveness. To determine success, Suchman has identified the following questions. What is the nature of the content of the objective, that is, do we want to change knowledge, attitudes and/or behaviour? Who is the target of the programme? When is the desired change to take place? Are the objectives unitary or multiple? What is the desired magnitude of effect? How is the objective to be attained? Are there any unintentional effects?[28] To account for why the programme did or did not work, Suchman suggests another set of considerations. What attributes of the programme itself contributed to success? Who were the recipients of the programme and to what extent were they affected by it? What were the conditions (locale, timing, auspices) under which the programme worked? What different effects were produced?[29] The following section considers some of the opportunities and problems which arise when applying these considerations to evaluation of a resource management programme.

HINDSIGHT REVIEWS:
PRINCIPLES AND PRACTICE

Attention is directed towards research design, measurement, validity and reliability, and timing. For each of these aspects, general principles are presented and examined with reference to the B.C. salmon licensing programme.

PLATE 28
Gill Netter

B.C. Archives Photo

Research Design

Experimental design represents the ideal for structuring hindsight reviews. Campbell and Stanley have described in detail a range of such designs.[30] Although numerous designs exist, they all derive from a basic model. This design stipulates that people be assigned randomly into two groups. One group is exposed to the programme being assessed. The other group, referred to as the control, does not experience the programme. Observations are taken before and after implementation of the programme. Any differences between the two groups in the post-programme observations are attributed to the effect of the programme. The purpose of this design, of course, is to isolate and control the impact of the stimulus or programme. In order to ascertain the effect of a programme, it is necessary to control all other effects which might affect the behaviour, attitudes or knowledge of its recipients.[31]

To place this ideal design in perspective, a number of alternatives may be considered (Table 5,7) Using Campbell and Stanley's terms, an "X" indicates the exposure of a group to a programme whereas an "O" represents an observation or measurement of effects. The X's and O's in the same row refer to the same group. Time is interpreted from left to right. An "R" designates individuals assigned to groups on a random basis. In Table 5,7 Design 4 (pretest-posttest with random assignment) represents the classical experimental design.

The first alternative (one-shot case study) represents the design frequently used in resource management hindsight reviews. Observations are made after a programme has been introduced. No baseline data are available against which to contrast the post-programme experience. Furthermore, no comparison is made with a control group. In Campbell and Stanley's words, "...such studies have such a total absence of control as to be of almost no scientific value. ...Securing scientific

162

TABLE 5,7

RESEARCH DESIGNS
FOR HINDSIGHT REVIEWS

Pre-Experimental Designs

1. One-shot case study — $X \quad O$

2. One-group pretest-postest design — $O_1 \quad X \quad O_2$

3. Static group comparison — $X \quad O_1$
   O_2

True Experimental Designs

4. Pretest-posttest control group design
   $R \quad O_1 \quad X \quad O_2$
   $R \quad O_3 \quad \quad O_4$

5. Solomon four-group design
   $R \quad O_1 \quad X \quad O_2$
   $R \quad O_3 \quad \quad O_4$
   $R \quad \quad X \quad O_5$
   $R \quad \quad \quad O_6$

6. Posttest - only control group design
   $R \quad \quad X \quad O_1$
   $R \quad \quad \quad O_2$

Quasi-Experimental Designs

7. Nonequivalent comparison group design
   $O_1 \quad X \quad O_2$
   $O_3 \quad \quad O_4$

8. Time-series design
   $O_1 \quad O_2 \quad O_3 \quad X \quad O_4 \quad O_5 \quad O_6$

9. Multiple time-series design
   $O_1 \quad O_2 \quad O_3 \quad X \quad O_4 \quad O_5 \quad O_6$
   $O_7 \quad O_8 \quad O_9 \quad \quad O_{10} \quad O_{11} \quad O_{12}$

Source: CAMPBELL, D.T. and STANLEY, J.C., op.cit.

evidence involves making at least one comparison."[32] The next design
(one-group pretest-posttest) improves upon the first by incorporating
baseline or preprogramme information. This procedure allows one comparison over time. However, it does not isolate the impact of the programme. It is possible that factors other than the programme under review
could have caused any observed differences between 0_1 and 0_2. Without a control group, it is difficult to ascertain the role of such other
intervening variables. The last design of the pre-experimental type
attempts to reduce the "conditioning" which may be caused by repeated
observations over time. If it is suspected that recipients of a programme
will not behave naturally if they are observed before and after introduction of a programme, the design circumvents this problem. But it
resolves the problem by forfeiting the opportunity to analyze change
over time. Moreover, this and the previous designs do not randomly
assign individuals to the various groups.

The next three designs all represent those which are based upon
true experimental principles. Alternative 4 represents the classical
model. As Suchman states

> The logic of this design is foolproof.
> Ideally, there is no element of fallibility.
> Whatever differences are observed between
> the experimental and control groups, ...,
> must be attributable to the program being
> evaluated.[33]

One source of possible error, the conditioning of respondents by
pre-programme observations, is handled by the fifth design. The Solomon
four-group design controls both the experimental and interaction effects
arising from the observation process. If circumstances do not allow
breaking of programme recipients into four groups, the next design permits the potential effects from observation to be controlled while satisfying the need to randomly assign individuals to groups.

The quasi-experimental designs violate at least one of the conditions required by true experimental designs and yet offer advantages. If control and experimental groups can be established but random allocation is not feasible, the seventh alternative may be used. The essence of the next alternative is the presence of a periodic measurement process. This design may be desirable if it is anticipated that attitudes may change with respect to a programme and/or that there may be short-, immediate- and long-term effects. These can be monitored only by making a series of observations over time. If a control group is included, then the ninth alternative may be utilized.

Concerning evaluation of the B.C. salmon licensing programme, its impact relative to other factors must be isolated if its success is to be judged. For example, one stated objective of the licensing programme was to increase fishermen's incomes. Incomes definitely have increased since initiation of the programme (Table 2, 7) However, many factors other than the license programme have influenced incomes. Hatchery programmes (Capilano, Big Qualicum) and spawning channel projects (Babine Lake) have contributed to large runs which in turn lead to increased catches and income. For native fishermen, the Indian Fishermen's Assistance Programme, initiated in 1968, has invested nearly $15 million in an attempt to enhance the role of natives in the commercial fishery. Prices for fish have risen substantially. These and other factors have acted alone and in combination to affect the income of fishermen.

If it is important to isolate the impact of the licensing programme, what opportunities are presented by the alternative research designs (Table 5, 7)? Unfortunately, while the true experimental designs represent an ideal against which hindsight reviews may be judged, the opportunities for applying them to control the numerous variables are slight. As Rossi states, "...controlled experiments - the most desirable

165

model - are not frequently used in evaluation."[34] The reason for their

lack of use, in the words of Weiss and Rein, is that "...experimental

design creates technical and administrative problems so severe as to

make the evaluation of questionable value."[35]

Administrative and technical problems are interwoven with each

other and with ethical questions. First, the experimental design assumes

control and experimental groups. Administrative and ethical consider-

ations prohibit applying a programme such as salmon licensing only to

some fishermen while excluding others. Second, experimental designs

assume random allocation of individuals to one or more groups. If it is

not possible to break the fishermen into control and experimental groups

it is not possible to utilize random allocation methods. Third, the

strongest designs require pretest and posttest data. Records of pre-

programme vessel quality and management effectiveness are not avail-

able although data are available on incomes and fleet value. On this

basis, designs requiring control groups or pre-programme data are quest-

ionable and should be eliminated. The alternatives left are designs 1

and 8 (Table 5, 7)

These alternatives fit Weiss and Rein's comment that when ex-

perimental designs cannot be used then "a more historically oriented,

more qualitative evaluation has greater value."[36] Whether the impre-

ssionistic or survey approaches are used, hindsight reviews of the salmon

licensing programme are limited to either one-shot case studies or long-

itudinal analyses without the presence of control groups. The latter is

preferable since the effects of, and attitudes toward, the licensing

programme will be spread over a span of time.

<u>Measurement</u>

Measurement of programme success requires identification of the

objectives and development of criteria, standards or indicators against

which to judge whether or not the objectives have been realized. It
should be relatively simple to identify the objectives. Nevertheless, as
Hyman and Wright caution, it is unwise to

> ...take such goals as given....Nothing
> could be more wrong. Most social action
> programs have multiple objectives, some
> of which are very broad in nature, ambiguously
> stated, and possibly not shared by all persons
> who are responsible for the program.[37]

Weiss states the dilemma in slightly different terms. In her words

> Programs often have multiple goals.
> Some are more important than others; some
> are more accessible to study; some may be
> incompatible with others. The evaluator
> has to have a sense of goal priorities in
> order to study the most significant issues.[38]

If Suchman's general questions about programme objectives are
adapted, it is possible to describe the licensing programme objectives
and consider the significance of Hyman and Wright and Weiss' observations.

The first question asks what is the content of the objectives, or
what change is desired? When the licensing programme was announced
in September 1968, three objectives were identified: increase fishermen's incomes, reduce overcapitalization and improve management of
the fishery. Subsequently, the Minister announced that additional
objectives were to improve the quality of landed fish through requiring
holds to be upgraded. Regarding the targets of the programme, several
are identified. Fishermen are the primary target given the desire to
increase incomes and reduce overinvestment. The resource managers
are another target relative to the objective of improving overall management of the fishery.

A question which follows is whether the objectives are unitary or multiple. The licensing programme clearly has multiple objectives. Furthermore, some of the objectives conflict. Indeed, whereas the requirements to upgrade holds has contributed towards better quality fish, this objective has not been met without additional investment. Data between 1966 and 1974 show that the average value of vessels has increased sharply (Table 2, 7). Campbell reached a similar conclusion in 1973, noting that overcapitalization had become worse whereas the "...higher values are not justified in relation to the increased returns that can be obtained because of the fewer number of fishing vessels."[39] In this instance, satisfying one objective (upgrade vessel quality) has been a factor working against achievement of another (decrease overcapitalization). Of course, other aspects have led to further investment in addition to the need to meet the requirements of Phase 3.

Two of Suchman's questions raise new considerations. To determine the desired magnitude and timing of effect, it is necessary that criteria, standards or indicators be established. It is essential that criteria be made explicit rather than implicit as "...depending upon criteria which are picked, different conclusions may be drawn..."[40]

Unfortunately neither when the programme was announced nor during implementation was any indication given as to what the Minister intended to use as criteria. He did not specify when the objectives were expected to be achieved. He also did not indicate how much incomes had to increase or overcapitalization decrease before the programme would be judged a success.

Several examples illustrate the lack of criteria. The intention of the licensing and buyback phases was to reduce the number of fishermen in the salmon fleet. In turn, this reduction would decrease congestion on the fishing grounds and thereby contribute to higher earnings as well as facilitate management. A key issue is to define the ideal size of the fleet. Without such a definition, the reduction of the fleet occurs in a relative vacuum. When asked what the final fleet size would be, the Minister replied

> I really don't have a particular figure
> in mind, nor has the department, ...I have
> said time and again it was originally 8,000
> and now it's down to 5,000. Depending on
> how the salmon runs come back and if we are
> able to increase them sharply in the next few
> years, we could bottom out at 4,500. Don't
> take any figure like 4,000 as gospel - I don't
> know what it is going to be.[41]

Another example arises from phase 3 which introduced quality standards. As one fisherman explained, when the programme was first implemented no guidelines were established as to exactly what quality standards were required. The vagueness is indicated by the following guidelines distributed by the Fisheries Service. Boats were required to have "facilities for protecting fish from sun, weather, bilge and other contamination". "Fish holds, pen boards and shelf boards must be smooth, nonporus and easy to keep clean." "Where necessary fish pens must be shelved to prevent crushing of fish."[42] Details were not given concerning what represented "well insulated", "easy to clean", "smooth" and so on.

Answers need to be provided for the following questions. For the programme to be considered a success by the government, what percentage increase in incomes is required? What reduction in overcapitalization is needed? What improvements in managing the resource are expected? At another level, what change in income and source of livelihood after their departure is required for the marginal fishermen who were pushed out by the programme? These are the types of questions for which the government must provide answers if the merits of the programme are to be assessed. The five criteria offered by Suchman suggest the general categories of criteria for which information is needed (Table 6,7).

Reliability and Validity

The concepts of reliability and validity are related closely to the issue of measurement. If evidence is to be assembled relative to a set of criteria, it must be reliable and valid. If either of these aspects is not satisfied, the evidence becomes of questionable value. Reliability refers to consistency of measurement. In other words, reliability indicates the probability of obtaining the same results upon repeated use of the same measuring instrument. Validity relates to whether the observation chosen to reflect a characteristic actually measures that characteristic.

For hindsight reviews in general, and the licensing programme in particular, substantial problems may arise. Concerning reliability, one complication is to determine reliability when actual change has occurred. That is, if a series of observations in a longitudinal study reveal different patterns, the evidence may be interpreted in several ways. One interpretation would be that real change has occurred. On the other hand, the change may be a result of the type of measurements taken or the influence of the investigator. As Suchman has noted

> A measure which produces different results upon repetition may indicate that a change has taken place and not that the measure is unreliable. Thus, a reliable evaluative instrument measuring valid change might appear unreliable.[43]

On the other hand, if observations are concentrated over a relatively short period, problems still emerge. As Gergen has noted, when a study relies upon responses from individuals over the short-term, "there

TABLE 6,7

SUCHMAN'S FIVE EVALUATIVE CRITERIA

CRITERIA	DEFINITION	EXAMPLE
1. Effort	The quantity and quality of activity that takes place regarding a programme. This represents an assessment of input.	The number of times a bird flaps its wings.
2. Performance	What was accomplished relative to objectives. A measure of output.	The distance flown by the bird.
3. Adequacy	The relative effectiveness of a programme. Measures how adequate is performance relative to the total amount of need.	How far the bird has flown in relation to its destination.
4. Efficiency	Concerned with evaluation of programme relative to alternatives. A measure of the performance/effort ratio.	Could the bird have arrived at his destination more efficiently by some other means than flying the way he did?
5. Process	How and why the programme works or does not work.	Investigation of the anatomy of the bird and the principles of flight to explain effort, performance, adequacy and efficiency.

Source: SUCHMAN, op.cit. pp. 61-67

is no way of determining the extent to which observations reflect either simple inconsistencies in the measuring device or temporary and fluctuating behaviour on the part of the individual being studied."[44] A related point also must be considered. In the interests of ensuring confidentiality, researchers normally do not reveal the identity of respondents. This practice is desirable and essential to ensure candid responses. Nevertheless, it makes reliability checks difficult since subsequent investigators are unable to interview the same respondents.

Validity generates problems which may be particularly acute. After criteria have been identified (effort, performance, adequacy, efficiency, process), it is necessary that they be operationally defined and that indicators be established. Immediately a question arises as to whether or not the investigator actually is collecting data which measures such abstract concepts as adequacy or efficiency. For example, are increases in incomes a valid measure of "adequacy" relative to the objectives of the licensing programme? Moreover, the investigator must establish thresholds which delineate when the criteria are satisfied. Failure to identify such thresholds was cited earlier as a basic flaw in the federal governments' attempts to judge the success of the licensing programme. Without knowing how much incomes should rise, capitalization decrease or management improve it is difficult to draw conclusions about the programme. The federal government, as architect of the programme, has an obligation to clarify this aspect in order that the reliability and validity of any evidence used in evaluations may be judged.

Timing

The timing of hindsight evaluations is a contentious matter involving several questions. When should an assessment be undertaken? Immediately after implementation or after several years have elapsed?

172

A trade-off must be made. If unintended negative results are to be modified, it is sensible to review programmes immediately after implementation. Unfortunately, outcomes often do not become noticeable for some time. And yet, if too much time is allowed to elapse, these negative outcomes may become too solidly established to alter.

The licensing programme was initiated in September 1968, and the fourth and last phase was announced in February 1972. The report resulting from the fourth phase was completed during April 1973. By May 1973 six of the seven buyback auctions had been held. By the summer of 1973, the licensing phase had operated for 3 fishing seasons. During June 1973 when the author started the first of two seasons of field work on reviewing the impact of the programme, he was told by federal fisheries officials in Vancouver that evaluation was premature. It was suggested that "several more years" should be allowed to pass before conducting a review. No indication was given as to how many more years were required. To date, one internal review has been completed under contract to the Fisheries Service, but has not been made available for public examination. Another study, available to the public and published during 1976, concentrates on incomes and capitalization but does not present evidence relative to effectiveness of management. As a result, a comprehensive evaluation available to the public has yet to be done.

It is unfortunate that evaluation has not been conducted on the licensing programme when a review of the Indian Fishermen's Assistance Programme (IFAP) has been completed. IFAP was approved in principle by the Treasury Board on May 15, 1968, and funding was authorized on September 10, 1968, two days after the licensing programme was announced. The position of the Indian people in the commercial fishery had shown a steady decline since 1945, and IFAP was designed to assist them by providing funds to construct new vessels or to purchase

older vessels, to convert, reconstruct or modify vessels, to purchase
gear and equipment, and to mount fisheries training courses. A series
of Treasury Board minutes allocated up to $4.5 million to support IFAP
over 5 years. The programme subsequently was extended for a second
five-year period with a budget of $10.2 million.

Before the second phase was approved, a review was conducted.
A four-man team was established drawing upon individuals from the
Fisheries Service and Department of Indian Affairs. The terms of ref-
erence for the review included comparing the results against the orig-
inal objectives, comparing changes in income of Indian fishermen under
IFAP with all other fishermen, and assessing the individual parts of
IFAP. [46]

The assessment was conducted in three phases. First, relevant
statistical information was assembled from Fishery Service records.
Next, administrative aspects were examined through interviewing management as well as analyzing records and allocation of funds. The
third stage involved interviews with Indian fishermen on all parts of the
coast. Fifty-one Indian fishermen assisted by IFAP were interviewed
as well as 40 other Indian fishermen, and 17 other Indian people.
Fifty-six non-Indians were interviewed, making a total of 164 people
who were contacted.

Based upon its investigations the Review Team concluded that
the "benefits expected by the first Programme have not materialized,
but, nevertheless, some progress has been made." A number of administrative weaknesses were discovered. Many of the problems were
attributed to "...misunderstandings regarding the delineation of responsibilities and the breakdown of communications between the two
participating departments."[47] Nevertheless, it was recommended that
the programme be renewed for a second five years.

To facilitate a review, continuous monitoring of the impact of the licensing programme should be initiated. The Fisheries Service has data for gross returns from commercial fishing vessels over the period 1966 to 1974.[48] Other studies provide data on the importance of the commercial industry to selected remote coastal communities, socio-economic background of commercial fishing, economic aspects, vessel owner investment, and socio-economic aspects of commercial fishermen in Northern Regions.[49] As a result, considerable data already are available concerning incomes of fishermen and the capitalization of the fleet. This information needs to be systematically integrated into analysis of overall effectiveness of management.

To determine the relative success of the licensing programme, longitudinal monitoring should be implemented. Ideally a sample of commercial fishermen and individuals who left the industry after licensing was introduced should be monitored for changes in income, capitalization in vessels and general satisfaction with the programme. Obvious problems would arise, however; the programme started in 1969 and finding individuals who quit fishing could be difficult. Even maintaining information on continuing fishermen could be onerous. Consequently, it is more likely that any such investigation would have to use a random selection of commercial fishermen rather than relying upon the same respondents over a period of years. Whichever way is adopted, monitoring should be done as the licensing programme has generated short, intermediate and long-term effects. Furthermore, viewpoints and attitudes will change with time. A series of loosely related economic surveys will not be as valuable as a set of related reviews covering economic, social, ecological and management aspects over time.

PLATE 29

176

IMPLICATIONS

The British Columbia salmon licensing experience provides a
number of lessons. The programme itself has brought mixed benefits.
Since its introduction, fishermen's incomes have risen. However, the
role of the licensing programme relative to other management practices
(hatcheries, spawning channels) is not clear. The quality of the fleet
also has improved, as vessels have been upgraded to satisfy increased
standards. On the other hand, meeting these quality standards in conjunction with improvements to enhance catching capacity has led to
increased investment in the fleet. This outcome runs counter to one
of the stated objectives of reducing capitalization. Regarding the third
objective of improving management effectiveness, little systematic
analysis appears to have been done.

Other issues are still unanswered. While the absolute benefits
appear to have risen, little attention has been given to the incidence
of benefits and costs. This aspect deserves attention, since by freezing
and then reducing fleet size, the programme has resulted in individuals
leaving the industry voluntarily or involuntarily. A question arises as
to whether those who left the industry are better or worse off than before
they left it. This question gains substance when viewed in the context
of Pearse's observation that

> ...its adverse effects will be felt most
> by the casual, part-time and low-income
> fishermen, while the major private bene-
> fits will accrue to the owners of licensed
> vessels. In view of the objective of en-
> hancing the meagre incomes of fishermen
> it is unfortunate that those who will gain
> least are likely to include those with the
> lowest incomes and fewest employment
> alternatives.[50]

Further equity concerns arise relative to the status of individuals who no longer can rent company boats as firms retire small gillnetters and replace them with large seiners. The seiners are more productive. But to meet the ton-for-ton replacement rule, six to seven gillnetters have to be retired in order to introduce one seiner. The result is fewer fishing jobs. Since many of those who rent boats have traditionally been native Indians, this aspect raises an issue with deeper historical and cultural ramifications.

At a more general level, the licensing programme illustrates the basic research issues which arise in hindsight reviews. The discussion of research design addressed the matter of isolating the impact of one variable in an multiple variable environment. It becomes clear that current research methodology in the social sciences is unable to handle this aspect of control. The outcome will be the necessity of relying upon case studies, usually without the benefit of control groups, examined longitudinally using a mix of qualitative and quantitative techniques.

Measurement arose as another fundamental issue. Different criteria can be and are used in judging the impact of the programme. Two people with the same data may reach conflicting judgements because of different criteria or values. As Suchman states, the "crucial issue is simply not one of "right" versus "wrong", not of "objectivity" versus "subjectivity", nor even of "standards" versus "expediency", but a rather complex mixture of differing values, purposes, and resources."[51] It is this aspect which makes validity and reliability so important, since different interpretations not only may occur between different evaluators but also among different groups interested in the commercial fishery – politicians, resource managers, companies, unions and individual fishermen. Such a programme affects all these interests, for as Tussing remarks

> Instituting a program of license
> limitation in most fisheries constitutes
> a literally revolutionary reform, in-
> volving substantial redistribution of
> fishing income, of wealth in the form
> of rights to the resource and in the
> value of existing vessels and gear,
> and of management and regulatory
> power. Such a revolution does not
> proceed out of a bio-economic model
> or a cost-benefit-analysis.[52]

Timing emerges as a key consideration as well. A normal programme involves one or more phases: planning, implementation, operation, abandonment/termination. Review of each of these phases is
needed. Work has been done on the planning and implementation
phases.[53] Continuous review of the ecological, economic and social
impact now is required of the operation phase. Some of the data (ecological, economic) can be collected on an annual basis. Other information (social) is more appropriately gathered at selected time periods
but on a regular basis. Only in this manner will a complete picture
emerge of the benefits and costs of the licensing programme.

Given the many methodological problems encountered in hindsight review, it is easy to be discouraged.[54] As Morehouse remarks,
"if research results do not support program aims and agency commitments, they may be either simply ignored or, if acknowledged, criticized
as methodologically unsound."[55] Elaborating, Schick has observed that

> ...all evaluation is vulnerable to challenge
> on methodological grounds. Tests stand
> accused of cultural bias; the sample was
> improperly drawn or just too small; the
> stated goals are not the real ones; the
> true results were ignored by the resear-
> chers; and so on. ...

Given the complexities of social life and
the improbabilities of methodological per-
fection, the safest course often seems to
be to avoid evaluation. Once an evaluation has been attacked, the grounds have
been laid for justifiable disregard of its
findings.[56]

Conversely, the same complexities assure that most programmes

will be imperfect. If hindsight reviews help to identify the nature and

extent of such imperfections, and constructively suggest how they might

be resolved, then such reviews have a positive role in natural resource

management.

REFERENCES

1. The author would like to thank Canada Council for financial support during 1973 and 1974 for research on the licensing programme.

2. "Questions and answers on Davis Plan," The Fisherman, April 3, 1970, p.6.

3. Prince Rupert Fishermen's Co-operative Association. Annual Report, 1971. Prince Rupert, B.C.: PRFCA, 1971, p.4.

4. CAMPBELL, B.A. Limited entry in the salmon fishery: the British Columbia experience, PASGAP6, Vancouver: University of British Columbia, Centre for Continuing Education, Fisheries Programmes, May 1972, p.1.

5. CAMPBELL, K.M. "B.C's salmon licence control programme," Paper presented to the Meeting of the Association of Pacific Fisheries, April 2, 1973, p.2.

6. MOREHOUSE,T.A. "Limited entry in the British Columbia salmon fisheries," in TUSSING, A.R., et al., Alaska fisheries policy. Fairbanks: University of Alaska, Institute of Social, Economic and Government Research, 1972, p. 413.

7. HEDLIN MENZIES AND ASSOCIATED LIMITED. The economic potential of the West Coast fisheries to 1980. Winnipeg-Toronto-Vancouver: Hedlin Menzies February 1971; MOREHOUSE, op.cit.; P.A. PEARSE, "Rationalization of Canada's West Coast salmon fishery," in Economic aspects of fish production. Paris: Organisation for Economic Co-operation and Development, 1972, pp. 172-202; B.A. CAMPBELL, "Salmon licence control: the first three phases," Western Fisheries, 84(July 1972) pp. 13-16, 31-35.

8. MITCHELL, B. "Decision-making and consultation in resource management: the B.C. salmon fishery," Journal of Environmental Management, 4, No. 3 (1976), pp. 211-223

9. MITCHELL, B. and ROSS, W.M. "Problems of evaluation in resource management as illustrated by the British Columbia salmon licence programme," Geographical Inter-University Resource Management Seminars. Waterloo: Wilfrid Laurier University, Department of Geography, Vol. 4, 1973-1974, pp. 82-93.

10. CAMPBELL, B.A. "Problems of over-expansion in the salmon fleet," Western Fisheries, 81 (October 1970), Part I, pp. 14-24; 81(November 1970), Part II, pp. 22-28; 81(January 1971), Part III, pp. 15-24.

11. SINCLAIR, S. Licence Limitation - British Columbia: a method of economic fisheries management. Ottawa: Department of Fisheries, 1960; SINCLAIR, S. "Licence limitation - British Columbia," in HAMLISCH, R. Economic effects of fishery regulation. Rome: FAO, 1962, pp. 306-345.

12. "New regulations for B.C. salmon fishing industry," Fisheries News. Vancouver: Department of Fisheries, Information Branch, September 5, 1968, p. 1.

13. HSU,H.S.Y.An analysis of gross returns from commercial fishing vessels in British Columbia 1971-1974. Technical Report Series No. DAC/T-76-5, Vancouver. Fisheries and Marine Service, Pacific Region, Special Economic Programs and Intelligence Branch, 1976, p. 30.

14. "Phase III quality control standards extended 1 year," Fisheries Information, I, No. 2 (December 1971), p.1.

15. WEST COAST SALMON FLEET DEVELOPMENT COMMITTEE, Report. Vancouver: Fisheries Service, April 1973.

16. "American Buyback boats not legal in Canada," Western Fisheries, 92(May 1976), p. 11.

17. Personal Communication, C.H.B. Newton, Manager, Special Economic Programs and Intelligence Branch, Fisheries and Marine Service, Vancouver, March 17, 1976.

18. WEISS, C.H. "Evaluating educational and social action programs: a "treeful of owls"," in WEISS, C.H. (ed) Evaluating action programs: readings in social action and education. Boston: Allyn and Bacon, 1972, pp. 3-4.

19. CARO, F.G. "Approaches to evaluative research: a review," Human Organization, 28, No. 2 (1969), p. 88.

20. SCHICK, A. "From analysis to evaluation," Annals of the American Academy of Political and Social Science, 394 (1971), p. 60.

21. WHOLEY, J.S., et.al. Federal Evaluation Policy: analyzing the effects of public programs. Washington: The Urban Institute, 1970, p. 19.

22. SUCHMAN, E.A. Evaluative research: principles and practice in public service and social action programs. New York: Russell Sage Foundation, 1967, pp. 31-32.

23. WHOLEY, et.al. op.cit., pp. 24-26.

24. PAUL, B.D. "Social science in public health," American Journal of Public Health, 46 (1956), pp. 1390-1396.

25. WEISS, op.cit., pp. 5-6.

26. SHIPMAN, G.A. "Measurement of agency effectiveness," Public Administration Review, 29, No. 2 (1969), p. 207.

27. WEISS, op.cit., p. 6.

28. SUCHMAN, op.cit., pp., 38-41

29. Ibid., pp. 67-68

30. CAMPBELL, D.T. and STANLEY, J.C. Experimental and quasi-experimental designs for research. Chicago: Rand McNally, 1963.

31. For a discussion of other factors which may jeopardize internal and external validity, see CAMPBELL and STANLEY, op.cit. pp. 5-6.

32. Ibid., p. 6.

33. SUCHMAN, op.cit. pp. 95-96.

34. ROSSI, P. "Evaluating social action programs," Transaction, 4, No. 7 (1967) , p. 51.

35. WEISS, R.S. and REIN, M. "The evaluation of broad-aim programs: experimental design, its difficulties, and an alternative," Administrative Science Quarterly, 15 (1970), p. 97.

36, Ibid., p.97

37. HYMAN, H.H. and WRIGHT, C.R. "Evaluating social action programs," in LAZARFELD, P.F. et al (eds.) The uses of sociology. New York: Basic Books, 1967, p. 756.

38. WEISS, C.H. op.cit., p. 21

39. CAMPBELL, B.A. Licence limitation regulations: Canada's experience. Paper presented to the Food and Agriculture Organization Technical Conference on Fishery Management and Development, Vancouver, 13-23 February 1973, 12 pp.

40. MITCHELL, B. "An investigation of research barriers associated with institutional arrangements in water management," in MITCHELL, B. (ed) Institutional arrangements for water management: Canadian experiences. Waterloo: University of Waterloo, Department of Geography Publication Series No 5, 1975, p. 268.

41. "Questions and answers by Jack Davis," The Fisherman, February 16, 1973, p. 6.

42. Phase III quality control standards extended 1 year," Fisheries Information, 1, No. 2 (December 1971), p.3.

43. SUCHMAN, op.cit., p. 117

44. GERGEN, K.J. "Methodology in the study of policy formulation," in BAUER, R.A. and K.J. GERGEN (eds.). The study of policy formation. New York: Free Press, 1968, p. 210.

45. HSU, op.cit.

46. HAMEL, A.B., HAYES, F.E., ROTHERY, T.F. and HUNTER, M. Review of the B.C. Indian Fishermen's Assistance Program, October 1972.

47. Ibid., p. 3.

48. CAMPBELL, B.A. Returns from fishing vessels in British Columbia, 1966, 1967 and 1968. Vancouver: Department of Fisheries and Forestry, Pacific Region – Fisheries Service, September 1969; HUNTER, M. An analysis of gross returns from fishing vessels in British Columbia 1969 and 1970. Vancouver: Department of the Environment, Pacific Region, Fisheries Service, October 1971, HSU, op.cit.

49. SINCLAIR, W.F. The importance of the commercial fishing industry to selected remote coastal communities of British Columbia. Vancouver: Department of the Environment, Fisheries Service, Pacific Region, 1971; WILSON, W.A. The socio-economic background of commercial fishing in British Columbia. Vancouver: Department of the Environment, Fisheries Service, Pacific Region, August 1971; ECONOMICS BRANCH. Some economic aspects of commercial fishing in British Columbia. Vancouver: Department of the Environment, Fisheries Service, Pacific Region, June 1971; WILSON, W.A. A survey of vessel owner investment in British Columbia. Vancouver: Department of the Environment, Fisheries Service, Pacific Region, September 1971; SINCLAIR, W.F. and BOLAND, J.P. A socio-economic survey of commercial fishermen living in the northern regions of British Columbia. Vancouver: Department of the Environment, Fisheries and Marine Service, Pacific Region, June 1973.

50. PEARSE, op.cit., p. 201.

51. SUCHMAN, op.cit., p. 74.

52. TUSSING, A.R. "Introduction: economics and policy in Alaska fisheries," in TUSSING, A.R. et al (eds). Alaska fisheries policy. Fairbanks: University of Alaska, Institute of Social Economic and Government Research, 1972, p. 10.

53.   MITCHELL, op.cit.

54.   CARTER, R.K. "Client's resistance to negative findings and
      the latent conservative function of evaluation studies,"
      American Sociologist, 6, No. 2 (1971), pp. 118-124.

55.   MOREHOUSE, T.A. "Program evaluation: social research versus
      public policy," Public Administration Review, 32, No. 6
      (1972), p. 868.

56.   SCHICK, op.cit., p. 70.

CHAPTER 8

LIMITED ENTRY IN ALASKA

Allan Adasiak
Executive Director

Alaska Commercial Fisheries Entry Commission

INTRODUCTION

Limited entry is not an exclusively economic notion. When Alaska's current limited entry programme was a bill before the Alaska Legislature in 1973, one question that was asked repeatedly was, "Is this an economic programme or a conservation programme?" The answer of course, is "Yes". Considerations of economics and conservation in connection with a commercial fishery are inseparable. The notion of "efficiency" is felt by some to be primarily an economic touchstone. Yet what do the bulk of the fisheries regulations in effect anywhere do? They nibble away at the efficiency of the fleet: shorter nets, bigger mesh, smaller areas, shorter periods – anyone can continue the catalogue. As engines replace sails, synthetic nets replace linen, drums replace shoulder power, more and more "conservation measures" must be implemented to give the fish the needed chance to escape and reproduce. Man's own ingenuity causes him to be more and more managed in the interest of "conservation."

But steps to reduce efficiency also reduce a fisherman's economic performance. Now, while the genesis of the idea of limited entry has been in economics, in Alaska at least, the impetus for implementation of the State's current limited entry law has come primarily from the biological condition of the fisheries. Or, more specifically, it has come because traditional management techniques have been breaking down under the pressure of more and more units of gear in a fishery. The traditional techniques have not done anything as dramatic as collapse. As gear has increased, managers have continued to lose the precision with which catch and escapement can be determined. In other words, as the number of units of gear increases, so does the risk of overharvest.

EARLY MANAGEMENT STRATEGIES

Many management biologists in Alaska have recognized since territorial days the difficulties of managing a fishery with a large number of units of gear operating in it. One of the lasting efforts in the direction of entry limitation was the establishment of area registration, which began well before statehood was granted in 1959. Area registration was a response to the flood of fishermen into areas where the fishing was good or was expected to be good. Under it, an operator of salmon net gear was required to license by April 15, two months or more before the start of the fishing season, and to declare the single area in which he would like to fish. Area registration is still in effect, although consideration is being given now to doing away with it since the entry permit system limits the amount of gear in any salmon fishery management area.

After statehood, Alaska made a direct attempt at limited entry by legislation in 1968. This, however, failed in the courts for various reasons and was subsequently repealed. In the course of analyzing this aborted attempt at limited entry, two considerations mandated by the United States Constitution were spotlighted, and, for some at least, it started to become clear that they would have to be recognized in future limited entry efforts.

First, Alaskans quite normally like to put Alaskans first, but that is not legally acceptable when it runs against the United States

188

Constitution. A limited entry programme that discriminates unreasonably in favour of Alaskans and tends to exclude non-residents meets with the disfavour not only of the non-residents but of the courts. When there are too many people fishing, limited entry means some form of exclusion from fishing and it was politically far easier to pass a limited entry law which, if you had to exclude someone, excluded non-residents to a high degree. However, the United States Constitution does not permit that.

Second, there was substantial concern that a simple moratorium allowing only those who fished in the past to continue fishing in the future, would violate the equal protection clause of the State and Federal Constitutions. The idea again has a certain amount of political charm. No one would be excluded under a licence freeze, only no one new would be allowed to fish until illness, death, retirement, lack of skill, hard luck and other forces reduced the gear level to some optimal point. Similarly, a strict apprentice system for new entrants was believed to be tainted, although the notion of a system where people could "work their way up" had strong popularity with the fishermen, and many other citizens. The legal difficulty, somewhat abbreviated, is that a conservative judiciary does not favour apprenticeship programmes believing that if captains can select who the apprentices will be and who will be advanced to full-scale gear operator level, there is a strong possibility for the development of a closed class situation.

These two legal considerations figured prominently in the shape that the current Alaskan limited entry law was to take. First, to avoid unreasonable discrimination problems, decisions on who would continue to participate in a fishery would have to be made by applying the same set of impartial standards to residents and non-residents alike. Second, to avoid the closed class problem, permits to fish would be made "freely transferable." Since they could be bought or sold, bartered for, given

189

away, or otherwise transferred, there was a clear way for new people to
get into a fishery; at the same time since someone new entered only
when someone else left, the gear levels would not change.

Meanwhile, the sense of need for limited entry continued, and
legal concern in the late 1960's and early 1970's turned also to Alaska's
constitution. Since statehood in 1959, Article VIII, Section 15 of the
Alaska Constitution read: "No exclusive right or special privilege of
fishery shall be created or authorized in the natural waters of the State."
Some people argued that the notion of limited entry was not contrary
to this since it did not create an exclusive right, but to remove any
doubt, the Legislature proposed an amendment to add a sentence to
Section 15, reading: "This section does not restrict the power of the
State to limit entry into any fishery for purposes of resource conservation, to prevent economics distress among fishermen and those dependent
upon them for a livelihood and to promote the efficient development
of aquaculture in the State." The amendment was approved by the
Alaskan electorate on August 22, 1972 by a majority of 70 percent.

ALASKA'S LIMITED ENTRY PROGRAMME

In January 1972, Governor William A. Egan had sought and
received an appropriation to fund a limited entry study group, which
was charged with producing not "another ivory tower study" but a
workable plan to limit entry in Alaska's fisheries. The efforts of the
group lead to the introduction of "the Governor's bill" on limited
entry in January 1973. Following quickly on the introduction of the
bill, the study group's research was published in the report "A Limited
Entry Programme for Alaska's Fisheries," and was presented to the
State Legislature in February 1973.

The dual nature of limited entry as something dealing with

both conservation and economics is made clear in the statement of purpose in the law, which is "to promote the conservation and the sustained yield management of Alaska's fishery resource and the economic health and stability of commercial fishing in Alaska."[1] The job is to be accomplished "by regulating and controlling entry into the commercial fisheries in the public interest and without unjust discrimination".[2]

As finally adopted, Alaska's limited entry law differed from the original bill in these major respects:

1.   It was broadened to apply to all commercial fisheries in Alaska, not just the salmon fisheries;

2.   A "maximum number" of entry permits to be issued was defined by statute, and a formula for determining the optimum number of entry permits was created, along with a buy-back programme to reduce the number of permits to the optimum;

3.   The salmon drift gill net fisheries of Bristol Bay, Cook Inlet and Prince William Sound were declared "severely impaired," so that even interim-use permits were restricted there in 1974, while in all other fisheries interim-use permits were available to anyone prepared to fish, until such time as entry limitation was imposed.

4.   Eligibility criteria were established requiring that a person must have harvested the resource commercially as a gear license holder prior to January 1, 1973 to be eligible to apply for an entry permit in those fisheries placed under entry limitation before January 1, 1975; and

5.   Permit issuance criteria were elaborated and the idea of ranking applicants on the basis of the hardship they would suffer by exclusion from the fishery was introduced.

In other major aspects, the final bill remained practically identical with the original version:

1.   Permits were to be issued to individuals, not vessels, as a use right allowing the holder to personally operate a unit of gear in a particular fishery;

2.   Only one permit would be issued to a person in a given fishery;

3.   The permits would be freely transferable but not subject to encumbrance, attachment, or other forced transfer;

4.   The programme would be administered by a full-time, quasi-judicial regulatory commission with three members.

Canadians like Mr. Douglas Bell, who administered the British Columbia buy-back programme and was one of a very few persons who devoted their full-time efforts to Canada's limited entry programme, were surprised at the administrative scale of the Alaskan system, which in addition to three full-time commissioners had a staff of 23 and a budget of $763 thousand.[3] There are a number of reasons for the difference in the size of the programme. The number of potential applicants for entry permits in the salmon net fisheries alone was in excess of 17,000, while the number of permits to be issued might be half that. In addition, the programme was to deal with other fisheries as well. A research staff was needed as a part of monitoring the growth of gear in other fisheries and doing research necessary for tailoring limited entry programmes to the unique characteristics of those fisheries when such programmes became necessary. The definition of fishery was restrictive: "the commercial taking of a specific fishery resource in a specific administrative area with a specific type of gear," and while this eliminated the type of mobility problems that complicate fishing pressure considerations in British Columbia, it necessitated the work to formulate discrete regulations that recognized the individuality of each fishery. Finally, and perhaps most important, entry permits were to be issued to individuals, not to vessels, and were not to be issued just on the basis of landings over a fixed number of years. The standards for initial issuance represented a complex of criteria that had to be elaborated in regulations tuned to individual fisheries and functioning within the requirements of

PLATE 30
Seiner in Action

the law. The legal standards delineating the optimum number of units of gear to which fisheries would be reduced also required pioneering research.

The standards set forth in the law require the commission to adopt regulations establishing qualifications for ranking applicants for entry permits according to the degree of hardship which they would suffer by exclusion from the fishery. The regulations are to define priority classifications of similarly situated applicants based upon a reasonable balance of two hardship standards. Initially some members of the legislature were reluctant to give the Commission the broad authority to define specific priority classifications for individual fisheries. However, efforts to do so legislatively met with frustration as unique characteristics of individual fisheries were encountered that made broad legislative action seem impossible, and questions arose which it was recognized would require time consuming research to answer, although answers must be had before reasonable, fair classifications could be drawn.

Finally the Legislature provided the following two standards:

1.   degree of economic dependence upon the fishery, including but not limited to percentage of income derived from the fishery, reliance on alternative occupations, investment in vessel and gear; and

2.   extent of past participation in the fishery, including but not limited to the number of years participation in the fishery, and the consistency of participation during each year.

From January through April of 1973, when the limited entry bill was before the Alaska Legislature, almost no one in the state asked seriously whether limited entry was necessary, although various alternative systems were considered. People knew according to contemporary information that gear in the salmon fisheries had increased 74 percent between 1960 and 1972 and that catches had generally been declining. People knew that the drift gill net season in Cook Inlet used to be seven days a week, but that as gear expanded the season contracted to two 12-hour periods per week, some of which were suspended by in-season emergency regulations. The king crab fishery around Kodiak had dwindled from a three or four month season to one of 11 days.[4] Generally, gear was increasing, management was getting more difficult and less effective, and in many cases stocks were declining. Although the economic condition of the fishermen was a concern, and one which motivated commercial fishermen to support limited entry, the primary focus was on the future of the resource. Limited entry was needed immediately in three fisheries the Legislature characterized as "severely impaired;" it was undoubtedly needed almost as urgently in several other fisheries; and since growth in the number of units of gear in currently under-utilized fisheries seemed inevitable, limited entry would be needed elsewhere in the future.

The likely passage of a limited entry law caused gear licence sales between January and March of 1973 to rise between 80 and 100 percent over the comparable period in 1972 as people apparently sought to be "grandfathered in."[5] Seeing the limited entry programme endangered by a last minute "gear rush," the legislature moved to block it by saying that in any fishery put under limited entry before 1975, no one would be eligible unless he had held a gear licence and harvested the fishery resource commercially before January 1, 1973.

The legislature recognized that in currently over-crowded fisheries some people would have to be cut out at the beginning of a limited entry programme. It also recognized that the annual turnover rate of fishermen in a fishery was too great to allow issuing entry permits to everyone who had fished, for example, in three of the past five years. In terms of salmon gear licence holders, that would have represented

195

approximately 14,300 people, while the highest number of units of gear that fished in any year during that period was then estimated at between 7,000 and 7,500, excluding the salmon fisheries of the Arctic-Yukon-Kuskokwim area.

Utilizing legal advice from a constitutional expert it had retained, the legislature worked out a system of ranking fishermen on the basis of economic dependence and past participation that would eliminate those eligible applicants who would suffer the least hardship. For "distressed" fisheries, where there was already more gear than the estimated optimum number of units, the legislature said that the maximum number of permits that could be issued would equal the highest number of units of gear fished in any of the four years preceding 1973. The maximum number could be exceeded only if denial of a permit would cause a significant economic hardship on an applicant. The commission later adopted the same formula for setting maximum numbers in the other salmon fisheries it was dealing with at the same time as the distressed fisheries, with the obvious consequence that a number of people who had fished as gear licence holders in the past in a fishery would not receive permits.

A "fishery" is defined as "the commercial taking of a specific fishery resource in a specific administrative area with a specific type of gear." Thus there are, for example, two salmon fisheries in Bristol Bay, the drift gill net fishery and the set net fishery.

The legislature and the administration opposed any standard that would sort out fishermen on some criteria such as catch. This opposition was based upon concern over the social consequences of such a standard. A device, for example, that would eliminate as applicants all fishermen who harvested less than 3,000 fish in recent years might work to eliminate some of the less effective fishermen in the fishery, but it would also cause serious economic dislocation by eliminating a

number of people who relied upon commercial fishing to provide a
major part of their cash income.

The administration, most legislators, and most fishermen also
supported the issuance of entry permits not to vessels but to individuals.
Their reasoning was that the individual who did the fishing should
benefit from limited entry, not the person who owned the vessel. In
addition, people believed that if vessels received entry permits, it
would be relatively easy for the processing industry to increase its ownership of vessels and thus its control over who fished. By contrast,
issuing permits to individuals would increase the independence and
bargaining position of the commercial fishermen, and reduce the possibility of greater processing industry control over a fishery.

In April 1973, a bill creating the first comprehensive limited
entry programme in the United States was enacted by the Alaska State
Legislature and signed into law by the governor.[6] The overall objective
of the legislation was to stabilize the number of units of commercial
gear in each fishery at a level that allows effective resource management
and provides an adequate livelihood for fishermen.

THE LIMITED ENTRY COMMISSION

Beginning in January 1974 all fishermen who wished to operate
a unit of gear commercially in Alaska were required to buy an interim-
use permit from the Commercial Fisheries Entry Commission. Permits
were not required for crewmen, nor for subsistence or sports fishing.
Under the law, a separate interim-use permit was issued for each fishery resource, area and gear type combination – for example, salmon
purse seining in Southeastern Alaska. The administrative areas and
gear combinations adopted by the Commission closely paralleled the
management areas in use by the Alaska Department of Fish and Game.

During the 1974 seasons there was no restriction on the number
of interim-use permits issued except in three fisheries: the salmon drift
gill net fisheries of Bristol Bay, Cook Inlet, and Prince William Sound.
In these three fisheries, an applicant must have fished as a gear licence
holder prior to January 1, 1973 to receive an interim-use permit. This
restriction was a part of the law, placed there because the legislature
felt that these three fisheries were already severely impaired and needed
some immediate gear limitation in the 1974 fishing season.

The Commission was directed by the law to examine all the
fisheries in the state prior to the 1975 fishing seasons and to identify
those fisheries which then had enough or too much gear. Those fisheries with too much gear were termed "distressed" fisheries. A distressed fishery, as defined in the law, is a fishery where the present
level of gear fished exceeds the estimated optimum level of gear that
can be managed with traditional management techniques, or where
there is too much gear to provide a reasonable average rate of return
to the fisherman for his labour and investment, considering the other
opportunities available to him. The commission was also to identify
"designated" fisheries, that is, those where the present level of gear
should not be exceeded, but does not need to be cut back in relation
to the estimated optimum number. These classifications, however, did
not preclude cut-backs in the future where the final determination of
an optimum number varied significantly from the earlier estimate, or
where changed conditions warranted gear reduction.

The commission was directed by law to issue entry permits to
individuals in those fisheries that it had identified as designated or
distressed. As noted earlier entry permits are similar to property in
that they can be bought, sold, inherited or traded. They cannot,
however, be pledged, mortgaged, encumbered or transferred with any
retained right of repossession or foreclosure, or attached or sold on

execution or judgment of a court order. This, combined with the restriction of one permit per person per fishery, was done to prevent one person or company from gaining control of several permits and dictating the conditions under which a fisherman could fish. A fisherman with a permanent entry permit must also be physically present on a vessel or set net site at any time gear is actually fished. Permits could be temporarily transferred to another individual in an emergency or special hardship situation only. Permanent and temporary transfers must be approved through the Commission.

The Commission identified the fisheries most likely to need entry regulation as the power troll fishery and all salmon seine and gill net fisheries in Alaska, except those in the Arctic-Yukon-Kuskokwim area. Using as the maximum number standard in these fisheries the formula of highest number of units of gear fished in any year between 1969 and 1972, it was estimated that between 7,300 and 7,500 entry permits would be issued. At the time, at least 12,000 applicants were anticipated for the 19 fisheries, and the commission knew that it would have to devise specific regulations to apply the statutory ranking standards of economic dependence and past participation.

The job of the commission beginning in late 1973 and continuing through 1974 was focused on three major areas. First, explaining the programme to fishermen and receiving testimony on how the programme should be applied fairly; second, background research necessary to make final determinations of which fisheries required limited entry and how applicants for entry permits in those fisheries should be ranked; and third, issuing interim-use permits in all fisheries and designing methods for handling entry permit applications. Each of those activities is described below.

Since limited entry was a new programme with a direct effect on many people in the state, there was a great need to disseminate

information about it. In 1974, this was done through radio and tele-
vision announcements, newspaper advertisements, posters, mailed
circulars, and public meetings.

A total of 29 information meetings and public hearings were
held between September 1973 and June 1974. In addition to providing
information on limited entry, the commission sought testimony and
comment from fishermen to help determine which areas they felt required
limited entry and how they though applicants for entry permits should
be ranked. Besides receiving specific considerations for individual
fisheries, the commission learned that fishermen generally preferred a
point system of ranking applicants; consequently point systems were
devised as a part of the regulations proposed on July 15, 1974.

Over 15 meetings were held with native organizations, fishermen's groups and other interested groups of individuals throughout the
state beginning in August 1973.

Additionally, there were 12 public hearings held in September
and October 1974 on the proposed regulations. The purpose of these
hearings was to obtain oral and written testimony from the fishermen
and other interested parties regarding the proposed regulations so that
the commission would have the benefit of the maximum amount of input
from the people who would be affected by the limited entry programme.

Supplementing the oral testimony, the commission received
hundreds of letters and comments on various aspects of the law and the
proposed regulations, and many more letters requesting information
about the programme. Questionnaires relating to the implementation
of the programme were distributed at many of the public hearings and
the responses were made part of the hearing record.

THE SOCIO-ECONOMIC RESEARCH
PROGRAMME

Much of the data needed by the commission to implement the limited entry programme had never been gathered, systematized and analyzed. This included data on the number of years fishermen actively participated in the fisheries and the degree of consistency within a given year. Other information had not been collected at all, such as costs and earnings of fishing operators, income dependence, and investment information.

As a preliminary step, data on computer files was corrected and edited. This involved checking hundreds of thousands of fish tickets and commercial licenses from 1969 through 1972. Much of the work had to be done clerically.

The research staff, which included a fisheries co-ordinator, an economist, a systems analyst, a research analyst, and a programmer, were employed full time in collecting and preparing the information needed by the commission to make decisions regarding the proposed regulations.

Research focused primarily on 1969–72 since testimony showed that fishermen generally favoured giving more weight to a person's recent years of economic dependence and past participation in a fishery and recency was limited by statute (in the 19 fisheries under consideration) to January 1, 1973.

Here are a few of the highlights:

Annual Participation of Fishermen

The number of years the average fisherman actually spent fishing in a particular fishery was used to provide an indication of the vocational labour force that is present. More than half of the fishermen participating fished two years or less as gear licence holders in all major salmon fisheries except the Southeastern purse seine fishery, where average participation was longer. Turnover tables were also developed to begin to identify trends of leaving and re-entering a fishery.

Consistency of Participation
During a Given Year

In addition to knowing the turnover in participation, the commission also needed data on how long fishermen actually fished during a given season. This was needed to determine the numbers of persons fishing only short periods of time, such as weekends, vacations, or salmon run peaks. Consistency was measured in terms of weeks during which at least one landing was made. The data suggested that there were a large number of short-time fishermen and it was used to produce histograms that were the basis for determining average rates of participation during a season.

Income Data

The other information developed suggested that a certain number of fishermen must receive a substantial portion of their income from activities unrelated to fishing. To test this hypothesis, the Internal Revenue Service agreed to study tax returns submitted by 2,400 individuals who fish in Alaska. The study included both residents and non-residents. Since IRS data is confidential, the survey was designed as a stratified sample that did not reveal individual identities to the commission. The survey compared gross earnings received from a fishery with non-fishing occupational income, or in other words, with income received from employment outside of fishing (investments, pensions, public assistance, etc. were not included). The actual formula used was gross earnings divided by the sum of gross earnings plus non-fishing occupational income. The results showed widely disparate income dependence percentage patterns between the various fisheries. Contrast, for example, the Southeastern purse seine fishery, where 83 percent of the fishermen showed an income dependence percentage above 80 percent with the Kodiak purse seine fishery, where 41 percent of the fishermen fell into the same category. Comparisons of different types of fisheries also demonstrated different income dependence dispersions.[7]

In addition, it was found that there is a statistically significant difference between the average dependence of those fishermen who have fished many years and those who have fished only a short time. For example, power trollers who had fished 3 or 4 years between 1969 and 1972 showed an average dependence of 76 percent, while those that had fished one year showed an average of only 50 percent.

This and other research conducted by the commission delineated significant differences between the various fishermen who participated in Alaska's commercial fisheries and between fisheries by both type and area. The results were used to draft and evaluate the effects of various point systems, and tests were run using fisherman-related data available on computer tape and from other sources. Hypothetical applicants were measured against the point system and the results of these and other tests used to set the number of weeks required to receive points for consistent participation, domicile requirements for availability of alternative occupations, and the income dependence percentages necessary to receive points for income dependence. The point system was also evaluated to ensure that the number of points potential applicants would receive was balanced between past participation and economic dependence, and to insure its fairness in each fishery. The results of this continuing effort showed up both in the proposed regulations and the regulations finally adopted by the Commission, which reflect significant characteristics of the various fisheries and give preference to those fishermen who would suffer greater hardship if they could not continue fishing.

The final point system had a variety of categories under which a person with proper evidence could receive maximum totals of 20 points for his past participation and 20 for his economic dependence. Points were weighted in favour of gear licence holders since entry permits would allow the operation of a unit of gear and gear licence holders, rather than crewmen, have held the primary responsibility for gear operation. Thus, for example, a gear licence holder could accumulate income dependence points while a crewman could not. This division was made since a crewman could continue being a crewman without an entry permit, but a gear operator would need a permit to continue in that line. Points were also weighted in favour of recent activity so that, to use the same example of income dependence, a gear licence holder could qualify in 1971 for zero, two or four points, but in 1972 for zero, three or six points. The point levels were kept the same in any category for all fisheries. Differences between fisheries were recognized by varying the threshold levels for consistency or income dependence it was necessary to reach to qualify for points. For example in 1972 in fishery A it might have been necessary to have a minimum income dependence percentage of 30 percent to qualify for three points and 60 percent to qualify for six points, while in fishery B the minimum thresholds might be 50 percent for three points and 90 percent for six points. These thresholds were set on the basis of historical analysis and public comment on the proposed regulations.

A level of 20 verified points was also adopted that would result in the automatic issuance of an entry permit. By law no one could be denied an entry permit who would suffer significant economic hardship. The commission determined through research that the categories of 20

PLATE 31
Brailing Seine

R.C. Dixon Photo

points or more would include those persons who would suffer such hardship as of the January 1, 1973 cutoff date the law imposed for considering a person's qualifications. The commission also established five or
less points as categories of "minor economic hardship," a designation
that would impose transferability restrictions on such permits if they were
in fisheries that required a buyback programme because of excess gear.

The complete point system included points for years of past
participation, back to 1960 in certain circumstances; consistency of
participation in specific recent years; availability of alternative occupations; investment in vessel and gear; and income dependence. In
one sense the regulations establishing the point system are the main
achievement of the commission in its first year and a half of operation.
The details of system's operation can best be inferred from an examination
of the regulations. They could be the subject of an exposition far longer than space allows here.

Costs and Returns to Fishing Vessels

In addition to the research described so far, the commission
studied costs and returns to fishing vessels in the state. The study was
accomplished by interviewing over 520 active commercial gear licence
holders from all four West Coast states.[8]

The study was the first large scale effort to examine the economic health of commercial fishing - one of Alaska's most important
industries. It covered 1973, the last year of unrestricted entry into
Alaska's commercial fisheries, and was undertaken both to set a bench-
mark for evaluating the limited entry programme and to help determine
the gear levels that can harvest the fisheries in the state and provide a
reasonable economic return to participating fishermen.

In addition to the 520 interviews, extensive use was made of
various computerized records. Completed interviews represented

approximately 7 percent of the fishermen in the fisheries studied. While generally valid, the results reflected the randomness of the sample picked for each fishery and the percentage and accuracy of completed responses.

To those familiar with the industry, some of the results may come as a surprise. One reason is that the figures are averages of all fishermen in a particular fishery, based on responses received. Obviously, some fishermen were doing better than the average, but many were doing worse. The study also did not attempt to measure the actual cash balance a fisherman might have had at the end of the season. Charges were also made for depreciation and costs of investment which are invisible on a ledger, but nevertheless are real costs of doing business. Among the general conclusions of the survey were the following:

1. A non-farm family of four living in Alaska in 1974 on an adjusted gross income of less than $5,250 per year would fall below Federal Poverty Guidelines. Without supplementing his income from other sources, the average gear operator in 15 of 18 salmon fisheries examined made less than that amount. In seven fisheries gear operators actually showed a net loss.

2. There was a very close relationship between the size of investment and level of gross earnings. There was also a close relationship between gross earnings and net earnings. Thus those fisheries which require a large capital investment such as purse seining, also appeared to be the most financially rewarding.

3. The most rapid growth of registered gear in the salmon fisheries occurred where a small initial investment was required, such as in the drift gill net fisheries. With the exception of the power troll fishery, the estimated market value of vessels and gear in those fisheries which showed a very rapid growth in the 1960's was under $16,000. Size of investment has not deterred growth in the shellfish fisheries, but these fisheries were essentially undeveloped at the beginning of the decade.

4.   There is evidence that the rapid growth in gear registration that
      took place in some fisheries during the 1960's contributed to sub-
      sequent low earnings. For example, the Southeast drift gill net
      fishery showed a modest growth of about two new units of reg-
      istered gear a year betweeen 1960 and 1970 and still had relat-
      ively good earnings. Bristol Bay, which showed an increase of
      78 new units of registered gear a year, and Cook Inlet, which
      showed an increase of 41 units of registered gear a year, showed
      poor earnings.

      In effect, those salmon fisheries that require a higher level of
      investment generally had barriers to entry during the 1960's that
      prevented their earnings from deteriorating as rapidly as those
      fisheries with low barriers to entry.

5.   In the survey, fishermen indicated what they felt they needed to
      gross in a year to pay all their expenses and have enough remain-
      ing to make a living for themselves. This value was closely
      correlated with the market value of their investment. Those with
      large investments felt they needed to gross approximately the
      market value of their investments each year, while those with
      smaller investments felt they needed more than this amount.

6.   Besides crew shares, the largest expense for most fishing vessels
      was for repairs and gear losses. Fuel was next.

Permit Application Procedures

During 1974 the commission issued over 18,000 interim-use
permits to over 11,000 commercial fishermen. All interim-use permits
were issued from the commission's offices in Juneau, rather than by
vendors in various areas, in order to ensure accurate and timely processing of applications. With four full-time employees the Commission
was able to handle up to 300 permits a day with a maximum turn-around
time of 5 working days.

Permit information was processed bi-weekly by computer and
reports were given to enforcement officers in the field. This led to
the apprehension of several violators of the limited entry law at the very

beginning of the salmon seasons when they attempted to make landings without an interim-use permit.

The limited entry law requires that a gear operator carry his permit while operating a unit of gear, and in 1974, the first year that permits were required, the permit was merely a paper form. However, data collection needs and convenience to the fisherman lead to the development of a new system for 1975. Starting that year, each fisherman who received an entry permit or an interim-use permit was given an embossed plastic card similar to a credit card. The card was used to imprint fish landing tickets each time fish were sold to a buyer or processor. The Alaska Department of Fish and Game continued to store fish ticket information, including that provided by the card, on computer files. The additional information provided a basis for detecting limited entry law violations, studying the effect of limited entry on fishermen's earnings, and doing other analyses with an ease not previously possible. Use of the card was made mandatory in 1976 by a Board of Fisheries regulation.

A process for handling entry permit applications with a minimum of difficulty for the fisherman was developed during 1974. Experience suggested that a number of fishermen would have poor or incomplete records and would have difficulty obtaining all the information necessary to complete an application. To assist the fishermen, the Commission compiled as detailed a record as possible for each fisherman, based on existing information in state files. Where such information existed, fishermen were not required to submit further evidence to support their claims.

A computer system was developed that consolidated licensing, fish ticket and vessel ownership information. Application request cards were mailed to all gear licence holders on state files between 1969 and 1972; additional request cards and blank application forms were made

available in the field. Application request cards that were completed
and returned were the source of mailings totalling 12,600 applications
on which the computer had printed an applicant's points known to be
supported by state records. Fishermen with 20 or more pre-printed
points fell into a category in which the law mandated that they be
issued an entry permit and they needed only to verify the points and
sign the application to be issued one. Fishermen with fewer points also
needed to verify them, but they needed to submit evidence only for
additional points they claimed. Various printouts of computerized data
were also used by Commission staff to help fishermen validate points.
In addition, those fishermen claiming special circumstances were examined on a case by case basis, by hearing officers when necessary.

The application period opened in December 1974, and for 19
commercial salmon fisheries in Alaska, 1975 was the year entry limitation began. The preceding year and a half of activity by the Commission, including research, public hearings, proposed regulations, and
more public hearings, was the prelude to the actual regulating of
access of some of the state's commercial fisheries.

Since the Commission must also look at fisheries that are threatened with the problems of excess gear, in 1975 it also turned its attention to the six commercial salmon fisheries of the Arctic-Yukon-Kuskokwim[9] area which it subsequently found to need entry regulation.
It continued issuing interim-use permits in non-limited fisheries in
1975 and 1976, and took steps toward the establishment of buy-back
programmes. In addition, it continued to investigate the need for
entry regulation in the state's other commercial fisheries, with particular emphasis on the shellfish fisheries. In 1976 it added certain
herring fisheries to the list of those in which a determination of the need
for limited entry would be made.

The Commission also found itself the object of a lawsuit chall-

enging the constitutionality of the Alaskan limited entry law, and it
saw opponents of limited entry gather sufficient petition signatures
to have a proposition that would repeal the law placed on the November
1976 ballot.

REVIEW OF THE PERMIT SYSTEM
TO DATE

In calendar year 1975, the Commercial Fisheries Entry Commission regulated entry into 18 of Alaska's largest commercial salmon net
fisheries and the power troll fishery. This comprised all of the salmon
fisheries in the state, except those in the Arctic-Yukon-Kuskokwim
area, and the hand gurdy troll fishery. As of December 31, 1975, a
total of 6,770 permits were issued, 73.1 percent to residents of Alaska,
and 26.9 percent to non-residents. [10] Table 1,8 compares those percentages to gear licenses issued to residents and to non-residents who
fished prior to the passage of the limited entry law in 1973.

This close parallel to the historic resident vs. non-resident
distribution of gear licenses illustrates with results the accuracy of the
point system in allocating permits in this respect. It also counteracts
with facts a brooding suspicion among some Alaskans that non-residents
were getting more permits than they "ought to".

The qualifications claimed by a number of applicants required
that these applicants receive individual treatment by the Commission.
During 1975, Commission hearing officers conducted more than 300
administrative hearings. The hearings, held at various locations, could
run as long as five hours, plus the time required for a hearing officer
to review the record, making additional information inquiries, and
develop a recommended decision. These hearings and subsequent
commission adjudications of the recommended decisions generally involved applicants with special or unavoidable circumstances that

211

TABLE 1,8

RESIDENCY COMPARISON OF PERMITS
AND GEAR LICENCES

	Resident	Non-Resident
1975 permits*	73.1%	26.9%
1972 gear licences**	70.8%	29.2%
1971 gear licences**	70.9%	29.1%
1970 gear licences	70.5%	29.5%
1969 gear licences	71.3%	28.7%

*   Determined by Commercial Licence File information on
    resident and non-resident licensing, only those issued as
    of December 31, 1975, excludes transfers.

** Excludes licences issued in fisheries closed during the
    full calendar year.

called for an individual evaluation of the applicant's situation in relation to the regulations and the law. Regardless of whether the applicant was represented by counsel, the hearing was conducted in a non-
adversary manner, the basic intention being to enable the applicant to
develop the greatest number of points to which he was legitimately en-
titled. By the Fall of 1976 some 360 hearings had been conducted by
the Commission's hearing officers, and commission adjudications of the
hearing officer's recommended decisions conducted on about half that
number. All of the remaining hearings may not have to be adjudicated
because of evidence developed during hearing follow-up work. Most of
the questions and other matters contained in the bulk of the 9,400
applications received were resolved without the need for an applicant to
go through the hearing process.

While this time-consuming process sometimes meant delays in permit issuance, these various application procedures were the only fair way to treat applicants who through no fault of their own had exceptional circumstances during the years that counted toward their qualifications for an entry permit.

Only two entry permit applicants have sought judicial appeals from Commission determinations. In both instances the Commission could not accept the person's application because the eligibility requirement of the law precluded such acceptance. The Commission could not accept an application if the applicant did not fish as a gear licence holder at some time between 1960 and 1972 in the fishery for which he was applying. No judicial appeals have been sought by eligible applicants.

Approximately 13.75 percent of the applications from eligible people will not qualify for entry permits. The actual number of people who will not qualify for a permit is less, since many people applied for more than one permit.

A total of 553 permits were permanently transferred in 1975. The transfer process has resulted in a net increase of permits in the hands of Alaska residents. Transfers, on the basis of residence, were as follows:

Resident to resident	285	(52%)
Non-resident to non-resident	166	(30%)
Non-resident to resident	79	(14%)
Resident to non-resident	23	(4%)

The transfer of a permit indicates someone new entering a fishery as a gear operator, and of course someone else dropping out. These transfer figures have served to dispel another Alaskan resident apprehension: namely, that non-residents, who are sometimes believed to

213

have easier access to money, would buy-up numerous entry permits.

A permit price survey conducted by the Commission indicates that in approximately 40 percent of the cases permits were transferred for free. Generally these transfers occurred between family members, although more distant relations were occasionally involved, as were skippers and crewmen. In a significant number of other cases the permit was transferred for nothing along with the sale of a vessel or set net site.

While specific prices covered a somewhat wider range, the average price paid for an entry permit varied from $750 to $11,035, depending on the type of permit. The average prices, where sufficient sales of entry permits occurred to prevent disclosure of information on an individual transaction, are set out for each fishery in Table 2,8.

In some fisheries the average prices at this writing may be somewhat higher, since the prices cited include all sales from the inception of the programme. Relatively healthy harvests in some fisheries in 1976 have tended to increase permit prices in those fisheries. In other fisheries, particularly where 1976 harvests were low, the prices may tend to be lower than the average prices given. Anticipation of 1977 harvest levels will also tend to influence permit prices, as will speculation on the success or failure of the effort to repeal limited entry prior to the November election.

The price survey also determined that in the majority of cases where financing is necessary, permit sales are financed by the transferor of the permit, or a bank. Of the respondents, only 7.5 percent indicated that a processor had financed the purchase. This would appear to counter the concerns of some fishermen that processors would attempt to take control of entry permits through financing.

The effect of reduced gear levels in 1975 and 1976 when compared to 1974 was varied. In most cases it resulted in additional fishing periods for the fishermen, although the amount of additional fishing

214

TABLE 2, 8

PERMIT SALES AND PRICES PAID
THROUGH AUGUST 1975

Fishery	Total Number of Sales	Average Price of Permit Alone
Southeast Purse Seine	16	$11,035
Southeast Drift Gill Net	26	$ 9,100
Yakutat Set Gill Net	2	$ 750
Prince William Sound Purse Seine	6	$ 7,600
Prince William Sound Drift Gill Net	9	$ 3,412
Cook Inlet Drift Gill Net	10	$ 2,190
Kodiak Purse Seine	7	$ 4,571
Bristol Bay Drift Gill Net	19	$ 1,004
Statewide Power Troll	53	$ 5,598

Average prices shown are for transactions of permits not sold with vessels, gear, or set net sites. Separate questionnaires were sent to each party in a transaction; the most reliable data is set forth above.

There are two reasons that price information on all 19 fisheries is not listed in Table 2,8. Either the number of responses from a fishery was too small to avoid the disclosure of information on individuals, or there were no transactions of permits alone.

215

PLATE 32
Handling Net

time varied according to the strength of the salmon runs. The greatest effect was probably in the Southeast Alaska salmon fisheries, where the majority of Washington State fishermen affected by the Judge Boldt decision would otherwise have fished.

The Optimum Number of Permits

During 1975 the Commission began determining the "optimum" number of entry permits for each of the 19 salmon fisheries operating under the entry regulation system that year. Establishing an "optimum number" is necessary in order to identify those fisheries that will require a "buy-back" programme.

The optimum number is defined in the law as a reasonable balance of the following general factors:

1.   The number of entry permits sufficient to maintain an economically healthy fishery that will result in a reasonable average rate of economic return to the fishermen participating in that fishery, considering time fished and necessary investments in vessels and gear.

2.   The number of entry permits necessary to harvest the allowable commercial take of the fishery resource during all years in an orderly, efficient manner, and consistent with sound fishery management techniques.

3.   The number of entry permits sufficient to avoid serious economic hardship to those currently engaged in the fishery, considering other economic opportunities reasonably available to them.

Work on item number one above, referred to in shorthand form as "economic optimum numbers," was completed in August of 1976 insofar as the development of a method of determination is concerned. While revisions in the method may be made as it is given a thorough empirical testing, it appears acceptable to the Commission.

That method has been described in a report prepared and submitted under a contract with the National Marine Fisheries Service. The report is titled Income Estimates and Reasonable Returns in Alaska's Salmon Fisheries.[11] In estimating expected returns, subjects considered included: the base period for determining total ex-vessel revenue, fixed and variable costs, labour costs, capital costs, outside earnings, and the fraction of issued permits that are used. Examples of estimates using the equations developed are also provided. In determining the number of operating units necessary to achieve "reasonable" returns, the report describes a method using three forms of comparison:

1. with wages earned in a similar industry;

2. with total annual earnings of non-farm workers; and

3. with estimates provided by fishermen themselves.

Empirical data from the Alaskan salmon fisheries have been used for purposes of exposition only to demonstrate the use to the methodological approach presented.

Work on optimum number criteria numbers two and three is still in progress. When it has been completed, a final integrated product, establishing optimum numbers of units of gear for Alaska's salmon fisheries (19) will be developed by the Commission for the application of another aspect of the State's limited entry law.

The law provides that in any fishery where the optimum number of entry permits is less than the number of entry permits in the fishery, a voluntary buy-back programme for the fishery will be instituted by the Commission. Under the programme the Commission would enter the market for permits, and vessels and gear where necessary, as another buyer. If a fisherman chooses to sell his permit to the Commission, it would be withdrawn from the fishery permanently.

Separate programmes are to be set up for each fishery requiring buy-back, and each programme is to be funded by the permit holders in the fishery for which it is established. Funding is to come from an annual assessment of up to seven percent on the gross catch of the individual permit holders. Preliminary research indicates that an assessment rate of considerably less than seven percent would be required to retire the necessary number of entry permits.

During 1975 the Commission investigated the need for entry regulation in the six commercial salmon fisheries of the Arctic-Yukon-Kuskokwim area of Alaska. The investigation was prompted by significant growth trends over the last five or more years in the amount of gear in those fisheries, and by recommendations for entry regulation advanced by fisheries management biologists and fishermen.

In addition to its research, the Commission conducted a series of hearings in nine villages before proposing regulations. Administrative hearings on the proposed regulations were later conducted in nine villages. The groundwork was also laid for providing application completion assistance to those in the area who might need it. Regulations to limit entry were adopted in early 1976, after changes as a result of public comments and Commission research. The end product was a modified point system, similar to the one used in the first 19 commercial salmon fisheries, but tailored to recognize the unique characteristics of the AYK fisheries.

The Commission mailed out approximately 3,200 applications to potential applicants whom state records indicated had held a gear licence and fished between 1970 and 1975. By the close of the application period in May 1976, the Commission had received some 2,700 applications for entry permits in the Arctic-Yukon-Kuskokwim commercial salmon fisheries.

As with the earlier set of applications, points were computer-
printed on those applications that were mailed out, to the extent that
they could be substantiated by computerized state records. Fishermen
needed to supply no evidence to support these points. In addition,
whenever an applicant's point total reached or exceeded the legal
minimum that required mandatory issuance of a permit the point total
was printed and flagged. Special instructions accompanying such
applications said that the only thing required for the applicant to be
issued a permit was for him to sign the application and submit the proper
fee. Such steps were taken to ease the burden of the evidentiary stages
of the application process.

As of September 1, 1976 in the Arctic-Yukon-Kuskokwim, the
Commission had issued approximately 1,664 entry permits. In addition
it issued some 1,360 interim-use permits to those eligible applicants
who might eventually qualify for entry permits. Based on application
information received and a review of records available to the Commission
information requests were sent out to all applicants who appeared to
have a possibility of substantiating further points. The Commission anticipated that the process of helping fishermen perfect their applications, then classifying the applicants, will continue through 1976.
Hearing officers are expected to begin conducting hearings in early
1977 for those applicants who are claiming special or unavoidable
circumstances which call for an interpretation of the regulations. Since
application processing and permit issuance continued during the fishing
season, many applicants received both an interim-use and an entry
permit.

As indicated above, interim-use permits are issued to applicants
in a fishery under entry limitation who may eventually qualify for an
entry permit. This allows fishermen to continue fishing while administrative determinations are made. Such permits were issued in the

220

1975 fishing season in the 19 fisheries then under regulation. A total
of 469 such interim-use permits were issued in those fisheries through
August 1976.

Interim-use permits are also issued to gear operators in those
fisheries in which a regulated entry programme has not been established.
Their use on fish tickets allows certain fisheries conditions to be monitored, as well as establishing key parts of a data base that would have
to be drawn upon should changed conditions indicate a need for entry
regulation in the future. The Commission issued approximately 10,000
interim-use permits in those fisheries not under entry regulation in 1975,
and approximately 8,500 permits in those fisheries not under entry
regulation in 1976. The apparent drop is accounted for primarily by
the issuance of entry permits in the Arctic-Yukon-Kuskokwim area in
1976 rather than interim-use permits.

Unconcluded Action 1976

Meanwhile, toward the close of 1976 the Commission awaited the
outcome of two events, one of which could affect its future far more
drastically than the other. It awaited the final result of a court challenge that would affect entry permit issuance procedures, and it awaited
the results of the November 2nd general election in which the state's
voters would decide whether to repeal Alaska's limited entry law,
abolishing the programme.

The constitutionality of that portion of Alaska's limited entry law
restricting the applicant pool to those individuals who participated as
gear licence holders at some time from 1960 to 1972 (barring those who
first acquired gear licences in 1973 or 1974) was being tested in the
Alaska court system in 1976 in Isakson v. Rickey, 550 P.2d 359
(Alaska 1976). In the Superior Court, Judge Thomas B. Stewart ruled

that the limited entry law was constitutional in all respects, placing considerable emphasis in his decision on the unrestricted transferability of entry permits. While the State Supreme Court reversed Stewart on the portion of the law mentioned above, differing interpretations of the decision as it affects the form of the court order necessary to implement the decision could bring the matter before the State's highest court again for, in effect, a clarification of its initial decision. Such a decision could affect entry permits already issued; it is expected at the least to create a new potential applicant pool of an estimated 3,200 persons otherwise not eligible to apply for entry permits.

Initiative petitions to repeal the limited entry law were first circulated in the Spring of 1975. A push starting in the late fall of that year resulted in some 16,000 signatures, at least 10,000 of which satisfied the requirements for a legally valid petition signature. That number was more than sufficient to put the question on the November 1976 general election ballot. Those sponsoring the petitions included disgruntled applicants who did not receive permits, persons who (even though they might have received permits) felt that anyone should be able to operate a unit of fishing gear commercially, and a number of shellfish fishermen, based principally in Kodiak, many of whom apparently believed erroneously that the system of entry limitation used in Alaska's salmon fisheries would be applied to the shellfish fisheries.

The largest organized group of supporters of the limited entry law comes from the United Fishermen of Alaska, an umbrella organization for more than 20 commercial fishermen's groups across the state, including thousands of members. These people have formed the Committee to Save Alaska's Salmon, whose sole purpose is to work for the retention of limited entry. The State Board of Fisheries and Board of Game passed a joint resolution in April 1976 urging the retention of the present limited entry programme in regard to salmon. The Alaska

Chapter of the American Fisheries Society has also drafted a resolution in support of limited entry, and public endorsements have been made by a committee of the Alaska Federation of Natives and by the Rural Alaska Community Action Programme.

CONCLUSION

In conclusion it must be stressed that while limited entry can take a variety of forms, it means far more than a step toward integrated management. It means social and economic change, with all of the consequences, bad and good, that such change provokes.

POSTSCRIPT

Organized as the "Committee to Save Alaska's Salmon," Alaskan fishermen raised nearly $170,000 and conducted an intensive battle to retain the state's limited entry programme. As of November 5, 1976, with most of the vote in after the November 2nd election, the results showed 59,963 ballots for retention of limited entry and 34,500 for repeal. While it was generally recognized that the law may need amendments, the 63.4 per cent margin of victory should be sufficient to establish limited entry as a continuing management tool.

REFERENCES

1. State of Alaska, Limited Entry Act of 1973, AS 16.43.010(a).
    Juneau: Legislative Affairs Agency

2. State of Alaska, Limited Entry Act of 1973, AS 16.43. loc. cit.

3. State of Alaska, Fiscal Year 1974 budget, Office of the
    Governor, Commercial Fisheries Entry Commission.

4. Personal Communication, Roy A. Rickey, former director,
    Commercial Fisheries Division, Department of Fish and Game,
    State of Alaska, Juneau, Alaska, January 1973. c.f.
    management records, Commercial Fisheries Division,
    Department of Fish and Game, State of Alaska, Anchorage
    and Kodiak regional offices respectively for Cook Inlet
    and Kodiak information.

5. "Grandfathered in" "Grandfathering" refers to provisions in a
    law that establish a cutoff date and recognize certain pre-
    existing rights. In implementing Alaska's limited entry law
    in the first 19 salmon fisheries, eligibility to apply for an
    entry permit was such a right for those fishermen who held
    a gear license and harvested the fishery resource commercially
    prior to January 1, 1973, in the fishery for which they were
    applying.

6. State of Alaska, Limited Entry Act of 1973: AS 16.43. Juneau
    Legislative Affairs Agency.

7. State of Alaska, Commercial Fisheries Entry Commission, un-
    published working documents based upon United States
    Internal Revenue Service reports.

8. OWERS, J. Costs and Earnings of Alaskan Fishing Vessels : An
    Economic Survey. Juneau : State of Alaska, Commercial
    Fisheries Entry Commission, September 1974.

9. "Arctic-Yukon-Kuskokwim," or "AYK" refers to the Alaska fish
    and game management area made up of those watersheds north
    of Bristol Bay draining into the Bering Sea, the Chukchi Sea
    and the Arctic Ocean, including St. Lawrence, St. Mathew,
    and Nunivak islands. Generally speaking, "Arctic" refers

to the area north of the Brooks Range. The Yukon and Kuskokwim are the major rivers south of the range and within the management area.

10. State of Alaska, Commercial Fisheries Entry Commission, unpublished computer run. Permits were sorted on the basis of address ZIP code.

11. United States Government, National Marine Fisheries Service, Alaska Region, Income Estimates and Reasonable Returns in Alaska's Salmon Fisheries, Contract No. 03-4-208-262 as amended. Juneau, August 1976.

PLATE 33
Return From the High Seas

SECTION III

THE FUTURE

"Unless there is a public will, echoed by a political
commitment, honestly to attempt to understand and
balance environmental gains and losses, resource
managers will be unable to fulfill their
potentially most exciting and valuable
role in making the world a pleasanter
place in which to live."

"Nor is the experimental evaluation procedure a substitute
for imaginative interpretation of existing data or an
automatic mechanism to create better plans. It is
simply a format for helping to bring imaginative
thinking out into the open."

"Perhaps men and salmon cannot live together, and
salmon will survive only where men cannot.
Like Cousteau's splendid penguins swimming
under the Antarctic ice they will abide...
in inhospitable waters until
man's day is passed."

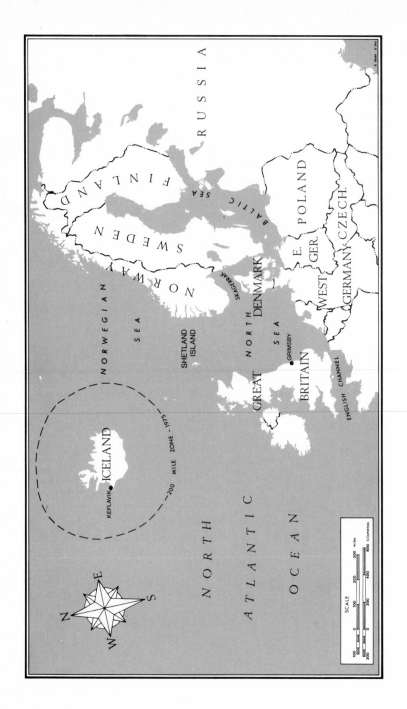

PLATE 34 Iceland's Impact on Global Commons

CHAPTER 9

RESOURCE MANAGEMENT IN A
GLOBAL COMMONS

Timothy O'Riordan

School of Environmental Sciences
University of East Anglia

INTRODUCTION

There was a time, not so long ago when resource management
was regarded largely as a technical economic accounting exercise to
determine how much and when to extract resources at least cost.[1]
Admittedly pure economists would talk of a goal of maximising long
run net social welfare, but most paid only lip service to the difficulties
of ascertaining all the relevant social effects of resource development
programmes, so agreed that to maximise net economic gains was a
reasonable approximation.[2] In this context, resources were regarded
as 'neutral stuff' which 'became' valuable with the growth of economic
development and technological advance.[3] Underlying this was the
simple proposition that resource development today meant not only
economic wealth tomorrow, but the improved ability to extract more
raw materials from the globe to produce even greater prosperity the day
after. 'The scientific age differs in kind, and not only in degree from
the preceding mechanical age', noted Barnet and Morse, in their
classic neo-Ricardian analysis of this topic.[4]

> Not only ingenuity but, increasingly, under-
> standing; not luck but systematic investigation, are
> turning the tables on nature, making her subservient
> to man... Thus the increasing scarcity of particular

229

resources fosters discovery or development of
alternative resources, not only equal in economic quality but often superior to those replaced.

These were the heady days of neoclassical welfare economics
where property rights in resource ownership were either defined or
tacitly assumed and when externalities were regarded as peripheral
allocative distortions that could readily be corrected either by a suitable bribe or by the knowledge that compensation to losers could be
paid so that nobody should be worse off and at least somebody was
better off. Despite the protests from some economists that interpersonal
utilities were not comparable,[5] these important distributive (not to say
ethical) matters were conveniently subsumed within the vaguely applic-
able theory of Pareto optimality, that had little relation to the real
world.[6]

AN EMERGING PARADIGM : ECOLOGICAL ECONOMICS

Today these assumptions are under attack not merely from environmentalists but from other economists, who seek a return to
the emphasis in resource management theory backwards to the original
notion of social wellbeing and onwards to a new concept of ecological
protection.[7] Let us call this new approach 'ecological economics',
for it no longer takes for granted the marvellous restorative powers of
nature or the seemingly infinite tolerance of certain sections of the
public to accept environmental discomfort. The prime target of this
paradigm attack is the oft challenged allocative tool of the resource
management profession, benefit cost analysis.[8] But it should be
stressed that the whole theory of neoclassical economics is under fire,
not merely its accountancy handmaiden, for the premises upon which
this theory was based are no longer regarded as acceptable.

Criticisms of Neoclassical Economics

The cost of environmental nuisance

The new resource management theorists no longer regard environmental disamenities as mere allocative distortions which can suitably be corrected by adjusting the price mechanism. For one thing there are few property rights for environmental bads, so sufferers have neither economic nor legal resource to seek relief. 'Medicines are proprietary, but germs are free'. observed Schelling.[9] 'I can have you arrested if you steal my electric amplifier, but help yourself to the noise'. In the absence of any reform in legal rights, pricing mechanisms cannot work because the form and amount of interparty compensation depend on the law of property rights – which tend to favour the nusiance generator over the nuisance receiver.[10]

The matter of ill defined property rights for environmental bads is an important one, because it is now apparent that such bads are joint products of the production and consumption of environmental goods (see Figure 1,9) which are not necessarily suffered or paid for by those who produce or consume the products of that activity. In Figure 1,9 the upper graph shows the conventional Supply (S) – Demand (D) relationship for the production and consumption of a good, and its price Pg. The lower graph shows the associated production of nuisance (bads) first in absolute terms (Na), then as known about (Nk) – this may be 'controlled' by information made available by the nuisance generator – and finally as 'perceived' (Np) by the public. The willingness to pay to avoid nuisance (Pb) varies according to knowledge and awareness – concern. In the past, the suffering public was seemingly largely content to suffer, because many accepted the apparent personal gains from economic development as worth the costs, and in any case few were so

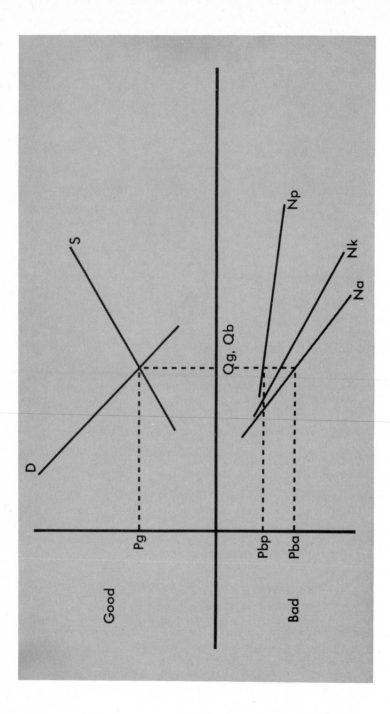

FIGURE 1,9. Determining Optimum Levels of Resource Production in Relation to Environmental Nuisance

politically organised or legally supported as to create any counter-
vailing political pressure to the powerful forces promoting resource
development.[11]

Today, a sizeable number of people are reaching the conclusion
that the 'social optimum' of Pareto influenced neoclassical economics
will never be achieved unless the nature of economic development and
the allocative theories upon which it depends recognise the pervasive
influence of environmental nuisances and ensures that these are either
eliminated or that the third party losers are adequately and fairly
compensated. It will be clear that if this proposition is accepted then
resource management theories move beyond the realm of economics
into ambits of politics and law. For it carries with it radical notions
of participatory democracy and redefined property rights in law, including the possibility of legally enforceable rights to a minimum level
of environmental quality, and even to the protection of a particular
way of earning a living.[12]

The question of determining optimism levels of resource production in relation to environmental nuisance is now most controversial.
The underlying theoretical basis for much of the discussion is illustrated
by Figure 2,9. In this diagram W represents the amount of waste generated with the increasing production of good X. Ao is the assimilative
capacity of the environment before pollution occurs; A_1 is the assim-
ilation capacity of the environment as degraded by pollution. The
curve TB –TIC is that of total benefits minus total input costs outside
of costing for any nuisance. Thus it relates to Pq – Qq function in
Figure 1,9. The curve TPC_0 is the value of pollution costs (equivalent
to Pb in Figure 1,9) when the assimilative capacity of the environment
is not degraded. The curve TCP_1 is the value of pollution costs as the
environmental quality worsens and is more cherished.

233

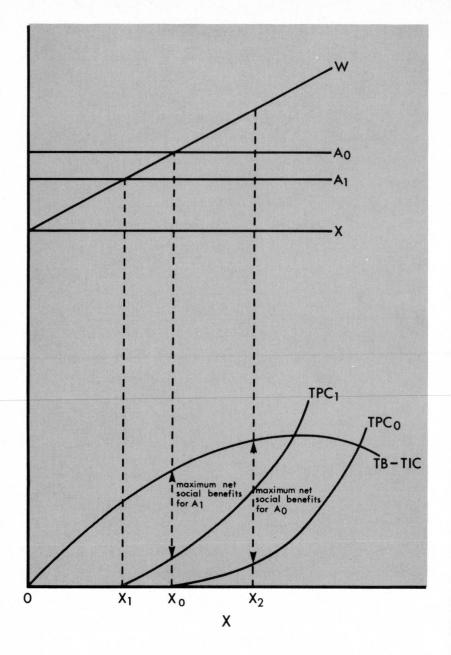

FIGURE 2,9. Neoclassical Model for Determining Optimum Level of Production

Looking at Figure 2,9 based on some work by David Pearce,[13] it will be seen that under the neoclassical rubric, the optimum level of production would be at X_2 where net social benefits are maximised. But this is at a point beyond the assimilative capacity of the environment (including minority groups) to absorb (tolerate) the nuisance, so if output is sustained at this point, the environmental nuisances will relatively worsen (because they will become less assimilated more noticeable and more resented) requiring a new social optimum at point X_0. But this is still an unstable situation given a degrading environment and a less tolerant public and the optimum point of maximising net social benefits could shift further to X_1. Pearce contends that the ecological optimum and the economic optimum should be fixed from the start at X_0, that is, where environmental nuisance is all but eliminated. This approach, however, depends on two crucial assumptions, neither of which can be properly proven:

1. that the assimilative capacity of the environment degrades once it is exceeded and can never be restored, (and of course can be calculated in the first place), and

2. that public recognition and hostility to environmental nuisance increases as the nuisance worsens even if economic output is slowing up.

The writer is not convinced of either of these assumptions, though the reader may have different views. But whatever the outcome, resource allocation theories and methods will have to change to accommodate this challenge.

The notion of limits

The second component in the emerging paradigm of ecological economics is the explicit inclusion of 'ecological limits' into economic analysis. As indicated earlier, most neoclassical economists were quite content to assume away the notion of scarcity or resource limits on the grounds:

1. that man's technological inventiveness has enormous, if not infinite, capability to devise new resource exploiting and resource conserving techniques,

2. that the sobering impact of real price increases would bring (1) about, and

3. that the ability of groups of individuals, interested parties or nations, threatened by a scarcity of commonly owned resources, would, in their collective self interest, determine successful organisational and political means to control wasteful resource exploitation in order to guarantee resource availability and a productive economy simultaneously.[14]

Today this ideological faith in man's communal protective powers is also being challenged. This challenge takes two forms:

1. a demand for an adequate theory of ecological limits into which can be adjusted traditional concepts of waste and inefficiency, and

2. a belief that any new theory of resource management must incorporate an adequate distinction between needs (that are commonly regarded as essential for a civilised people) and wants (that are less commonly viewed as unnecessary but which are demanded for reasons of status, self indulgence, and sheer avarice).

Figure 3,9 links the relationship between the two components of the new approach to resource management. The reader will recognise the importance of the interactional relationships portrayed on the figure as these form the essence of social and political dynamics.

The distinction between needs and wants takes us once again into the world of politics (which determines moral judgements which are politically acceptable) and philosophy (which deals with ethical judgements which are viewed as socially desirable irrespective of a particular

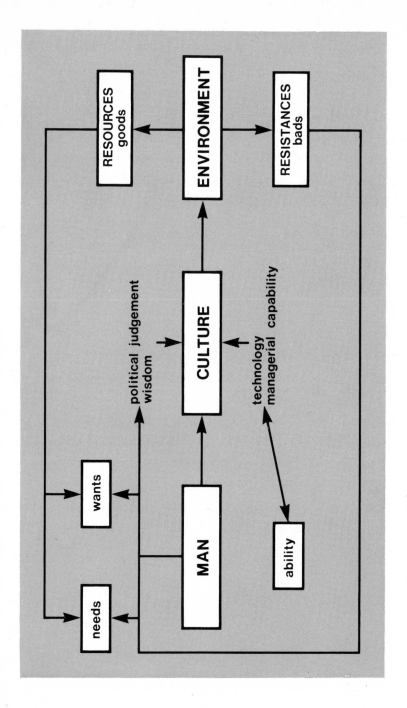

FIGURE 3.9.   New Model for Resource Management

237

political ideology). When these matters are brought into the framework of limits, the moral and ethical implications of resource management practices come very much to the fore, since in a zero sum game (necessary if one accepts the notion of limits), either everyone has to lose a little, or someone's gain is someone else's loss. In the world of renewable resources that are jointly owned (such as the ocean fishery), this problem is now very significant as these resources cannot meet the rising demand for them yet there are only imperfectly developed economic, legal and political mechanisms for allocating the fixed stock fairly.

The zero-sum game problem becomes even more troublesome if we view the world as a global commons with accepted but ill-defined limits to its exploitable environmental resources, because in the global context, whole nations stand to win or lose when resources are utilised. And at present there are few mechanisms for arbitrating transnational environmental rights and wrongs.[15] It is in this context that the case study which follows should be viewed, for it is the writer's belief that the twin challenge to traditional resource management theories becomes far more demanding when political and social procedures for allocating commonly owned global renewable resources are considered. And unless there is fairly substantial political and legal reform, there is a danger that their resources may be allocated by brute nationalistic force rather than through a faith in fair play. So the political and legal response to the international management of global resources should be worth watching.

PLATE 35
Whose Fish?

B.C. Archives Photo

239

A CASE STUDY :
THE ANGLO-ICELANDIC COD WAR

On June 1 1976 the Foreign Secretaries of Britain and Iceland signed a treaty that concluded the second, and hopefully the last, Anglo-Icelandic cod war. As the issues are possibly not too familiar to the North American reader, the relevant details will be outlined before analysing the case in the light of the new approaches to resource management.

The British have long prided themselves as a seafaring nation, with a powerful tradition in commercial fishing despite its very modest contribution to national wealth (around 0.001 percent). In recent years, along with many other fishing nations, the fishing fleet has travelled further and further afield because inshore stocks are largely depleted, and because the use of increasingly expensive and technologically sophisticated fishing vessels has made the lucrative deep sea fishing economically viable. Before 1972 about two thirds of all Britain's deepwater fishing took place within 50 miles of the Icelandic coast, and even though this accounted for only one fifth of all the UK fish catch by weight, it produced one third of all the edible fish and one half the total value of fish caught. The most popular (and profitable) species was the cod, admired for its white, fleshy appearance and its ease of filleting. Over one third of all fish eaten (6 lbs of an annual national per capita average of 17.5 lbs) is cod, which is also the mainstay of the nations 'fish and chips' industry.

As predicted in well known economic theory, the economic optimum for a common property fish catch exceeds the biological optimum, so depletion of stocks is inevitable.[16] In 1972 Iceland sought to defend her precious stocks of cod and herring by extending unilaterally her rights to those species over a zone 50 miles from her shores.

International convention allows states only to extend such rights to
12 miles, though there were precedents for extending economic sovereignty over oceanic resources over a 200 mile zone.[17] The British
protested on correct but technical legal grounds and sent in frigates
to defend her trawlers. After a protracted negotiation the two countries
signed a two year pact limiting the number of British trawlers eligible
to fish in the disputed zone from 139 to about 80, and restricting their
fishing areas to a number of selected areas. Similar agreements were
made between Iceland and other European countries, notably Denmark,
Norway and West Germany.

This Anglo-Icelandic pact ended on November 13 1975, before
which the British Government did very little either to compensate its
deepwater trawler industry or to encourage it to fish for alternative
species in British coastal waters. Yet, the fishing industry suffered;
of a total of 600 medium and long distance trawlers, 137 were laid up,
25 of which were removed from the 139 trawlers fishing off the Icelandic coast.

On October 15 1975, again unilaterally and again without
prior consultation, Iceland announced its de facto ownership of the
fishing resource over a 200 mile zone. In this action it proclaimed
that it was merely anticipating the agreement of the sixth Law of the
Sea Conference that was held in March 1976: nevertheless its decision
was again technically illegal - a fact that Britain recognised when she
once more sent in naval frigates to protect her fishing vessels. This
time, however, the Icelanders meant business and instructed their gunboats to harass the trawlers and ram the thin skinned frigates - a task
they performed with the utmost skill and devastating effect.

Why were the Icelanders so determined in their resolve? The
answer lies partly in the Icelandic character, partly in her conservationist zeal and partly in her internal politics.

The Icelandic Character

The Icelanders are a proud independent people with over a thousand years of tradition who cherish their way of life and support each other during grim times. They are a pleasant affable people whose mild manners disguise a toughness and grim determination that is shared by other northern peoples such as the Shetlanders and the Norwegians. They do not give in easily, especially where convinced they are right. As bargainers they really are in a class of their own.

The Conservation Issue

When it comes to protecting their fish stocks, the Icelanders are most zealous. The Icelandic marine research institute had advised its government that the cod stocks were seriously threatened by over-fishing, that control by catch quotas was unenforceable and in any case the quotas were too high and that the total fishable catch for 1976 should be 230,000 tons (c.f. 360,000 tons in 1975). They recommended that the United Kingdom's take be reduced to 65,000 tons (from 130,000 in 1975), and certainly no more. The British assumed this was a bargaining position, argued just for 110,000 then for 85,000 tons but found only an entrenched and unplacable opposition and a growing political demand to reduce the figure of 65,000 tons still further.

The Political Issue

Fishing is not only a way of life to the Icelanders, it is their economic lifeblood. Between 75 and 80 percent of her foreign revenue comes from fish exports, notably cod for the United States fish finger market. During the world recession of 1974-75 when demand for processed foods fell (amongst many other things), the Icelandic economy suffered a severe setback as increased oil prices soaked up her dwindling

242

foreign revenue. Inflation was rife, the working population was growing restless over high prices, so the coalition government was forced to devalue the krona twice in 1974, once by 17 percent and subsequently by a further 20 percent. As a consequence, the ruling party was under attack from both left and right, and hence could not afford to show any sign of weakness toward the British. Its final ace was the genuine threat to close the NATO air base at Keflavik which is considered of vital strategic importance in monitoring Russian naval activity.

So the British had to lose because both the dictates of marine biology and world public opinion was on the side of the Icelanders. The June agreement replaces the present ineffective method of catch quotas, with an easily policed limit of 24 licensed trawlers confined to clearly specified fishing zones. This means the loss of income for some 7000 trawlermen and their dependents, plus unemployment for another 25,000 to 35,000 in the fish packing and processing industries – not a pleasant outcome for the British Foreign Secretary to contemplate, especially as his political constituency is Grimsby, one of the hardest hit Yorkshire fishing ports. The pact will also cause the price of cod to rise fourfold as most of it will now have to be imported from Iceland and Norway, and obviously there will be an adverse impact on Britain's long-suffering balance of payments.

RESOURCE MANAGEMENT IN THE FUTURE

In the light of the cod war case study, let us look at the future of resource management in a zero-sum world where the environmental disruptions caused by economic development give rise to increasing alarm.

PLATE 36
Final Fishery

The Scientific and Political Dispute over Limits

To the average western mind the notion of resource limits is an unfamiliar one that is instinctively rejected. Certainly neither scientists nor politicians like to talk in these terms, preferring instead to discuss the challenge to technological and organisational ingenuity brought on by apparent resource scarcity.

No-one likes to put a figure on limits. In the cod war dispute, British and Icelandic fisheries biologists disagreed by a factor of two as to the maximum sustainable yield of cod, and each criticised the other's sampling methods and models of population dynamics. In this connection it is interesting to record that while the matter of fish conservation was regarded as the most important issue by the Icelanders, the British press and politicians concentrated on the illegality of the Icelandic action, the devastating economic impact on the home fishing industry and the naval histrionics of the gunboats and frigates.

Here we have a fundamental dispute over the nature of the problem. Looking again at Figures 2,9 and 3,9 it will be seen that resource management involves a package of gains and losses that link in to a variety of political goals. So problem definition and the stress given to different components of the problem by various pressure groups will become a more complex business for resource managers in the future. Holt[18] observes that the well tried technique of devising a maximum sustainable yield figure to guide world fisheries management is now under attack from all sides. To the biologists it is a dangerously simplified index of an intensely complex dynamic process, while to the economist it bears little relationship to the costs of fishing effort: to both there is always the possibility of underestimation of MSY which could result in species extinction. To define suitable stock size and appropriate catch limits is a treacherous business on which a variety of legitimate interests have quite fundamentally opposing views.

It is in this kind of context that traditional concepts of benefit-cost analysis as a resource allocative device run into difficulties,
since single discount rates cannot reflect societies different preferences
for a variety of benefits and costs. Some economists[19] are now calling
for a weighted discount rate to reflect the values people place in preserving options for the future. It is clear that these distorted rates will
involve political value judgements, but the economic implication of
this new approach is to encourage governments to place a 'social rent'
on the depletion of an exhaustible resource in order to dampen demand
pressures ahead of absolute scarcity. This social rent, or depletion
tax, would be a kind of insurance against irreversible destruction of
a resource, the possibility of which is not fully reflected in normal
market pricing.

In political terms, the matter of limits has equally dramatic
implications because, if accepted, it might render meaningless the
usual procedures of give and take bargaining. The British genuinely
thought the Icelandic figure of 65,000 tons was the prelude to bargaining; the Icelanders did not. So the politics of negotiation and
compromise gave way to the politics of confrontation and aggression.
This is a sobering prospect for resource managers to contemplate, but
one which is all the more probable if cherished values are at stake.
For compromise in values notes Crowe,[20] is not a form of rational
behaviour, but 'is rather a clear case of either apostasy or heresy'.
In the absence of well defined rights and respected arbitrating tribunals
the use of force and bluff may become the principal tools of resource
allocation to the detriment of world political stability and social
fairness. It is therefore not surprising that a number of respected
international lawyers are calling for an independent judicial tribunal

backed up by an international scientific research secretariat to advise
political judgements over the allocation of transnational resources.[21]

The current proposal before the Law of the Sea Conference to
extend coastal state economic sovereignty to a zone 200 miles offshore
(the 'exclusive economic zone' (EEZ) concept), perhaps advanced with
the best of conservationist intentions, is nevertheless an example of
aggressive expropriation that continues to be resisted by the have not
nations. For the EEZ notion will grant the resources of one third of
the global oceans to a mere handful of nations, ten of which will
control over a fifth of the world's marketable fish stocks. Even if the
non coastal states delay this proposal, it seems that the major nations
will legislate 200 mile EEZ's anyway.[22] Even Britain is finally getting
in on the act, her trawler lobby arguing in favour of a 100 mile zone
though the European Commission plans to grant her only a variable zone
of 6-50 miles.[23]

If the well equipped, long distance fishing vessels are forced
to turn to nationally controlled waters, the consequences for the
world's inshore fisheries could be catastrophic. These boats must operate on a massive scale and continuously to remain profitable, so any
pattern of quotas of maximum allowable catch would in all probability
be disregarded. The only feasible enforceable solution will be to limit
the number and size of vessels operating in these waters and possibly
to zone fishing areas for different categories of boat.[24]

Wants versus Needs

The wants-needs issue will also become more troublesome for
resource managers, who will need to turn to criteria other than purely
economic ones to determine gains and losses. In the cod war case,
while the British public could survive with no fish protein at all, what

247

fish protein they do require doesn't have to be cod protein. In any case, looking at protein consumption data, it appears that the fuss over the reduction of cod is made more by the cod producers (including the big processing firms)[25] than the consumers. Fish accounts for only 4 percent of the average British family's food budget, the average British family eating 3-5 times as much meat as fish and more eggs and cheese than fish by weight. From Table 1,9 it will also be seen that fish consumption is declining as prices rise and supplies dwindle, though fish prices have not risen as fast as those of meat or cheese (Figure 4,9). Prima facie there appears to be a shift to cheese (which is subsidised) and away from fish and meat (which are not).

TABLE 1,9

ESTIMATED HOUSEHOLD FOOD CONSUMPTION

Food Items	Ounces per person per week		
	1966	1970	1974
Cheese	3.11	3.59	3.94
Eggs	4.77	4.60	4.09
Meat	17.17	15.88	14.22
Fresh Fish	4.18	3.67	2.76
Frozen Fish	0.74	0.99	0.96

Source: Annual Abstract of Statistics, Central Statistical Office H.M.S.O. p. 242.

However, how far people will continue to be willing to switch to other proteins if fish prices rise is open to question. Certainly substitutes for cod are available - blue whiting and coley for example. But coley is a grey-coloured fish that is best cooked as a casserole that takes time

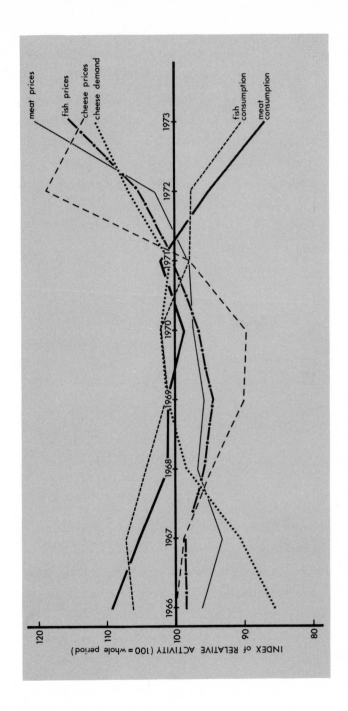

FIGURE 4.9. Food Consumption and Price Changes

249

and trouble. And the British consumer seems to prefer fleshy white fish that is easy to cook – as indicated by the fish price elasticities listed as Table 2,9. (In this table figures indicate the percentage drop in consumption for a 1 percent rise in price all other things being equal. Note the surprisingly low elasticities of eggs and fresh white fish). In any case, the fish processing industry dislikes the blue whiting as it is a difficult fish to fillet, requiring expensive imported machines, and in addition its short period of availability means that the industry would have to invest in expensive cold storage facilities.

TABLE 2,9

PRICE ELASTICITIES FOR FISH AND OTHER
PROTEINS, 1973

Uncooked white	-0.20
Frozen white	-1.50
Frozen fish products	-0.98
Canned salmon	-2.66
Eggs	-0.09
Meat	-0.62

Source: Ministry of Agriculture, Fisheries and Food:
Household Food Consumption and Expenditure,
1973. H.M.S.O. 1975.

Yet the average Briton eats between two and three times his daily protein requirement, so in terms of needs, this fuss is really over nothing important. It is only in terms of wants that it becomes a significant political and economic matter, and here the issue is contaminated by questions of industrial organisation, habit and custom, and the vast intellectual, cognitive and spatial separation of raw material in situ, producer, middleman and consumer. So the argument becomes not

250

whether the British consumer can or ought to be prized away from cod
(this is in part already happening), but whether the fish marketing
organisations will willingly permit it and the extent to which the government will actively support them. The fish finger manufacturers who
have recently spent $500,000 on a cod promotion campaign, are not
likely to give up without a fight. In the long run, price and resource
availability will determine the answer, but the resource manager is
interested in the short term and policies to promote change. How
consumers respond to scarcities in cherished goods and how these goods
should be appropriately allocated will certainly become important
matters for the resource manager of the future to contemplate.

The Balancing of Resource and Resistance

Resource and resistance fuse in environmental impact assessment.
There really isn't a theory of environmental impact assessment and
probably there never will be one, because in many ways it is a political
process of accounting that makes use of interdisciplinary scientific
analysis. The almost insuperable problems here are those of risk assessment and the weighting and balancing of incommensurables. So
environmental impact assessment can never be a technique so much as a
process of political judgement that involves professionals, resource
development and monitoring agencies and interested members of the
public communicating with and understanding each other.[26] This will
certainly mean, in the long run if not sooner, radical changes in the
relationship between elected offices and their constituents, and possibly
quite novel consultative procedures among various interested and affected groups before policies are determined, let alone specific resource
development proposals. This in turn will require a virtual revolution
in the education of a citizenry sensitive to the legitimate demands of

251

minorities and cognizant of the limits to technological prowess. And in turn again, this will mean   adequate guarantees for all affected parties to be able to present their case and be heard.[27]

IMPLICATIONS FOR PACIFIC SALMON

Many of the points raised by the Atlantic cod issue are pertinent for any discussion of the politics of pacific salmon. In 1970 the industry was worth some $37 million to the British Columbia economy, or approximately one tenth of its gross provincial product. It was rapidly becoming overcapitalised with too many small boats running at the margin of profitability while the processing companies were centralising the total industry. Of the 6600 vessels licenced to fish, 34 percent accounted for only 3.4 percent of the total catch and most of their skippers earned a pittance for an annual income. Most of the 1200 or so boats owned and/or operated by Indians fell into this category. So here was the classic situation of increasing concentration of effort, diminishing marginal returns to the additional small operator and of course a growing threat to the conservation of the species.

Since then, the Federal Government has acted to control the addition of new small boats through a new system of licensing based on tonnage. This has had the effect of eliminating many of the marginal operators whose vessels went up for sale to the non-fishing market. This was a bold move motivated by the interests of economic efficiency and presumably of the future of the salmon. However it did result in two classes of boat, the 'A' (larger and more capital intensive) vessel which enjoyed a de facto guarantee to fish in a more profitable market, and the 'B' (smaller) vessel which was slowly being phased out. Given a relatively fixed stock of salmon, it is natural that the 'A' boats will improve in value and further intensify their fishing effort: for although the 'B' vessel will slowly disappear since it is generally inefficient, the net effect on catching success will be negligible. So the federal policy has not really addressed itself to the conservation issue.

Socially, the new policy was disastrous since it put out of work the marginal operator who was not readily suited to alternative employment. Since Indians have historic rights to fish and were even more threatened by the new policy, they successfully petitioned to have 'A' licences, even though most of their boats fell into the 'B' category.

So the pressure on the salmon stocks continues and it is now politically even more difficult for the government to curtail the number or catch quotas of the existing vessels suffering from the burdens of large capital investment and high running costs. The Canadian government has sought to protect its pacific salmon stocks by promising a 200 mile exclusive zone for the west coast fishery to control fishing by other nations, particularly the Russians. Meanwhile the price of salmon rises and the consumer demand, always fairly low, falls. Canadians are not noted for their fish-eating tradition while the price elasticity for canned salmon is very high.[28] In the long run, the pacific salmon may be saved by the reflexes of the market place rather than by the dictates of conservation, but there could well be a long political argument over how best to regulate an over-efficient industry that has little room for manoeuvre if control must come through the price mechanism.

CONCLUSIONS

Many of the suggestions for future resource management strategies made in this chapter are distant visions, but they are the cynosure for the far sighted resource manager of today, who is aware not simply of national responsibilities but of international and transcultural obligations. There are signs in the wind that these reforms are in the air, but it is barely a breeze at present. Environmental impact assessment is working in many guises in the United States, but it is still resisted by the governments of Britain and Canada, probably because they fear the consequences.[29] Improved rights of legal redress over environmental nuisance are now evident in the United States and a small breakthrough is apparent in Canada, though there is still little response in the United Kingdom.[30] Meanwhile, there are promising attempts to provide aggrieved citizens with enforceable legal rights to protect themselves against transnational pollution,[31] though again, the emphasis to date has been on talk rather than action. But the courts can only prod the mischievous into a semblance of honesty and responsibility. Unless there is a public will, echoed by a political commitment, honestly to attempt to understand and balance environmental gains and losses, resource managers will be unable to fulfill their potentially most exciting and valuable role in making the world a pleasanter place in which to live.

REFERENCES

1. The theory was based on well developed concepts of neoclassical welfare economics. For a good statement, see ECKSTEIN, D. Water Resource Development: The Economics of Project Evaluation. Cambridge Mass: Harvard University Press, 1950, pp. 15-20. Also HERFINDAHL, D.C. and KNEESE, A.V., Economic Theory of Natural Resources. Columbus, Ohio: Messill, 1974, pp. 222-281.

2. To do this, economists had to assume some connection between preferences for a certain bundle of goods and willingness to pay. They maintained that through the mechanism of price, preferences could be ordered along a measurable scale.

3. The classic statement here can be found in the introduction to ZIMMERMAN, H.W. World Resources and Industries. New York: Harper and Row, 1951.

4. BARNET, H.D. and MORSE, C. Scarcity and Growth: The Economics of Natural Resource Availability. Baltimore: John Hopkins Press, 1963, p. 10.

5. H.C. Robbins pointed out in 1932 that preferences and disutilities cannot be compared because peoples ideas about what they like and dislike are unique to each individual. See ROBBINS, H.C. The Nature and Significances of Economic Science. London: Macmillan, 1932.

6. Economists have tried to bypass this important conceptual road-block by producing the theorem that if gainers could compensate the losers and still be better off, then this new arrangement would improve total economic wellbeing. The trouble is that in the real world this transaction is very rarely made, and even if compensation is awarded it is rarely paid by the beneficiaries, but mainly by the taxpayers at large. In any case, the very nature of compensation is not simply determined as a function of worth of loss, but of distribution of property rights. Se MISHAN, E. "The economics of disamenity" Natural Resources Journal, 14 (1974), pp. 55-86.

7. The most prominent members of this new school are Herman Daly in the U.S. and David Pearce in the U.K. See DALY, H.E. (ed). Toward a Steady State Economy. San Francisco: Freeman, 1973 and PEARCE, D.W. Environmental Economics, London: Longmans, 1976.

8. For a review of the criticisms of benefit cost analysis and efforts being made to revise it, see O'RIORDAN, T. Environment-alism London: Pion, 1976, pp. 171-178. See also PEARCE, D.W. Cost Benefit Analysis. London: Macmillan, 1971, and SELF, P.O. Econocrats and the Policy Process: The Politics and Philosophy of Cost Benefit Analysis. London: Macmillan, 1976.

9. SCHELLING, T.C. "On the ecology of micromotives" The Public Interest 25 (1971) pp. 61-98.

10. This theme is well developed by MISHAN (1974) op. cit. (see note 6).

11. For a readable, and largely accurate review of these forces, see WEISBERG, B. Beyond Repair: The Ecology of Capitalism. Boston: Beacon Press, 1971. There is no single equivalent volume in the Canadian context, though the reader will get the flavour by reading MITCHELL, D. The Politics of Food. Toronto: Lorimer, 1975 and GUTTSTEIN, D., Vancouver Ltd. Toronto: Lorimer, 1975.

12. This is a large subject area which cannot be developed in the limited context of this article. See LUCAS, A.R. "Legal foundations for public participation in environmental decision making" Natural Resources Journal 16 (1976), pp. 73-102.

13. PEARCE, D.W. "Are environmental problems a challenge to economic science?" Ethics in Science and Medicine 2 (1975) pp. 79-88.

14. Much of the criticism levelled at Limits to Growth argues these points. The best single critique is COLE, H.S.D. et al. Thinking about the Future. Brighton: Sussex University Press, 1973.

15. The interested reader will find useful material in the symposium on international law in Natural Resources Journal vol. 13 No. 2.

(April 1975), and in various issues of the relatively new journal Environmental Policy and Law.

16. This theorem was first propounded by GORDON, H.S. "The economic theory of a common property resource: the fishery" The Journal of Political Economy (1954) reprinted in DORFMAN, R. and DORFMAN, N. Economics of the Environment. New York: Norton, 1972, pp. 88-89.

17. In 1948 President Truman declared that the U.S. was recognising a 250 mile economic interest over its coastal seabed, and since 1970 more than 7 nations have announced a national economic interest over ocean resources out to 200 miles. See JOHNSON, B. "Third World and Environmental Interests in the Law of the Sea", London: Institute for Environment and Development, 1975.

18. HOLT, S.S. "Objectives in conserving the living resources of the sea" in STEIN, R.E. (ed). Critical Environmental Issues on the Law of the Sea", London: International Institute for Environment and Development (1975).

19. KRUTILLA, J.V. and FISHER, A.C. The Economics of Natural Environments: Studies in the Valuation of Community and Amenity Resources. Baltimore: John Hopkins Press and PLOURDE, C. "Conservation of extinguishable species" Natural Resources Journal 15 (1975) pp. 791-798.

20. CROWE, B.L. "The tragedy of the commons revisited" Science, 166 (1969) pp. 1103-1107.

21. See especially TECLAFF, L.A. "The impact of environmental concern in the development of international law" Natural Resources Journal 13 (1973) pp. 357-390.

22. Canada, Norway and the United States have already indicated that they will extend economic sovereignty over 200 miles by mid 1977 regardless of the outcome of the next Law of the Sea Conference.

23. This issue is still very contentious within the EEC. The most likely outcome is an elastic zone of fishing rights allocated to certain countries and the European Community jointly, but

the adverse outcome of the cod war may cause the British
Government to alter her bargaining tactics.

24.   For a good discussion of the effects on the English Channel
mackerel fishery see ALLABY, M. "The mackerel war"
The Ecologist 6 (1976), pp. 133-137.

25.   Two firms account for 65 per cent of the 40 million frozen fish
finger industry in the U.K. Birdseye (40 per cent) and
Findus Foods (25 per cent).

26.   There are few good analyses of environmental impact assessment,
as it is a procedure that is only in the United States.
A good bibliography is contained in MUNN, R.D. (ed.)
Environmental Impact Assessment:Principles and Procedures:
Toronto: SCOPE Report No. 51975. See also MORLEY,
C.G. (ed.) Proceedings of the National Conference on
Environmental Impact Assessment: Philosophy and Method-
ology, Winnipeg: Agassiz Centre for Water Studies (1974)
and O'RIORDAN, T. and HEY, R.D. (eds.) Environmental
Impact Assessment, Farnborough, Hants D.C. Heath, 1976.

27.   For a good coverage of the question of citizen participation in
resource management, see the symposium in the Natural
Resouces Journal Vol. 16, January 1976, and ELDER, P.S.
(ed.) Environmental Management and Public Participation.
Toronto: Canadian Environmental Law Association, 1976.

28.   In 1969 all fish products amounted to only 2% family food
expenditure (4.7% in 1974), the total weight consumed was
only 0.38 lbs in 1969 and 0.34 lbs per family in 1974.
Linked to the change in the consumer price index for the
two years this gives a price elasticity for all fish of 0.05.
This appears to mean that Canadians are low fish consumers
but changes in price do not significantly shift demand.
Salmon demand as a percentage of all fish consumed was
9% in 1969 and 14% in 1974, a very small proportion and
similar to cod in weight consumed for both years. Data
from Statistics Canada.

29.   For a study of British reaction see O'RIORDAN and HEY (1976),
op. cit. (note 26). For a review of the Canadian government's
reaction see LUCAS, A.R. and McCALLUM, S.K. "Looking
at the environmental impact assessment" Alternatives,5

258

(1976), pp. 33-39.

30.   For a general review of the status of environmental law in these
      countries, see O'RIORDAN (1976) op.cit. (note 8
      pp. 264-299. The status of legal standing to sue for
      environmental protection is well covered in ELDER (1976)
      op.cit. (note 28).

31.   SEIAL-HOHENVELDERN, I., "Alternative approaches to
      transfrontier environmental injuries," Environmental
      Policy and Law 2 (1976), pp. 6-10.

PLATE 37
Kildonan Cannery, Now Abandoned

B.C. Archives Pho

CHAPTER 10

MANAGEMENT UNDER UNCERTAINTY

Carl J. Walters

Institute of Animal Research Ecology
University of British Columbia

INTRODUCTION

A key feature of almost all fisheries management situation is
uncertainty. Rarely do we see decision or plans whose consequences
can be predicted with great accuracy; even after allowing for essentially unpredictable effects of random environmental factors, we often
find that the average response remains uncertain due to lack of understanding about basic functional mechanisms and interactions.

The intent of this chapter is to pinpoint some major uncertainties
about Pacific salmon enhancement, and to suggest a procedure for
taking these uncertainties explicitly into account in the evaluation of
alternative plans. By enhancement I will mean improvement of production through manipulation of spawning escapements and through
capital investments for habitat restoration and provision of artificial
production facilities (spawning channels, egg incubation boxes and
hatcheries). With the scale of development currently contemplated for
British Columbia, enhancement planning is obviously a very complicated
problem for which it would be foolish to attempt a single comprehensive
overview or recipe for success. I will attempt to review here only those
areas of uncertainty that have surfaced repeatedly in a series of modeling workshops sponsored at the University of British Columbia during
1973-1975 by Environment Canada. The procedure recommended here

261

for doing something about uncertainy is a product of discussions between our research group at the University of British Columbia and several decision theorists at the International Institute for Applied Systems Analysis, Vienna.

This chapter will suggest an approach to enhancement planning that is quite different from, but perhaps complementary to, the approach taken so far by Environment Canada. Our understanding from discussions and existing documents is that project selection will take place in roughly four stages:

1. an initial survey of possible development sites (drainage areas, spawning and rearing waters) and types of facilities (hatcheries, spawning channels, habitat rehabilitation);

2. calculation of benefit-cost ratios assuming that each site-facility combination will operate in a "vacuum" (contribute a marginal return to the total fishery that is independent of other stocks and facilities, without costly engineering difficulties);

3. filtering of the best possibilities from step (2) so as to eliminate high risk cases where there is danger of stock interaction (competition, predation) or where harvest from the enhanced stock is not manageable separately from other populations. It is hoped that simulation modeling will be a valuable tool to help identify such cases;

4. time phasing of the proposals surviving step (3) so as to provide experimental feedback from the first few projects that will help guide later planning and investment.

My suggestions relate primarily to steps (2) and (3); the benefit-cost and filtering procedures will not adequately take account of the less likely but potentially very costly outcomes that may result from enhancement, nor will these procedures properly measure the experimental value of some projects that may at first glance appear uneconomic or too risky. I argue that an essentially experimental or adaptive approach to management is needed. Instead of demanding that the planner pretend to understand what will happen, I would ask that he take more of the possible consequences (uncertainties) into account from the outset, so as to better design the time phasing of Step (4) above.

SOME MAJOR UNCERTAINTIES

Salmon management operates with a wealth of accumulated experience and research information, yet some major uncertainties remain: enhancement will generate a variety of essentially novel situations that are outside the range of recorded past experience, and there is a great danger in simply extrapolating from existing research data. The naive argument is often voiced that enhancement will simply restore stocks to their historical levels of abundance, thus creating no special problems; but high abundances do not signify high potential net production or sustainable yield.

We find six classes of uncertainties to be of particular importance. These classes represent a very broad spectrum of concerns, from engineering difficulties to economic and political problems and fundamental biological issues.

"Mechanical" Failures of Artificial Facilities

Recent difficulties with spawning channels and hatcheries in British Columbia indicate very clearly that engineered facilities and the artificial populations that they support are not to be trusted as economical sources of production in the near future. The Pinkett River spawning channel (Babine Lake), for example, has had problems with bank erosion and washouts while the Capilano hatchery had a large mortality of juvenile fish apparently due to a dose of chlorinated water from a treatment plant upstream. While particular engineering problems

263

are not likely to reoccur (once recognized they can be remedied and prevented in the future), the broad range of problems that have already occurred suggests that there may be many more "trouble points" that will continue to generate periodic production failures over at least the next decade or two.

The British Columbia and Washington experience with artificial facilities should be examined much more carefully with a view to developing some sort of failure probability rating curves (Figure 1,10). This analysis should deliberately not try to itemize all the particular problems (chlorine poisoning, washouts, clogging, etc.) that have been recognized; instead it should provide empirical guidelines for how often to expect unrecognized difficulties.

Political Irreversibility of Bad Decisions

Suppose a large enhancement facility turns out to be excessively costly or creates serious problems in managing rather less productive stocks. Any plan to shut down this facility would almost surely be moved into the arena of political decision making: protests would come from commercial interest groups who might profit (in the short term) from the facility in spite of its side costs, and it is not likely that the engineers and managers of the facility would enjoy having their efforts billed as mistaken.

Vested interest and personal commitment do not provide a very good seed bed for rational thinking and decision making. Considering how difficult it has been in the past to implement new management policies for salmon in the face of these pressures, it is not at all certain that bad decisions could be reversed quickly enough to prevent long term or irreversible damages. This problem is apparently very common

264

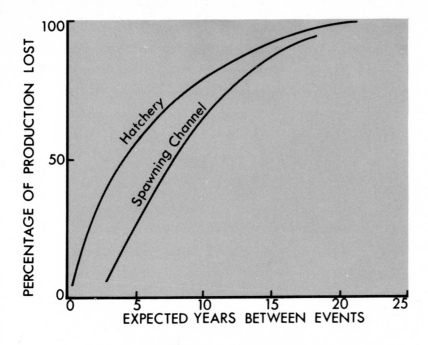

FIGURE 1,10. Failure Rating Curves for Enhancement Facilities.

in natural resource development and management; a variety of examples are presented in Walters.[1]

Future Control of Fishing Efforts and Investment

Any net economic benefits from the enhancement programme will be partially lost if increased salmon abundance results in higher commercial profits and if these profits trigger unmanageable political pressure to allow additional investment (more licences) or changes in technology (particularly replacement of trolling and gill net boats by purse seining equipment). If too many new boats enter the fishery, employment will increase but net profit from the industry might remain

265

stable or even decrease. More total boats and/or more purse seiners would also make it increasingly difficult to control the fishery on a day-to-day basis within each season so as to reach target escapements and protect less productive stocks. Walters and Buckingham[2] have tried to quantify the increased "control errors" that might occur, but there are some very large uncertainties in such calculations.

Ocean Limitation of Production

A general assumption in enhancement planning is that salmon production is limited by freshwater factors (spawning and rearing conditions). The evidence is strong that this assumption is correct in southern waters (from the Fraser River south) at least for coho, chinook, steelhead, and some sockeye stocks. For northern waters the picture is less clear. Figure 2,10 shows ocean survival rates (smolt to return) for a southern sockeye stock (Chilko, Fraser system) and a northern stock (combined Babine area, Skeena system). The northern data suggest some sort of asymptote or upper limit for the number of adult fish that will return, no matter how many smolts head out to sea. The Skeena shows this particularly well; it appears that the ocean will return 1-3 million adults (with very high "random" variation) whenever the smolt output exceeds 20-30 million. Returns in 1976 and 1977 will provide the critical test for this conclusion, when adults return from the very large smolt outputs (generated by spawning channels) of 1973-74.

The major salmon producing area in the gulf of Alaska is no more than 4×10^6 km^2. From various marine productivity studies as summarized by Parsons[3], zooplankton production for continental shelf areas should be about 10^7 gC/km^2/year, so an optimistic estimate of the total zooplankton production of the gulf would be 4×10^{13} gC/year. The total annual output (catch plus escapement) of planktivorous salmon

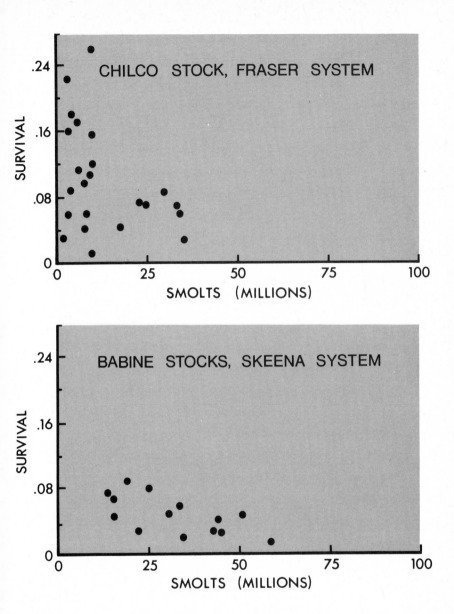

FIGURE   2,10.   Ocean Survival Rates in Relation to Smolt Output for Two Sockeye Populations. Skeena Data from Ricker and Smith [4]; Fraser Data Provided by D. Blackbourn, Int. Pac. Salmon Fish. Comm.

from the gulf (pink, chum, sockeye) is currently about 10^8 fish, each of which must have eaten at least 600-1000 gC of zooplankton (2 kg growth per year times 3 kg food consumption per kg growth times 0.1 kg C per kg wet weight). Thus the total zooplankton consumption by salmon must be at least 10^{11} gC/year. If we include the food consumption by salmon that enter the gulf but do not survive the full growth period to become output, the total zooplankton consumption per year is probably at least 10^{12} gC. Thus salmon now appear to be consuming 5-10 percent of the total zooplankton production. Since much of the total zooplankton production goes into maintenance and to other predators, this percentage may be near the limit that can be sustained: the ocean is not an infinite resource for salmon. An obvious recommendation based on this fact would be that no new enhancement facilities for sockeye be initiated along the North Coast, unless these facilities are directed at currently unproductive stocks that have distinctive times of seaward migration and/or oceanic migration patterns.

Considering this uncertainty, it might appear wise to initiate oceanic production studies as special prerequisites for additional development. However, additional research now would likely produce only suggestive but inconclusive results; witness Parker's[5] studies that point to the estuary as a critical bottleneck in salmon production. Research efforts should instead be conducted in conjunction with (not before) fairly large scale but essentially experimental increases in smolt production for distinctive stocks.

Interactions Between Stocks

It appears that four categories of biological interactions may be important determinants of enhancement programme success:

1. Cyclic dominance: interactions between year classes within stocks.

2. Interactions between stocks of the same species within a river system.

3. Interspecies interactions, particularly predation.

4. Large scale interactions among stocks sharing the Gulf of Alaska.

The cyclic dominance problem as defined by Ward and Larkin[6] has been widely discussed, most recently by Ricker and Smith[7]. For some reason, the presence of a large juvenile population in one year tends to be followed by poor juvenile survival in subsequent years; the prevalent hypothesis is that predator (trout, squawfish, whitefish, cestode parasite) populations or diseases are "stimulated" by the large cohort. A dramatic example may be emerging on the Skeena: based on the success of spawning channels in producing large smolt runs for 1973 and 1974, it was expected that about 90 million smolts would leave Babine Lake in 1975; the actual output was apparently under 40 million.[8] If this trend holds up, it may stimulate a madcap series of corrective investment decisions involving attempts to control the predator populations (which provide an important sport fishery), attempts to reduce parasitic infestation, and so on.

Existing data on interactions between stocks in the same river system is confusing. In the Skeena some natural sockeye populations have decreased since the introduction of spawning channels. On the other hand, the fertilization experiment on Great Central Lake (Vancouver Island) indicates an opposite possibility.[9] Fertilization during

269

1970-73 apparently caused a 4-6 fold increase in sockeye production,
but production also increased in Sproat Lake. Though not connected
in series, Great Central and Sproat share the same watershed and estuary,
and J. Manzer suggests that the increased Great Central smolt population may "buffer" the Sproat smolts from intensive predation.[10] The
mechanisms behind these examples may eventually be sorted out, but
for the present any predictions or generalizations about stock interaction
should be viewed with great suspicion.

Beyond the stimulus to natural predator populations that may
occur through enhancement, there is a possibility of significant predator-
prey interaction between enhanced populations. Coho, chinook and
steelhead all feed on the fry and smolts of other species. There may
also be competition among these predators, and among the other (plankton feeding) species.

Finally, there are strong suggestions of large scale interactions
in the Gulf of Alaska. Populations from Bristol Bay and the Skeena
River appear to be negatively correlated,[11] and ocean survival rates
appear to decrease with total abundance of fish in the Gulf of Alaska
as measured by total catches (Figure 3, 10).

Differential Impacts of Fishing

Even if enhancement programmes cannot increase the total number of returning adult fish available for harvest each year, they may
well reduce the number of spawners needed to produce these returns.
Thus the sustainable commercial exploitation rates (catch per returning
adult) may be increased unless mechanical facility failures occur quite
frequently. Less productive natural stocks will obviously suffer, as
well as the species that are prized for recreation.

270

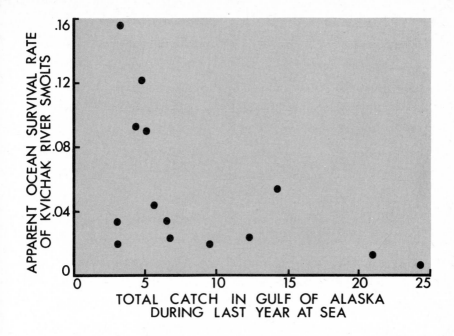

FIGURE 3,10. Ocean Survival Rate of an Alaska Sockeye Population in Relation to Total Gulf of Alaska Catches During Third Year of Ocean Life. Data Provided by Dr. Ken Parker, Alaska Dept. Fish & Game.

From a biological point of view it would seem obvious that great care should be taken not to destroy natural populations that can provide a cushion to fall back upon in the likely event of frequent enhancement facility failures; in the extreme, one might view artificial facilities only as a quick means to rebuild natural stocks after years of overfishing or poor natural production. The trouble is, as previously discussed, economic and political pressures will likely have a strong influence on policy.

Also, it is not certain that successive generations of fish can be switched back and forth between artificial and natural spawning and rearing areas, as would be required in a remedial enhancement programme.

271

R. Ginetz reports that some fish returning to the Fulton and Pinkett Channels on Babine Lake may die without spawning if denied entrance to the channels, rather than spawn in the adjacent natural stream. There is a large literature on homing and on the response of salmon to diversion from their target spawning areas; this literature suggests that most fish will show adequate flexibility in their choice of spawning location.

ELEMENTS OF EXPERIMENTAL
POLICY DESIGN

In looking at the uncertainties outlined above, one's first reaction might be a bad case of "paralysis through analysis": any action might result in serious problems, and there is a temptation to demand that nothing at all be done. It is not the intent here to make or support such demands; almost all human enterprise involves risks, and the real issue is: how can we objectively take some account of the risks so as to make decisions that are neither too conservative nor too optimistic, and that will provide information to better guide future decisions?

This section develops one reasonably simple procedure for comparing alternative enhancement plans in the face of uncertainty. The procedure is somewhat analogous to cost-benefit analysis, but takes into account a much wider variety of factors such as risk aversion and the experimental value of investments. The procedure involves five basic steps:

1. Assessment of risk aversion in terms of a "utility function" that measures the degree of satisfaction achieved with different levels of catch or economic return when the returns are uncertain.

2. Identification of alternative models or predictions or hypotheses about biological and economic responses.

3. Assignment of subjective probabilities or "degrees of belief" for the alternative models identified in step (2).

4.   Identification of alternative plans or experiments, some of
      which would allow discrimination among the alternative models
      identified in step (2).

5.   Cross-evaluation of the alternative plans and models so as to
      select that plan which has the best expected performance
      across the possible models, i.e., the plan which holds up
      best when several possible outcomes are considered.

In standard benefit cost analysis, step (1) is normally represented only through the assignment of some discount rate that reflects
uncertainty about future returns; step (2) is represented only through
selection of one model or hypothesis about returns (usually an optimistic possibility); step (3) is not considered at all; and step (5) is
reduced to a comparison across plans for the single model that is
considered.

Two simple examples will be used to illustrate the thinking and
calculations involved at each step. The first example is the situation
with sockeye salmon in the Fraser River; if we pool all of the stocks in
the system to give a composite total population and eliminate the data
for "cycle years" (every fourth year from 1974 backward), then an
overall stock-recruitment relationship can be plotted (Figure 4,10).
In this figure the data shown is for the years 1939-1973, omitting every
fourth or cycle year beginning in 1942. This overall relationship does
not show a clear pattern of density-dependent decreases in relative
production (recruits per spawner) when spawning stocks are increased.
Thus a simple enhancement plan might be to allow increased escapements in hopes that relative production would remain high. But two
major risks are involved: overspawning might occur as represented by
the model or hypothetical curve n_1, in figure (4,10), and/or cycle
year production might be inhibited.

As a second example, consider the relationship illustrated in
Figure (2,10) between smolt output and returning adults for Skeena

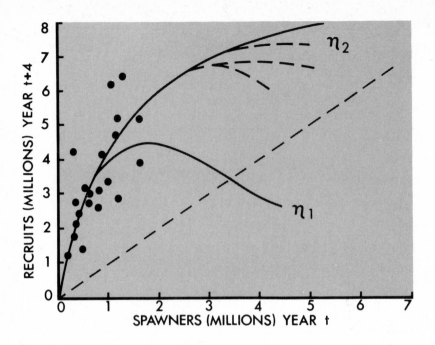

FIGURE   4,10.   Alternative Stock-Recruitment Models for Fraser River
Sockeye Salmon, Off-Cycle Years.

River sockeye (Figure 5,10). While there is some indication from this
data that there is a limit on ocean production, the evidence is certainly
not conclusive.   Enhancement through provision of two spawning
channels has already increased the smolt output by various amounts, and
it is relatively easy to construct alternative predictions as to the mean
results that will occur (curves n_1, n_2 and n_3 in Figure 5,10). This
example points out especially well the need to consider "random" variation around expected results in evaluating alternative experimental
plans: it would take several years of high enhancement output in order
to be confident about which (if any) of the alternative curves is correct

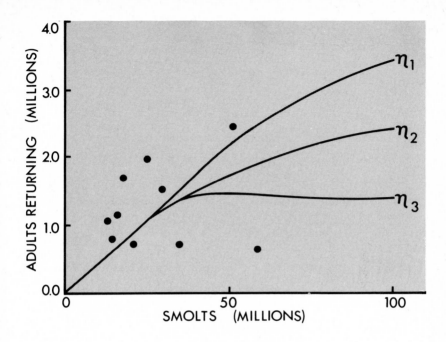

FIGURE 5,10. Total Ocean Returns of Skeena Sockeye in Relation to Smolt Output from Babine Lake.

and the costs over this "discovery period" must be taken into account. In the analysis that follows, we will try to determine in hindsight whether the existing Skeena enhancement facilities were a good investment.

ASSESSMENT OF RISK AVERSION

Detailed discussions of utility functions and risk aversion for salmon management have been presented by Keeney[12] and Hilborn.[13] Only the general idea will be reviewed here, and it can be introduced with a simple example. Suppose a wealthy relative offers you a choice between receiving a $2000 gift for sure or a "lottery" in which he would toss a coin and give you $10000 if the coin comes up heads and nothing at all if it comes up tails. The expected value of the lottery is (0.5) (0) + (0.5) ($10000) = $5000, but many of us would prefer the $2000 sure return instead: we are then said to be risk averse. In such situations it is simply inappropriate to use dollars directly to measure our relative satisfaction with the lottery; in developing a utility function we seek to transform from dollars into some other units such that expected values, when measured in these other units, do reflect our relative satisfaction with choices involving gambles or uncertainty. Now suppose that your relative starts lowering the size of the sure return that he would offer and you discover that you can no longer make a decisive choice when the sure offer is about $1,000; you are then said to be indifferent to the sure thing and the lottery, or in other words the two choices have equal utility (give equal satisfaction) for you. Symbolically, if we let U (X) mean "the utility index corresponding to X dollars," we can say

$$U (\$1,000) = (0.5)\ U (\$0) + (0.5)\ U (\$10,000).$$

By scaling the utility index such that

$$U (\$0) = 0 \text{ and } U (\$10,000) = 1,$$

we can then calculate U ($1,000):

$$U (\$1,000) = (0.5)\ (0) + (0.5)\ (1.0) = 0.5.$$

By asking about other gambles (for example, heads you get $1,000, tails you get nothing) and finding for each the corresponding equal satisfaction (or indifferent) sure return, we can eventually develop a full curve or utility function (Figure 6,10). Then this function can be used to calculate relative satisfaction with any lottery or gamble, and thus to compare various gambling situations to one another as well as to sure returns. The steep rise and bending over of the function (as in Figure 6,10) automatically measures risk aversion: satisfaction drops off sharply when the dollar returns get small.

Unfortunately the problem of utility assessment becomes much more difficult when time streams of returns rather than single gambles

PLATE 38
Blocked Salmon

Vancouver Sun Photo

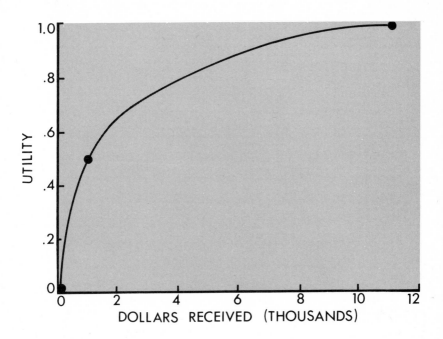

FIGURE 6,10. My Utility Function For Money From Rich Relatives.

are to be compared. The simplest approach is to calculate discounted total returns in dollars, over time (sum of annual discount factors times annual returns), then estimate a utility value for each possible total. This approach is better than just using the discounted total directly as a measure of relative satisfaction, but it does not reflect aversion to variability of returns within each time stream. For example, the highest total returns from salmon fisheries can be obtained by keeping escapements fixed, but such policies also result in maximum variability in catches from year to year.[14] Some manageable methods are being developed for time stream evaluation[15] but the simple approach will be used in the remainder of this paper.

Without referring to specific plans or policies, let us develop utility functions for the Fraser and Skeena examples. Off-cycle sockeye catches for the Fraser are never likely to exceed an annual average of 6 million fish; assuming a $3.00 price per fish and a 1 percent annual discount rate, the total future return from the fishery would then be at most $1500 million. This is also a reasonable upper limit for the Skeena sockeye. Thus we can assign an arbitrary utility scale with U ($0) = 0 and U ($1,500M) = 1.0. We then go through a questioning process as in the simple example above, and the results would probably be roughly as shown in Figure 7,10. Notice that the Skeena function is steeper, representing higher relative satisfaction with lower catches than in the Fraser system; this difference is expected considering that the Skeena fishery has historically operated at a lower level of capital investment, so that lower catches than in the Fraser could be tolerated without creating serious economic problems and dissatisfaction.

To show how the functions in Figure 7,10 are used, let us pretend that two alternative policies have been recommended for the Fraser. Suppose that it has somehow been estimated that policy 1 has an 80 percent chance of producing total future return equal to $150 million and

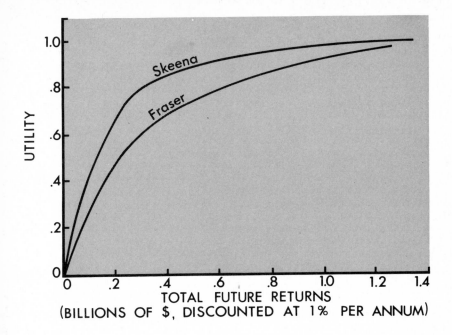

FIGURE 7,10 Hypothetical Utility Functions for Discounted Total Dollar Returns from Skeena and Fraser River Sockeye.

a 20 percent chance of producing $1,000M, while policy 2 has a 30 percent chance of destroying the fishery entirely ($0 future value) and a 70 percent chance of producing $1,000M over the future. We first estimate the utilities for these returns from Figure 7,10:

$$U(\$0) = 0$$
$$U(\$150M) = 0.4$$
$$U(\$1,000M) = 0.93$$

Then the expected utilities are taken by summing probabilities times component utilities:

policy 1 expected utility = (0.8) (0.4) + (0.2) (0.93) = 0.51
policy 2 expected utility = (0.3) (0) + (0.7) (0.93) = 0.65

Policy 2 looks best, even though there is a 30 percent chance of total destruction; if this conclusion seems unreasonable in hindsight, then we know that the utility function has been incorrectly estimated: most likely a higher utility should be assigned to $150M relative to $0, thus making policy 1 look better in comparison to any case where total loss is possible.

IDENTIFICATION OF ALTERNATIVE MODELS

Any assessment of the likely (or unlikely) impacts of a policy necessarily involves some sort of extrapolation model or preconception. It is frequently argued that preconceptions should be brought out into the open in the form of mathematical and simulation models; such precision is helpful but not necessary to apply the methodology outlined here. The basic requirement is to identify the range of possible outcomes that may result from every policy or plan to be considered. This identification is made easier if we first identify a series of alternative functional models such as the curves $n_1 - n_3$ in Figures 4,10 and 5,10; these models can then provide predictions about a wide range of plan alternatives without devising a new set of models for each plan. Besides being "plan independent," functional models usually provide a better grasp on whatever biological and economic processes are involved, and better predictions about responses over time to the uncontrolled environmental variation that is certain to occasionally shift system state away from planned averages.

When all of the uncertainties outlined in the previous section are considered simultaneously, a host of alternative predictions can be generated. Suppose each major class of uncertainties is represented by three alternative models, for example:

ocean production:	no limits	moderate limits	severe limits
depensatory predation:	no increase with salmon enhancement	moderate increase after enhancement	severe increas after enhancement
economic development:	full investment control	partial investment control	no control by government

Then if there are six major classes of uncertainties, we could generate $3^6 = 729$ alternative models of response to any plan. Each alternative model would involve selection of one "submodel" for every uncertainty class:

model #1 :	ocean unlimited,	no depensation, ...,	full effort control
model #2 :	ocean unlimited,	moderate depensation, ...,	full effort control
⋮			
model #729 :	ocean severely limited,	severe depensation, ...,	no effort control

When "random" environmental variation is also considered, many outcomes are possible for each of the 729 models. If we use three random or "Monte Carlo" simulation trials for each model to find the expected return for some plan, then a total of 3 X 729 = 2187 simulations would be necessary. Computers can handle problems of this size with no difficulty.

To illustrate the numerical calculations for comparing models and plans in the Fraser and Skeena examples, we will ignore the economic and political uncertainties and assume that the biological possibilities are adequately represented by curves n_1 - n_3 in Figures 4,10 and 5,10.

PLATE 39
The Controversial Hatchery

ASSIGNMENT OF SUBJECTIVE PROBABILITIES
TO ALTERNATIVE MODELS

There is considerable literature on the concept of subjective
or judgemental probabilities.[16] When we wish to compare a series of
models such as the curves in Figures 4,10 and 5,10, it is usually unreasonable to assume that all the possibilities are equally likely. Based
on intuition and past experience, we might for example believe that
curve n_1 in Figure 4,10 is twice as likely to be correct as curve n_2, and
we may consider curve n_3 to be only half as likely as curve n_2. We
would then assign approximate subjective probabilities or relative
degrees of credibility to the alternatives as follows:

$$p^*(n_1) = 0.57$$
$$p^*(n_2) = 0.29$$
$$p^*(n_3) = 0.14$$

(The symbol $p^*(X)$ is to be read "the subjective probability of X.").
Though the subjective probabilities might be assigned on the basis of
prior statistical experience (for example, we might know that 7 out of
10 sockeye populations appear to follow recruitment curves more like
n_1 in Figure 5,10), there is no reason not to include pure biological or
economic "gut feelings" that are difficult to quantify. The key point
to keep in mind is that subjective probability assignments and risk
aversion are not the same thing, though a risk averse manager is likely
to assign higher probabilities to the more pessimistic outcomes. Wanting
to avoid low return situations is not the same as believing that such
situations are very likely.

For complex predictions involving several uncertain submodels,
subjective probabilities can be assigned across the possibilities within
each submodel, then the probability for any overall combination is the
product of the probabilities making up the combination. For example,

suppose the following table of probabilities has been constructed:

	optimistic	moderate	pessimistic
ocean production	0.9	0.1	0.0
depensatory mortality	0.3	0.4	0.3
economic development	0.1	0.4	0.5

Thus the overall model consisting of (ocean production unlimited, depensation, no economic development control) would be assigned $p^* = (0.9)(0.4)(0.5) = 0.18$. Across the 27 possible models that could be constructed from the table, the overall probabilities will sum to 1.0 if the probabilities across each row sum to 1.0.

Note that different decision makers will assign different subjective probabilities, just as they will have different risk aversions. It is doubtful that any purely objective procedure could be devised that would simultaneously capture such variation and still lead to complete consensus about the best plan to follow. The analysis tries to help find the best plan given some feelings; it is not a normative procedure for deciding what feelings are "best" in some broad psychological, social or economic sense.

DEVELOPMENT OF ALTERNATIVE
EXPERIMENTAL PLANS

Given a set of alternative models with associated probabilities, the next step is to identify some alternative development plans. As a basis for comparison, there should always be some "plan 1" that involves no changes or new investments. Presumably plan 1 would involve holding stock sizes at present levels and would thus produce little or no information about the various uncertainties or alternative models.

Any experimental plan may be viewed as consisting of four operational stages over time:

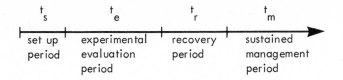

$$\begin{array}{c|c|c|c|}
 & t_s & t_e & t_r & t_m \\
\hline
\text{set up} & \text{experimental} & \text{recovery} & \text{sustained} \\
\text{period} & \text{evaluation} & \text{period} & \text{management} \\
 & \text{period} & & \text{period} \\
\end{array}$$

We will use t_s, t_e, etc. to refer to the length, in years, of the four stages (t_m can be considered infinite). Different plans may vary drastically in the lengths of the periods, which are defined as follows:

1. Set-up period: time required before any results or experimental data become available; includes engineering design, construction time, and lags due to biological life cycle. For the Skeena t_s has proved to be about 10 years: 8 years to bring the spawning channels to full production, plus two years before the first large smolt output begins to return as adults. For escapement increases on the Fraser, $t_s = 4$ years (the dominant life cycle length) plus any time required to politically sell the plan.

2. Experimental evaluation period: the operating time required in order to become reasonably certain about which model is correct. High random variation will tend to increase the required period, while the period will be shorter for plans that involve more drastic manipulations (for example, very high smolt outputs for the Skeena, or very high escapements on the Fraser). The length of the period for any plan may be determined by a gaming procedure in which a modeller secretly selects one alternative model and generates noisy "data" from it until the manager can recognize it.[17]

3. Recovery period: If the experimental manipulation proves unsuccessful (i.e., a pessimistic model turns out to be correct) then there will be a period of recovery before sustained management is possible. The beginning of the recovery period represents an

adaptive decision point, beyond which future actions and returns
are geared to whichever model proves correct. For the Skeena,
the recovery period would involve loss of catches if the enhancement facilities cannot increase ocean production and if natural
stocks have been depleted. For the Fraser, the recovery period
might actually involve increased or bonus catches in order to reduce escapements to historical levels. Note that length of the
recovery period can only be estimated if both plan and model
have been specified, in contrast to the experimental period which
should be the same for all alternative models.

4.   Sustained management period: Assuming that the experiment
     results in positive identification of the correct model, then
     expected returns over the long run can be calculated with re-
     lative ease for any plan-model combination.

This simple, four-stage view of experimental plans is an obvious
oversimplification. When many uncertainties are involved, the concept
of a single experimental period has little meaning; there will be several
decision or switching points where the plan might be modified or discarded. Even in simple examples like Skeena smolt enhancement or
Fraser escapement increase, it is difficult to predict the exact length
of the experimental period; about all that can be said for sure is that
more drastic or expensive experiments will require less time to produce
definitive results. Also the four stage view does not represent the
possibility of incremental experiments. For example, a good plan for
the Skeena might have been to put in one spawning channel to produce
75 million smolts for a few years, then add a second channel to increase
the output to 100 million if the first channel proved successful. This
chapter will not attempt to show how complex plans with many experimental stages and decision points can be precisely evaluated; our hope

PLATE 40
Will the Salmon Return?

I.H. Norie Photo

is that the four stage view will provide at least some improvement over benefit/cost estimates that do not reflect adaptive decision sequences at all.

Let us now devise simple plans for the Fraser and Skeena examples. After examining Figure 4,10, Walters and Hilborn[18] were able to devise four alternative plans for the Fraser:

Plan 1:   hold escapement around 1.0 million forever (do not experiment).

Plan 2:   increase escapements to 1.5 million for 15 years then manage according to whichever model proves correct.

Plan 3:   increase escapements to 2.0 million for 5 years, then follow the correct model.

Plan 4:   increase escapements to 3.0 million for 3 years, then follow correct model.

These plans represent progressively greater disturbances to the normal operation of the fishery. Note that the required experimental period would be shorter for the more drastic plans; the experimental periods were determined during a workshop gaming session in which Walters secretely picked either n_1 or n_2 from Figure 4,10, then generated noisy "data" until Environment Canada scientists could recognize which model had been chosen. Several gaming trials were conducted for each escapement plan, with different random errors in each trial, and the required experimental periods were found to vary considerably between trials.

After examining Figure 5,10 a similar series of plans were devised for the Skeena:

Plan 1:   no enhancement

Plan 2: a single spawning channel to increase smolt output to 75 million; shut down after 15 years if no increase in ocean production observed.

Plan 3: the existing plan, two spawning channels to provide a maximum smolt output of around 100 million; shut down after 5 years (of full smolt output) if no increase in ocean production (model n_3 correct).

The required experimental periods were determined by the same gaming procedure as used for the Fraser example. We rejected outright any plans for continuing spawning channel operation if ocean production does not increase. Even if the ocean can only produce 1.5 million adults on average, the spawning channels could still be used to increase sockeye catches from around 0.8 million to 1.2 million fish, since only about 0.3 million spawners (rather than 0.7-0.8 million) would be required to produce the 30-50 million smolts that are needed to insure 1.5 million adults (Figure 5,10). But the annual exploitation rate would have to be increased from 50 percent to about 80 percent of returning adults, which would likely lead to disastrous overfishing of less productive natural sockeye stocks and other species (particularly chinooks and pinks); this overfishing would more than balance the sockeye gains.

CROSS EVALUATION OF MODELS AND PLANS

Let us define the conditional utility U(plan i/model j) as the expected utility of following plan i given that model j turns out to be correct. Then the overall expected utility of a plan can be written as the sum of products of subjective model probabilities times conditional utilities:

$$\text{Expected utility of plan i} = \sum_j p^*(\text{model j}) \, U \, (\text{plan i/model j})$$

To find the overall expected utilities of all the plans to be compared we must estimate a matrix giving all possible conditional utility combinations:

"States of Nature"

	Model 1	Model 2 ... Model n
Plan 1	$U(plan_1/model_1)$	$U(plan_1/model_2)..U(plan_1/model_n)$
Plan 2	$U(plan_2/model_1)$	$U(plan_2/model_2)..U(plan_2/model_n)$
$\vdots$		
Plan $_m$	$U(plan_m/model_1)$	$U(plan_m/model_2)..U(plan_m/model_n)$

Each conditional utility element in the table represents the average result of following one four-stage plan (see subsection on plans above) into the future while assuming that one model is correct, and can thus be estimated rather easily by simulation. We take a plan and model, simulate them forward in time while including random effects and accumulating total dollar returns, and then associate a utility value with the resulting total; the simulation is then repeated several times with different random effects, and the average utility is calculated across the trials. If we use 10 simulation trials of 50 years each, then 500 simulated years go into the calculation of each conditional utility. This is not an excessive computational problem unless the model is very complicated.

Once the table above has been computed, then it is easy to select the best plan. We simply sum across the rows of the table, weighting each row element by the appropriate subjective model probability. The plan with the highest weighted row sum is (relatively) the best among the alternatives considered.

Two sample simulations of model-plan combinations for the Fraser example are shown in Figure 8,10. In both samples the escapement is increased to 2.0 million beginning in year 1; since recruits for

290

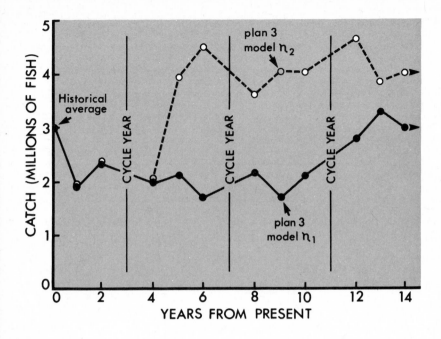

FIGURE 8,10. Hypothetical (Predicted) Time Series of Catches from the Fraser Sockeye Under Two Alternative Models and an Experimental Management Plan.

years 1-3 would come from past escapements (around 1.0 million) which have produced recruitments averaging 3-4 million (Figure 4,10), catches for years 1-3 would be around 2.0 million no matter which model is correct. Then in year 5 the results diverge depending on which model is correct; recruits in the n_1 case remain at about 4.0 million and produce catches around 2.0 million while the experimental 2.0 million escapement is maintained, and recruits in the n_2 case increase to around 6.0 million to produce catches around 4.0 million. Corrective action for the n_1 case takes place in Year 13, when a 3 million catch is taken to reduce the escapement back to 1 million; this policy is then continued in perpetuity.

By doing many simulations like Figure 8,10 for the Fraser, the following conditional returns table was constructed (entries are average discounted sums of catches over time, multiplied times $3.00/fish):

	"States of Nature"	
	Model n_1 fig. 4,10	Model n_2 fig. 4,10
Plan 1 (continue 1.0M escapement)	$231.6 million	$277.2 million
Plan 2(1.5M esc. for 15 years)	$233.4 "	$324.6 "
Plan 3(2.0M esc. for 5 years)	$226.2 "	$332.7 "
Plan 4(3.0M esc. for 3 years)	$215.1 "	$331.8 "

"Actions"

Using the utility function from Figure 7,10 to translate from dollar returns to satisfaction for each simulation trial, the analogous conditional utility table turns out to be:

	"States of Nature"	
	Model n_1	Model n_2
Plan 1	0.5	0.55
Plan 2	0.52	0.60
Plan 3	0.45	0.61
Plan 4	0.40	0.61

"Actions"

Note that the conditional utility elements are lower than would be expected if elements of the conditional returns table were plugged directly into Figure 7,10 to obtain expected utilities; each table element is calculated from several simulation trials, and those trials giving unusually low returns (due to chance) result in disproportionately low utility estimates which tend to pull down the average utility across trials. From the conditional utility table we can immediately reject plans 1 and 4, since plan 2 has better expected returns than either of them no matter which model is correct. The choice between plans 2 and 3 depends on the subjective probabilities for the two models; roughly, plan 2 is best if $p^*(n_1) > 0.5$ while plan 3 is best if $p^*(n_1) < 0.5$. In any case, it certainly appears that some experiment involving increased escapement should be seriously considered for the Fraser system.

For the Skeena example, a "back of the envelope" procedure was used to calculate the following conditional returns table:

"States of Nature"

	optimistic (n_1 fig. 5,10)	moderate (n_2 fig.5,10)	pessimistic (n_3 fig. 5,10)
Plan 1: no enhancement	$240 million	$240 million	$240 million
Plan 2: one channel	$564 "	$347 "	$235 "
Plan 3: two channels	$748 "	$472 "	$198 "

(left margin label: "Plans")

The elements in the first row were obtained by dividing the average annual catch (0.8 million fish X $3.00/fish) by the .01 discount rate. For the second row, it was assumed that 75 million smolts would produce about 2.8 million adults in the optimistic world and 2.0 million in the moderate world, and operating plus capital costs of $0.1 million/year were assumed. For the pessimistic model and plan 2 ($235 million), it was assumed that a five year period of very low harvests would follow the closure of the enhancement facility, in order to allow recovery of natural stocks. For the third row it was assumed that 100 million smolts would produce about 3.5 million adults for the optimistic case and 2.5 million for the moderate case; it was also assumed that escapements would be held at around 0.8 million in an attempt to preserve natural stocks. For the pessimistic case and plan 3 ($198 million), it was assumed that a ten year period of low harvests would follow closure of the spawning spawning channels.

When the crude return calculations for the Skeena are converted to utilities using Figure 7,10 the following table is obtained:

	"States of Nature"		
	Optimistic	Moderate	Pessimistic
Plan 1	0.73	0.73	0.73
Plan 2	0.92	0.83	0.72
Plan 3	0.95	0.88	0.68

It is immediately clear from this table that some sort of enhancement is justified unless a very high probability is assigned to the pessimistic model. If we assume that the optimistic and moderate models are equally likely, then by a simple algebraic exercise it can be shown that plan 3 is best unless $p*$ (pessimistic model) > 0.50. That is, the plan that has actually been followed would have been a bad choice only if the original planners had recognized a better than 50 percent chance that the ocean production would be severely limited; thus they acted wisely in view of the data available during the mid-60's, which gave no real hint of such limitation. With the data available now, the best future decision would be plan 1 or plan 2 (but hindsight is cheap).

Cross-evaluation of plans and models is obviously a tedious procedure, even for the simple examples presented above. But tedious calculations are just the sort of thing that computers are designed to do, and we hope that the procedure can be fully automated so as to readily handle a wide variety of models and plans. In any case, it at least provides a means to avoid the common pitfall of believing or relying upon a single model or preconception in evaluating alternative plans.

CONCLUSION

This chapter has presented a rather pessimistic outlook on Pacific salmon management. Even after many years of intensive management and research, there are still large uncertainties about biological and economic responses to new management regimes. It appears that more research work prior to enhancement investment will not resolve these uncertainties: it will be necessary to learn new lessons the hard way, by trial and error management. The decision procedure outlined in the last section is a means for evaluating some of the trials and errors more precisely, but it cannot provide a substitute for experience.

Nor is the experimental evaluation procedure a substitute for imaginative interpretation of existing data or an automatic mechanism to create better plans. It is simply a format or framework for helping to bring imaginative thinking out into the open. The framework does not generate single best predictions or best plans; it only tries to compare the performance of alternative plans in the place of alternative predictions. By demanding that plans be structured around an adaptive decision point, with experimental management up to the point and several options for sustained management afterward, the framework tries to measure the value of adaptive management planning in a simple way. Much work remains to be done on multi-decision adaptive plans.

REFERENCES

1. WALTERS, C.J. Foreclosure of options in sequential resource development decisions. International Institute for Applied System Analysis, RR-75-12. 1975.

2. WALTERS, C.J. and BUCKINGHAM, S.L. A control system for intraseason salmon management. International Institute for Applied System Analysis conference series CP-75-2. 1975.

3. PARSONS, T. and TAKAHASHI, M. Biological oceanographic processes. Permagon Press, Headington Hill Hall, Oxford. 1973, 186 pp.

4. RICKER, W.E., and SMITH, H.D. A revised interpretation of the history of the Skeena River sockeye salmon. J. Fish. Research Board, Canada, 32, 1975. pp. 1369-1381.

5. PARKER, R. Size selective predation among juvenile salmonid fishes in a British Columbia inlet. J. Fish. Res. Bd. Canada, 28, 1971. pp. 1503-1510.

6. WARD, F.J. and LARKIN, P.A. Cyclic dominance in Adams River sockeye salmon. International Pacific Salmon Fisheries Commission Programme Report No. 11, 1964. 116 pp.

7. RICKER, W.E. and SMITH, H.D. op.cit.

8. GINETZ, R. Personal communication.

9. PARSONS, T.R., STEPHENS, K. and TAKAHASHI, M. The fertilization of Great Central Lake. I. Effect on primary production Fish. Bull., U.S. No. 70, 1972. pp.13-23. See also MANZER, J.L. On the relation between Lacustrine growth and production of age 1.2 sockeye (Oncorhynchus nerka) in Great Central Lake prior to experimental nutrient enrichment. Fish. Res. Bd. Canada, No. 324. 1972. 31 pp.

10. Personal Communication, J. L. Manzer, Pacific Biological Station, Nanaimo, B.C., February 4, 1976.

11. WOOD, F.E.A. Personal Communication

12. KEENEY, R. A utility function for examining policy affecting salmon in the Skeena River. International Institute for Applied System Analysis memorandum series (in press). 1975.

13. HILBORN, R. Preferences for salmon management on the Skeena River. Institute of Animal Resource Ecology, University of British Columbia, Progress Report, PR-2. 1975.

14. WALTERS, C.J. Optimal harvest strategies for salmon in relation to environmental variability and uncertain production parameters. J. Fish. Res. Bd., Canada, 32, 1975, pp. 1777-1784.

15. BELL, D. A utility function for time streams having interperiod dependencies. International Institute for Applied System Analysis, RR-75-22. 1975.

16. RAIFFA, H. Decisions analysis: introductory lectures on choices under uncertainty. Reading, Mass: Addison-Wesley, 1968.

17. WALTERS, C.J. and HILBORN, R. Adaptive control of fishing systems. J. Fish. Res. Bd. Canada, 33 (in press).1976.

18. Ibid.

PLATE 41
Early Adaptation to Excess: Tree Caches

CHAPTER 11

CONCLUDING REMARKS: THE PROBLEM IN ITS SETTING

J.H. Mundie

Environment Canada

INTRODUCTION

Then said Evangelist, pointing with his finger over a very
wide field,....'Do you see yonder shining light?' He
said, 'I think I do.'

John Bunyan, The Pilgrim's Progress, 1678

The problem of Pacific salmon management is twofold:
the maintenance of a natural resource, and its allocation to people with
diverse claims.[1] The setting is the contemporary world of urban and
industrial growth, unemployment and inflation. The light which we
throw on the problem is the new understanding that issues cannot be
interpreted, nor decided upon, in isolation but must be seen in a broad
context of ramifying relations which we call a system. The origins of
the new understanding are multiple; it has roots in philosophy, engineering, warfare, business management and ecology. By recognizing that
problems cannot be understood unless viewed comprehensively, we can
hope to understand not only salmon management but apparently incom-
prehensible activities such as grand opera, spectator sports and morris
dancing.

MANAGEMENT IN PERSPECTIVE

The thought that a living resource should be maintained, let
alone promoted, emerges in the most recent seconds in the Day of Mankind. A strong western tradition of Greek and Christian influence has

insisted that man is free to deal with nature as he pleases, since it exists to serve his needs.[2] Capitalist and communist concur.

Man, as we all know, can indeed impose his conditions and
bend nature's rules. He does so, however, at a cost, for nature is
easily damaged; and he, being part of nature is himself penalized. A
strange analogy with the body/mind problem presents itself. The mind,
one may claim at least for everyday purposes, cannot exist without the
body. Yet it can make decisions which are detrimental to the body's
welfare, even disastrous to it. How can a part of the body issue orders
which are not in the body's best interest? How can man, a product and
part of nature, turn on it as depredator?

James Crutchfield describes how man as a predator of salmon
has failed conspicuously to maximize either the salmon populations or
his own gains. Stocks have declined, and labour and capital have been
grossly wasted. From the failure to put the fishery on a sound economic
basis stems the failure to reach the primary goal of salmon management-
"some composite measure of human well-being." The chief reasons for
this are the pursuit of immediate profit and conflicts of interest. Inadequate knowledge of the ecological needs of salmon has not been a
prime cause of their decline. Decisions have been made knowingly.

The mood of today, and it may be an ephemeral mood, is
tempered with restraint. The tradition of stewardship, traceable to
Plato has a voice. Man has responsibilities towards nature (and the
mind to the body?). Certainly the Pacific salmon must not attain the
status of the Atlantic salmon in Europe. At the same time, of course,
we want larger catches.

We, as this book brings out, are all sorts of people;
commercial fishermen, native people with a special dependence on
salmon, sports fishermen demanding excitement in unspoiled surroundings, and a host of others whose livelihood is linked to salmon. To

300

maintain the resource, and to allocate the benefits to us all, decisions
are necessary on a great array of issues: on restricting entry into the
commercial fishery; on limiting capital investment; on methods of fishing (at present these are absurd but they nevertheless allow some people
to earn their livelihood in a chosen way); on the redistribution of
rights of fishermen and powers of managers; on the needs of isolated
communities; on conflicts between recreational and commercial fishermen; on uncontrolled international fishing; on the constant insidious
(and not so insidious) encroachment of urban and industrial development
on salmon habitat; and on ways of increasing salmon production artificially. Many of these issues are acknowledged in the Canadian Government's policy for commercial fisheries[3] which works towards giving
Canadian society as a whole the best combination of benefits from the
fishery.

      Perhaps the gravest concern is the constant threat to the
salmon's environment. Competing uses such as generation of energy,
irrigation, deforestation, navigation, waste disposal, water-supply for
subdivisions, mineral removal from the sea floor, port development
in estuaries, all stand as today's examples of the historic process to
which salmon have succumbed in other parts of the world. Man and
salmon provide a problem in coexistence states Anthony Netboy, doyen
of salmon conservationists.[4] Perhaps men and salmon cannot live together, and salmon will survive only where men cannot. Like Cousteau's splendid penguins swimming under the Antarctic ice they will
abide (provided DDT does not reach them) in inhospitable waters
until man's day is passed.

      To tackle the complex questions of salmon management
(stock-recruitment relationships, the harvesting of mixed stocks, the
allocation of fishing intensity, selection of stocks for enhancement,
and the quantification of trade-offs) highly sophisticated techniques

of simulation and decision-making are being evolved, as Carl Walters
and his colleagues show. Laymen, and scientists whose experience is
in other areas, must take these techniques largely on trust. We are
in the hands of technocrats. We give two cheers to their ingenuity and
perseverance. Two only, because, as Walters stresses, a high element
of judgement must remain. Certainty is elusive. One reason for this
is the prohibitive cost and difficulty of obtaining precise initial information; another is the yearly variability of freshwater and estuary
environments; yet another is the urgency of many managerial choices
which dictates that partial evidence must suffice. Misjudgements and
errors, then, are likely. Science is to be trusted, but scientists nevertheless may make mistakes. Their science, as the thalidomide children
would remind us, may not be complete.

No amount of informed and wise decisions, of legislation,
fairness and justice can satisfy needs, to say nothing of wants, if the
resource steadily diminishes. Scarcity leads to confrontation and aggression, as Timothy O'Riordan shows. Hence management's concern
with enhancement. Here the decisions may determine the biological
and economic future of the fisheries. Of special interest, as Ron
MacLeod's chapter brings out, will be the balance of techniques designed to improve or restore habitats and major bioengineering facilities
of hatcheries, spawning-channels and incubation systems; for nature and
man have different strategies. The freshwater stages of salmon are
usually spent in highly variable environments subject to the vagaries of
climate. Nature's strategy is to be generous in her allocation of time
for migrating smolts and returning adults, and of numbers of eggs
spawned. Man's approach differs. He selects eggs and milt from a
few adults and imposes stable conditions of rearing and short times of
release. In doing so he reduces the genetic content of the stock and
its ability to adapt to change. Were he raising a purely domestic

302

animal this might be of little consequence, but he is raising a product
which must be fit enough to take its place in the wild. Should the
artificially reared stock hybridize with wild fish the genetic adaptive-
ness of the native salmon may be reduced. Clearly there are biological
questions here of major implication to managers.

Enhancement projects to produce more fish are part of the
general demand for economic growth. Belief in this has been so strong
that it has only very recently been called into question; the gross
national product has been, and is, the compass-setting of all governments. In a landmark of economic analysis Arthur Lewis[5] debated the
benefits and costs of economic growth. He conceded that wealth does
not bring happiness, but it increases the range of human choice. It
gives man greater control over his environment. In short, it brings
power. The poor have little power of redress. We may overlook the
economics of inequality whereby the proportion of the poor in an
expanding economy can remain unchanged. Presumably the benefits
of more salmon will be distributed across the community. In Lewis's
analysis, made only 21 years ago, there is little mention of the ecological costs of growth, although he notes that it is the richest nations
of the world which are using up the minerals and fuel most rapidly.

The ecological costs of growth have forced themselves upon
us in a mere two decades. Nowadays many analysts see mankind to be
entering a threefold crisis. Firstly, a crisis of numbers (there are,
simply, far too many of us); secondly, of scarcity (resources and time
are running out); and thirdly, of values (we have lost sight of how we
ought to live). If this crisis is to be met it can only be by the joint
efforts of the common man, technologists, educators, statesmen, economists, scientists and administrators. Crucial to their success will be
a spirit of co-operation and not confrontation; and equally crucial will

be concensus that "an attitude toward nature must be developed based on harmony rather than conquest".[5]

The problems of salmon management, then, represent in microcosm some great issues of our time. They call not merely for ecological economics but also for ecological politics. They are one test of whether man can make a civilization distinguished by restraint and a sense of place. This is the greatest issue in the pilgrim's wayward progress.

PLATE 42
Spawning; Death; Recycling

I.H. Norie Photo

REFERENCES

1. The author thanks Dr. Jon Schnute and Mr. Tom Bilton for valued comments on this chapter.

2. PASSMORE, J. Man's responsibility for nature. London: Duckworth, 1974.

3. ANON. 1976. Policy for Canada's commercial fisheries. Fisheries and Marine Service, Department of the Environment, Ottawa, Canada. 1976, 70 pp.

4. NETBOY, A. The salmon, their fight for survival. Boston: Houghton Mifflin, 1974.

5. LEWIS, W.A. The theory of economic growth. London: Allen and Unwin, 1955.

6. MESAROVIC, M., and E. PESTEL. Mankind at the turning point. The second report to the Club of Rome. New York: Dutton, 1974.

APPENDIX A

DISTINGUISHING FEATURES OF THE PACIFIC SALMON

Those readers who make the effort to see the salmon in their natural habitat will come up against the problem of knowing which species they are watching and at what stage in their life cycle. The diagrams following are a guide to the Pacific salmon, and the closely similar Pacific coast trouts, when in rivers and lakes.

The illustrations are arranged with distinguishing features of the fish indicated by a marker, and with a description of the features marked on the opposing page. The illustrations were drawn by Al Denbigh of the Nanaimo Biological Station, photography was by Charles Morley, and caption text by Derek Ellis.

PINK

MIGRATING – body spots present, side of body bears a broad, dark stripe, caudal fin spotted, ventral surface glaring white.

MALE – anterior dorsal surface distended into a prominent hump, body spots present, side of body bears a broad dark stripe, caudal fin spotted, ventral surface glaring white.

FEMALE (not illustrated) – resembles migrating form but darker.

CHUM

MIGRATING – male and female spawning forms often assumed during migration.

MALE – body spots absent, side of body bears vertical patterns of black, yellow and purple; prominent teeth.

FEMALE – body spots absent, side of body bears broad, dark stripe.

COHO

MIGRATING – nostrils white, body spots present, dorsal surface dark (i.e. counter-shaded), caudal fin spotted on upper lobe only.

MALE – nostrils white, body colour very dark, side of body with broad red stripe, caudal fin spotted on upper lobe only.

FEMALE (not illustrated) – resembles migrating form but overall colour darker, broad red lateral stripe.

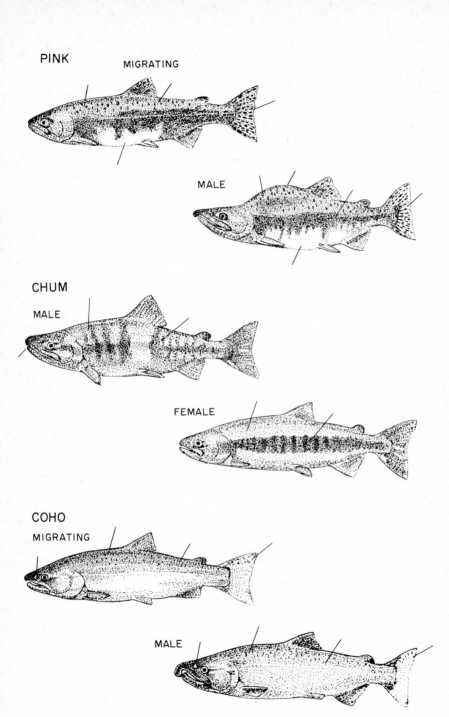

PINK

MIGRATING

MALE

CHUM

MALE

FEMALE

COHO

MIGRATING

MALE

309

SOCKEYE

MIGRATING – dorsal surface dark green, body spots absent but netlike scale pattern present, ventral surface silver, i.e. counter-shaded.

MALE – head green, anterior dorsal surface distended into a hump, body red.

FEMALE – head green, body red, side of body with broad, dark stripe.

CHINOOK

MIGRATING – dorsal surface dark, i.e. counter-shaded, body spots few and large, caudal fin spotted on both lobes.

MALE – anterior part of body may deepen considerably, body spots present, caudal fin spotted on both lobes.

FEMALE – body dark, body spots present, caudal fin spotted on both lobes.

CUTTHROAT TROUT

Body spots abundant, dorsal fin with white tip and spotted, sides without red stripe, caudal fin spotted, anal and pelvic fins with white tips.

RAINBOW TROUT

Body spots abundant, dorsal fin with white tip and spotted, side of body with red stripe, caudal fin spotted, anal and pelvic fins with white tips.

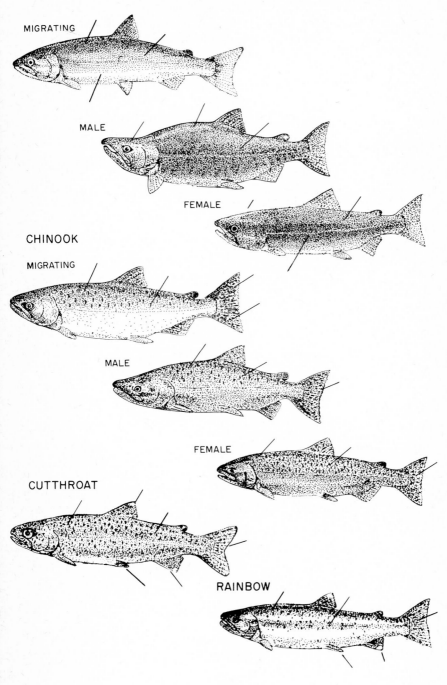

SOCKEYE

MIGRATING

MALE

FEMALE

CHINOOK

MIGRATING

MALE

FEMALE

CUTTHROAT

RAINBOW

311

PINK FRY

Length 1 inch (2-3 cms). Parr marks absent, dorsal surface dark green, ventral surface and sides silver, i.e. counter-shaded.

CHUM FRY

Length $1\frac{1}{2}$ inch (3-4 cms). Dorsal surface green, parr marks faint, ventral surface and sides silver, i.e. counter-shaded.

COHO FRY

EARLY - length 1 inch (2-3 cms). Dorsal fin with conspicuous white and black leading edge, parr marks prominent, anal fin with extended tip, and white and black leading edge.

LATE - length 3 inches (8 cms). Dorsal fin with black leading edge and white tip, parr marks prominent, anal fin with extended tip and white leading edge.

SOCKEYE FRY

Length 1 inch (2-3 cms). Body spots small, parr marks small and irregular.

CHINOOK FRY

Length $1\frac{1}{2}$-$2\frac{1}{2}$ inches (4-7 cms). Dorsal fin with dark leading edge and white tip, parr marks prominent, adipose fin with dark trailing edge, anal and pelvic fins with white leading edges.

PINK FRY

CHUM FRY

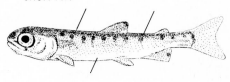

EARLY COHO FRY

LATE COHO FRY

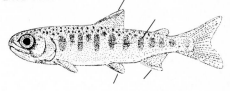

SOCKEYE FRY

CHINOOK FRY

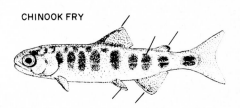

CUTTHROAT FRY

Length 1-3 inches (2-8 cms). Parr marks prominent, dorsal fin with white tip on three rays and spotted, adipose fin with dark marks on edge, anal and pelvic fins with white leading edges.

RAINBOW FRY

Length 1-3 inches (2-8 cms). Anterior dorsal surface with parr-like marks, parr marks prominent, dorsal fin with white tip on six rays and spotted, adipose fin with continuous dark edge, anal and pelvic fins with white leading edges.

COHO SMOLT

Length 4-6 inches (10-15 cms). Dorsal surface brown or green, dorsal fin with white tip and dark patch, parr marks faint or absent, caudal fin with dark patch at tip of each lobe, anal fin with white tip slightly extended, ventral surface silver, i.e. counter-shaded.

SOCKEYE SMOLT

Length 3-5 inches (8-13 cms). Dorsal surface brown or green, parr marks small, irregular and faint or absent, ventral surface silver, i.e. counter-shaded.

CUTTHROAT JUVENILE

Length 4-6 inches (10-15 cms). Body spots abundant, dorsal fin with white tip over three rays and spotted, caudal fin spotted, anal pelvic fins with white tips, parr marks may be present.

RAINBOW JUVENILE

Length 4-6 inches (10-15 cms). Body spots abundant, dorsal fin with white tip over 6 rays and spotted, red stripe on side of body, caudal fin spotted, anal and pelvic fins with white tips, parr marks may be present.

CUTTHROAT FRY

RAINBOW FRY

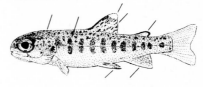

COHO SMOLT

SOCKEYE SMOLT

CUTTHROAT JUVENILE

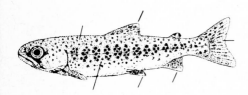

RAINBOW JUVENILE

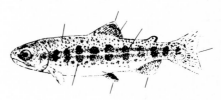

THE CONTRIBUTORS

Dr. James Arthur Crutchfield, Jr., was born in New London Connecticut in 1918. He received his Bachelor of Arts degree in economics in 1940 and his Master of Arts degree in economics in 1942 from the University of California, Los Angeles. Following service with the Office of Price Administration during World War II, he returned to graduate work at the University of California, Berkeley, and received his doctoral degree from that institution in 1954. After two years on the faculty of the University of California, he came to the University of Washington as assistant and later associate and professor of economics. He holds joint appointments in the Department of Economics, the Graduate School of Public Affairs, and the Institute for Marine Studies at the University of Washington. His major research areas have been in the field of natural resource economics, including fisheries development and management, water resources, water and air quality management, and the economic aspects of environmental management. He has been closely associated with fishery management problems at national and international levels in Africa, Latin America, and South-east Asia.

Dr. Derek V. Ellis, was born in Windsor, England, in 1930, and took his first degree in Zoology at the University of Edinburgh. Thereafter he followed graduate studies in McGill University's arctic programme which first introduced him to salmonids in the form of the arctic char. From 1957 through 1963 he was employed as a scientist undertaking research on salmon migrations at the Pacific Biological Station, Nanaimo, B.C. Since 1964 he has been Associate Professor of Biology at the University of Victoria, in which capacity he has continued salmon studies at intervals and each year presents a series of lectures on salmon to undergraduate students of Animal Behaviour.

Dr. Ray Hilborn was born in Red Oak, Iowa in the closing minutes of 1947. He received a B.A. in biology from Grinnell College in 1969. He received his Ph.D. in zoology from the University of British Columbia in 1974. The next year he was on the staff of the International Institute of Applied Systems Analysis in Laxenburg Austria, where he did research on applications of systems analysis and decision theory to resource management, with particular emphasis on Pacific Salmon. Since 1975 he has been jointly an employee of Environment Canada and on the faculty of the University of British Columbia. He has published scientific papers on genetics, population dynamics exploitation strategies, computer methodology, ecosystem simulation, and environmental impact assessment.

Dr. Randall M. Peterman was born in California in 1948 and received a Bachelor of Science degree from the University of California at Davis in 1970. He received a Ph.D. in 1974, after graduate studies at the Institute of Animal Resource Ecology, University of British Columbia, Vancouver, B.C. From 1974 to 1975, he was a National Research Council of Canada Postdoctorate Fellow. Since 1975 he has held a joint appointment with Environment Canada and the Institute of Animal Resource Ecology, University of British Columbia. His research has ranged from studies of forest and desert insects to work on fish behaviour and population dynamics. Since 1971, he has been involved with the application of systems analysis techniques to many areas of renewable resource management.

Mr. Philip A. Meyer was born in Telegraph Creek, British Columbia in 1941. He received his Bachelor of Arts degree in Economics and Political Science in 1962 from Victoria College, in affiliation with the University of British Columbia, and his Master of Arts degree in 1966 from the University of California at Santa Barbara. He has published a number of studies in the field of Natural Recreation and Natural Environments, and serves as a technical advisor to several agencies outside Canada. He is presently Chief Social Science Advisor to the Habitat Protection Directorate, Fisheries Management Service of the Federal Department of Fisheries and the Environment, for British Columbia and the Yukon.

Mr. Paul Fielding Scott was born in 1941 in Port Alberni, British Columbia. He received his Bachelor of Applied Science in Civil Engineering from the University of British Columbia in 1965. His professional career has included employment in both the consulting engineering field and the public service field. Since 1973, he has been employed as Senior Engineer with the Environmental Protection Service offices in Capilano 100, Park Royal, West Vancouver.

Mr. William J. Schouwenburg, a native of Edmonton, was born in 1936. He received his Bachelor of Science in Zoology from Florida State University in 1958. He accepted a position as Fisheries Biologist with the federal Fisheries Department in 1959. He has since specialized in environmentally oriented studies and evaluations relating to pollution control, estuarine alienation and hydro-electric developments. He is presently Acting Chief of the Water Use Division, Habitat Protection Directorate, Fisheries and Marine Service in Vancouver.

Mr. J. Ronald MacLeod was born and raised on the West Coast of Vancouver Island and was almost destined to become involved in either forestry or fisheries. As was his fate he became involved in many aspects of both industries in his early years, but fisheries was his choice when he turned toward a permanent career. He joined the Fisheries Department of Canada in 1956 as Fisheries Protection Officer stationed in Alert Bay. Because of his unique ability to understand and manage both fish and people he quickly assumed increasing responsibilities and moved through every level in the organization to his present position as the Director of the Salmonid Enhancement Programme.

Dr. Bruce Mitchell was born during 1944 in Prince Rupert, B.C., where he worked in the B.C. commercial fishing industry as a shoreworker and troller deckhand while in high school and attending university. He received an honours B.A. in geography from the University of British Columbia during 1966, and an M.A. from the same institution in 1967. His doctoral degree was obtained at the University of Liverpool in 1969. Research activity has focussed upon water and fisheries management, with emphasis upon institutional arrangements, decision making and public involvement. Current research includes a study of the evolution of sports fishery policy and practice in Ontario since 1945, as well as a study of institutional and physical adjustments to flooding and erosion hazards in Southern Ontario. He is an Associate Professor in the Geography Department, Faculty of Environmental Studies, University of Waterloo, Waterloo, Ontario.

Mr. Allan Adasiak is a United States citizen born in Rochester, New York in 1940. He studied at Princeton University and the University of California at Berkeley. He was Executive Assistant to the Attorney General for the State of Alaska for two years prior to becoming Executive Director of the Alaska Commercial Fisheries Entry Commission in 1973. He resigned from the commission in the fall of 1976 and is currently working as a consultant in Juneau, Alaska.

Dr. Timothy O'Riordan received his undergraduate and doctorate degrees in geography at the Universities of Edinburgh and Cambridge respectively. He taught in the Geography Department at Simon Fraser University from 1967 to 1974 during which period he also visited Clark University and the University of Canterbury in New Zealand. Since 1974 he has been Reader in the School of Environmental Sciences at the University of East Anglia where his research is primarily concerned with analyses of environmental policy making and the social psychology of recreational behaviour.

Dr. Carl John Walters was born in the United States in 1944. He received his Bachelor of Science degree in fisheries from Humboldt State College, California, in 1965, and his Master of Science and Doctorate degrees in fisheries from Colorado State University Fort Collins, in 1967 and 1969. Since 1969 he has been an assistant professor of Zoology and Animal Resource Ecology at the University of British Columbia, where he teaches courses in applied ecology and theoretical population dynamics. His research and publications cover a range of problems in applied ecology, from fish and wildlife population dynamics and alpine limnology to interdisciplinary research approaches in watershed management.

Dr. John Harold Mundie was born in Scotland in 1927. He received his Bachelor of Science Degree in Zoology at the University of Aberdeen in 1949 and his Ph.D. at the University of London in 1955. He spent ten years as a research scientist at the laboratory of the Freshwater Biological Association, Windermere, England. At this time he was seconded for a year to the University of Saskatchewan to work on northern lakes. He taught for two years at Leicester University, U.K. Since 1966, he has been a research scientist with Environment Canada at the Pacific Biological Station, Nanaimo, B.C., where his main interests are in the ecology of streams and freshwater phases of salmon.